Decentralizing Urban Policy

Decentralizing Urban Policy

Case Studies in Community Development

PAUL R. DOMMEL AND ASSOCIATES

John Stuart Hall Victor E. Bach Leonard Rubinowitz

Leon L. Haley John S. Jackson III

THE BROOKINGS INSTITUTION

Washington, D.C.

THE BROOKINGS INSTITUTION
1775 Massachusetts Avenue, N.W., Washington, D.C. 20036

Library of Congress Cataloging in Publication data:

Dommel, Paul R.
Decentralizing urban policy.

Includes bibliographical references and index.
Contents: Introduction—Decentralizing community development—Chicago, Illinois/Leonard Rubinowitz—Phoenix, Arizona/John Stuart Hall—[etc.]
1. Federal aid to community development—United States—Case studies. 2. Decentralization in government—United States. I. Title.
HN90.C6D65 361.6 81-70465
ISBN 0-8157-1888-8 AACR2
ISBN 0-8157-1887-X (pbk.)

9 8 7 6 5 4 3 2 1

THE BROOKINGS INSTITUTION is an independent organization devoted to nonpartisan research, education, and publication in economics, government, foreign policy, and the social sciences generally. Its principal purposes are to aid in the development of sound public policies and to promote public understanding of issues of national importance.

The Institution was founded on December 8, 1927, to merge the activities of the Institute for Government Research, founded in 1916, the Institute of Economics, founded in 1922, and the Robert Brookings Graduate School of Economics and Government, founded in 1924.

The Board of Trustees is responsible for the general administration of the Institution, while the immediate direction of the policies, program, and staff is vested in the President, assisted by an advisory committee of the officers and staff. The by-laws of the Institution state: "It is the function of the Trustees to make possible the conduct of scientific research, and publication, under the most favorable conditions, and to safeguard the independence of the research staff in the pursuit of their studies and in the publication of the results of such studies. It is not a part of their function to determine, control, or influence the conduct of particular investigations or the conclusions reached."

The President bears final responsibility for the decision to publish a manuscript as a Brookings book. In reaching his judgment on the competence, accuracy, and objectivity of each study, the President is advised by the director of the appropriate research program and weighs the views of a panel of expert outside readers who report to him in confidence on the quality of the work. Publication of a work signifies that it is deemed a competent treatment worthy of public consideration but does not imply endorsement of conclusions or recommendations.

The Institution maintains its position of neutrality on issues of public policy in order to safeguard the intellectual freedom of the staff. Hence interpretations or conclusions in Brookings publications should be understood to be solely those of the authors and should not be attributed to the Institution, to its trustees, officers, or other staff members, or to the organizations that support its research.

Foreword

IN AUGUST 1974, President Gerald R. Ford signed a bill establishing the community development block grant (CDBG) program, which consolidated a number of separate urban categorical grant programs and distributed the funds by formula. Block grants were part of the New Federalism advocated by President Richard M. Nixon as a way of giving state and local officials more discretion in the use of intergovernmental aid. Although this form of decentralization received wide support, its consequences were difficult to foresee. With support from the Department of Housing and Urban Development, a study group drawn from the Brookings Governmental Studies staff set up a network of field associates in sixty-one communities across the nation to assess the CDBG program. Brookings research extended through the sixth year (1980) of the program and resulted in four reports.

Decentralization has been emphasized again in President Ronald Reagan's proposals to convert additional kinds of federal aid into block grants. The CDBG experience reviewed in this book describes the problems faced by communities shifting from the rather rigid categorical grant system to more flexible block grants. Five case studies prepared by field associates constitute the core of the book. In the chapters preceding and following the case studies, Paul R. Dommel explains the background of the block grant program, summarizes its effects on local decisionmaking in community development, explains the political factors that make decentralization "a moving target," and speculates about the program's future. He combines the findings of the case studies with those of the Brookings field research project to show that although decentralized decisionmaking did indeed foster local diversity, many communities faced procedural and substantive difficulties in implementing the CDBG program.

Dommel, a senior fellow in the Brookings Governmental Studies program, joined the research team as the field associate for Worcester,

Massachusetts, and as the analyst of the CDBG formula. In 1977, he became director of the Brookings CDBG project. The case studies were written by field associates Victor E. Bach, formerly of the Lyndon B. Johnson School of Public Affairs, University of Texas, and now of the New School for Social Research; Leon L. Haley of the Graduate School of Public and International Affairs, University of Pittsburgh; John S. Hall of the Center for Public Affairs, Arizona State University; John S. Jackson III of the Graduate School, Southern Illinois University; and Leonard Rubinowitz of Northwestern University.

For reviewing and commenting on the case studies, the authors thank Roger Ahlbrandt of the University of Pittsburgh, David Berman of Arizona State University, Andrea Rozran of the Woodstock Institute, William L. Shade of the University of Scranton, and Lawrence D. Spencer of the Houston Council on Human Relations. They are also grateful to Frederick J. Eggers, John L. Gardner, and Harriet Newburger of the Department of Housing and Urban Development for their assistance in incorporating the case studies into the research project; to James L. Sundquist, director of the Governmental Studies program when this book was planned; and to his successor Martha Derthick, whose guidance and patience contributed much to its completion.

Tadd Fisher edited the manuscript. It was typed by Cynthia Cocke and Thomas T. Somuah; the index was prepared by Diana Regenthal.

The views expressed in this book are those of the authors and should not be ascribed to the Department of Housing and Urban Development or to the trustees, officers, or other staff members of the Brookings Institution.

BRUCE K. MAC LAURY
President

Washington, D.C.
January 1982

Contents

1. Introduction 1
Methodological Issues *5*
The Field Network Evaluation Study *7*

2. Legislating and Implementing a Block Grant 13
The Coming of the New Federalism *13*
Development of the Urban Block Grant *17*
Legislative Issues *25*
Targeting *34*
Implementation: A Hands-Off Policy *43*
Conclusion *45*

3. Phoenix, Arizona *John Stuart Hall* 47
Patterns of Growth *48*
Forging a Municipal Government *54*
Poverty in the Midst of Sun Belt Affluence *56*
Slow Acceptance of Federal Aid *59*
The Decision Process: Year One *62*
Year Two *71*
Focusing on Objectives *72*
Accent on Housing *74*
Wider Distribution of Benefits *77*
Conclusion *79*

4. Houston, Texas *Victor E. Bach* 84
The City's Profile *84*
The First Year of CDBG Planning *91*
The Second Year of the Block Grant *104*
Grant Allocations *106*
CDBG Program Shortcomings and Successes *111*
The Future *115*

5. Chicago, Illinois *Leonard Rubinowitz* 120
The People and Their Prospects *120*
Applying for the Block Grant: The First Year *129*

Year Two *146*
Plans, Allocations, and Benefits *149*
What Difference Has the CDBG Made? *158*
The Third Year and Beyond *161*

6. Allegheny County, Pennsylvania *Leon L. Haley* 166
The County's Vital Statistics *166*
Long Experience in Development Activities *169*
County-Municipality Cooperation in Getting Grants *172*
First-Year Planning *174*
Second-Year Planning *185*
Balancing Program Needs *188*
Social Targeting *191*
Overall Effects of the Block Grant *193*
The Future *194*

7. Carbondale, Illinois *John S. Jackson III* 195
A Small but Cosmopolitan City *195*
Beginning the Program *203*
Allocating CDBG Funds *212*
Social Targeting *218*
Conclusion *220*

8. The Process and Its Outcomes 223
The Changing Federal Role *223*
Local Decision Processes *225*
Continuity and Change *232*
Conclusion *240*

9. Decentralization: A Moving Target 243
Social Targeting *243*
Geographic Targeting *249*
The Effect of Targeting Policies *250*
Formula Changes *253*
Program Implementation *255*
The Effects of Changing Administrations *259*
The Effects of Fiscal Stringency *263*

Index 265

Tables

1-1. Key Characteristics of the Five Case Jurisdictions 10
2-1. Growth of Federal Aid, 1959–80 14
3-1. Allocation of the Community Development Block Grant in Phoenix, by Functional Program 76

7-1. Model Cities Activities Continued in Carbondale, Illinois, under the Block Grant 214
7-2. New Social Services in Carbondale, Illinois, under the Block Grant 215
7-3. Capital Projects in Carbondale, Illinois, Continued from Categorical Programs 216
7-4. Capital Projects Started in Carbondale, Illinois, under the Block Grant 217

CHAPTER ONE

Introduction

FEDERAL AID has evolved as a complex system of cooperation and sharing of functional responsibilities among the federal, state, and local levels of government. But within this cooperative framework, the federal government's imposition of policy and administrative requirements creates tension. State and local governments prefer discretion over the use of federal aid. As the amount and variety of federal grants have increased, so have the possibilities for tension within the intergovernmental system.

Between 1960 and 1980 the amount of federal aid increased from $7 billion to over $90 billion a year, and the number of assistance programs, mostly small, narrow-purpose grants, grew from approximately 160 in 1961 to more than 500 in 1980. With this growth has also come the imposition of many federal mandates requiring state and local officials to comply with various statutes and directives in such areas as environmental safeguards, affirmative action, and wage standards.[1]

As the grant system grew in size and complexity and became more regulated, governors, mayors, city managers, county executives, and organizations representing them pressed the federal government for major changes. They have urged the government to reduce the number of grants and to provide them in a way that will give state and local officials greater discretion in spending the money. They have further sought federal assumption of responsibility for certain functions, most notably welfare and medicaid.

The New Federalism of the Nixon administration was a response to these pressures. In some areas of governmental activity the Nixon admin-

1. For an analysis of mandates, see Catherine Lovell and others, *Federal and State Mandating on Local Governments: An Exploration of Issues and Impacts* (Graduate School of Administration, University of California at Riverside, 1979). For a view on the local impact of mandates, see Edward I. Koch, "The Mandate Millstone," *The Public Interest,* no. 61 (Fall 1980), pp. 42–57.

istration designed, or was willing to accept, centralization of programs.[2] Nixon's proposed family assistance program, which did not pass, would largely have federalized the income support function. The supplemental security income program, enacted in 1972 to provide federally guaranteed minimum incomes to the elderly poor, the blind, and the disabled, was a major centralizing measure. Environmental policy was another area where the federal role grew significantly during the Nixon administration. But the dominant direction of the New Federalism was decentralization. A new set of grant-in-aid programs was designed to shift authority and initiative toward the lower levels of government and to distribute funds through automatic formulas rather than allow federal officials to decide which projects or communities would receive aid.

The centerpiece of the New Federalism was general revenue sharing, enacted in 1972 to provide aid to state and local governments with virtually no strings attached to its use. Another important part was a set of proposals to consolidate a variety of narrow-purpose programs into block grants covering broad functional areas and giving local officials more discretion over the kinds of activities to be funded. Two block grants were established: one for training under the Comprehensive Employment and Training Act in 1973 and the community development block grant (CDBG) under the Housing and Community Development Act of 1974. In 1980 general revenue sharing and broad-purpose grants accounted for about one-fifth of the $91.5 billion in federal aid.

Besides shifting power downward in the federal system, the Nixon administration initiatives were supposed to shift power in the recipient governments from "specialists" to "generalists." Under some categorical programs, such as urban renewal, specialist agencies had been created in many communities. Frequently they were more responsive to the policy directions of their federal counterparts than to local elected officials. The New Federalism envisioned shifting more control and initiative to local chief executives and legislators who were generalists in the sense that they were either elected by the general population or served directly at the pleasure of those who were.[3] Program choices and the form and distribu-

2. For a discussion of the philosophic underpinnings of the New Federalism, see A. James Reichley, *Conservatives in an Age of Change: The Nixon and Ford Administrations* (Brookings Institution, 1981), pp. 165–68.

3. The term "generalist" has two related connotations. In the sense of constituencies, generalist officials are accountable to the local constituency as a whole. But the term also relates to functional considerations; that is, generalists have no vested interest in any specialized functional area, such as housing, social services, and so

tion of program benefits were to be determined by local actors operating in diverse local arenas, free from significant federal intervention or constraint. The local process of decisionmaking was expected to change, and quite possibly the decisions themselves, on the assumption that federal constraints had "distorted" local needs and preferences. With more local discretion in the use of aid funds and less specialist dominance, the money might be spent on different types of activities.

In this book five case studies are used to examine the transition to more local discretion under the CDBG, which consolidated several separate discretionary grant programs of the Department of Housing and Urban Development (HUD) into a single program that distributes grants on a formula basis to large cities and populous counties and provides discretionary grants to small communities. The programs consolidated were urban renewal, the neighborhood development program, model cities, water and sewer projects, neighborhood facilities, open spaces, and loans for public facilities.[4] These programs are collectively referred to through-

---

forth, but deal with the broad range of considerations that constitute general-purpose government.

4. The *urban renewal* program was established under title 1 of the Housing Act of 1949 and emphasized slum clearance and new construction. The Housing Act of 1954 modified the law to encourage rehabilitation and required a "Workable Program for Community Improvement," which among other things called for comprehensive planning and citizen participation. Restoring basically sound neighborhoods, installing adequate public facilities, improving public institutions, revitalizing central business districts, and providing proper sites for industrial plants were among the kinds of projects included in urban renewal.

The *neighborhood development* program, authorized by the Housing and Urban Development Act of 1968, replaced the conventional urban renewal program. It provided annual financing for specified renewal activities, unlike the reserve funding system of urban renewal in which all the money was set aside at the time the renewal application was approved. The original program frequently tied up large amounts of unspent funds, thereby limiting the number of new projects that could be approved and often resulting in project amendments as costs increased.

Title 1 of the Demonstration Cities and Metropolitan Development Act of 1966 was designed to coordinate and supplement federal grant programs in areas designated as *model cities.* It granted significant discretion to recipient localities and their residents in deciding how to spend the model cities funds to meet social, economic, and physical needs.

Section 702 of the Housing and Urban Development Act of 1965 allowed grants, usually not to exceed 50 percent of the development costs, to finance public *water and sewer facilities,* provided that any waste carried is adequately treated before it enters a public waterway. Section 703 of the act authorized grants for *neighborhood facilities* needed to carry out health, recreational, social, or similar community service programs.

Title 7 of the Housing Act of 1961 provided 50 percent matching grants to state out the book as categorical grants, although the model cities program gave much greater flexibility to local officials on activities to be funded than was the case with the other programs merged into the block grant. The CDBG legislation also provided for ending housing rehabilitation loans under the section 312 program, which was to end a year after the CDBG began but was extended and expanded in later legislation.[5] The block grant legislation authorized $2.5 billion in the first year and $2.95 billion in the second and third years to fund a wide variety of community development activities. The emphasis was on physical development projects, but some social service spending was permitted.[6] In 1977 the program was extended an additional three years and the authorization of funding was increased by stages until it was nearly $4 billion in the sixth year. A second three-year extension was enacted in 1980 but with only a slight increase in authorized funding. The level was reduced substantially in 1981 as part of President Reagan's domestic policy and budget changes.

The central questions of the case studies are how local governments responded to the block grant in establishing or altering their decision

---

and local governments to acquire *open space* or to develop recreation, conservation, and scenic areas in urban areas.

Public facilities loans were initiated under title 2 of the Housing Amendments of 1955, which authorized the federal government to purchase securities and obligations of, or make loans to, municipalities for financing public works or transportation facilities.

5. The section 312 program, passed in 1964 as part of the National Housing Act, provides loans to owners or tenants for rehabilitating homes or business properties in urban renewal or code enforcement areas. The original interest rate of 3 percent was changed in 1978 to allow variable rates, depending on income.

6. Section 105 of the Housing and Community Development Act of 1974 listed thirteen categories of eligible activities that could be funded with CDBG money. Generally, any activity eligible under the categorical grants, as well as some new ones, could be funded with the block grant. The only limitation was set on services provided under model cities; for the most part the legislation permitted only those services that supported concentrated physical development activities. The categories specified in the legislation appeared to cover almost any physical development activity a community might wish to carry out—for example: "the acquisition, construction, reconstruction, or installation of public works, facilities, and site or other improvements—including neighborhood facilities, senior centers, historic properties, utilities, streets, street lights, water and sewer facilities, foundations and platforms for air rights sites, pedestrian malls and walkways, and parks, playgrounds, and recreation facilities, flood and drainage facilities in cases where assistance for such facilities under other Federal laws or programs is determined to be unavailable, and parking facilities, solid waste disposal facilities, and fire protection services and facilities which are located in or which serve designated community development areas." In amendments enacted in 1977, two additional categories were added to promote economic development activities.

processes and what changes, if any, were made in local program priorities and funding choices with the more flexible block grant. Our aim is to tell what happened during the transition years—the first two years—of the CDBG program, rather than to evaluate the early performance of the program. As explained in the next chapter, it is difficult to distill clearly the primary intent of the program from among the ambiguous and sometimes conflicting goals embodied in the CDBG legislation (such conflicts are a common problem in American public policy). As discussed in chapter 9, the local decisions in the early years of the CDBG may indicate how local political and programmatic decisions will evolve under the Reagan administration's renewed emphasis on local discretion over federal funds.

As an instrument of intergovernmental aid, the CDBG program lies between the narrowly focused, more federally controlled categorical grant and the no-strings-attached approach of general revenue sharing. The CDBG program does not simply occupy a fixed midpoint between two extremes, however; it spans a policy range within which shifts may occur, reflecting the current balance of national and local program preferences and power. The local preferences are expressed by communities in their grant applications, which indicate both the scope of local problems and the outcomes of the local bargaining process. The national preferences are those of federal officials seeking to interpret the national goals of the legislation and thus to establish the policy framework to guide local decisions on how to spend the money.

As urban aid policy, we consider the CDBG a lineal descendant of federal programs to revitalize cities—urban renewal, model cities, and the neighborhood development program, grants that evolved in such a way as to broaden steadily the uses to which federal aid could be put. Thus the CDBG may be interpreted as a logical culmination of earlier trends rather than as a sharp new departure. But important discontinuities also appeared as development strategies shifted from the delineated project area approach of the earlier grants to a program with potentially communitywide application. The transition from the individual urban grants to the more flexible block grant had dimensions of both continuity and change.

Methodological Issues

Federal programs designed for decentralization pose a number of problems for the researcher attempting to draw conclusions about the national experience as a whole. The problems posed by the diversity implicit in decentralized decisionmaking are increased if the research focuses—as this study does—on the decision process. It is easier to tell how much money has been spent on, say, housing rehabilitation than to judge the relative roles and influence of generalist and specialist officials on program decisions.

Survey approaches using uniform information-gathering instruments applied to a large sample of local governments have the potential advantage of yielding statistically significant and therefore generalizable findings at the national scale. Large samples also have significant disadvantages, however, because the resultant data do not readily reflect the procedural and substantive diversity likely to be found in a decentralized program; that is, large-sample data are likely to be valid indicators of program realities in the aggregate but unrepresentative of particular communities. Moreover, because of the premium placed on uniformity the analytic framework can be adjusted only with great difficulty to accommodate new, potentially significant factors that emerge after the research has gotten under way. Most important, survey instruments and other uniform data-gathering techniques are limited, if not inappropriate, means for characterizing the complex forces that underlie local political behavior and shape decisionmaking.

In contrast, the case study approach has the advantage of providing an in-depth account of a program and its complex workings at the local level. Furthermore, it is sufficiently flexible to permit appropriate shifts in the research framework to accommodate newly uncovered factors and diverse configurations of events and actors in any given locale. But within the context of a national grant program that generates activity across a large number of communities, the problem of small numbers is a major limitation of the case study. Because of the small sample size of any case approach, the findings have very limited generalizability and are vulnerable to criticism concerning the idiosyncratic nature of the chosen site or sample and the inability to capture the national program experience.

The difficulty of steering a reasonable methodological course between the large sample and the case study while seeking credible conclusions about a nationwide yet decentralized program has been recognized for some time.[7] Both community action and model cities were federal programs that presumed much flexibility in local decisionmaking, and the processes of these programs were most effectively studied in the com-

7. For a discussion of these methodological issues, see Robert W. Weiss, "Alternative Approaches in the Study of Complex Situations," *Hainou Organization,* vol. 25 (Fall 1966), pp. 207–20.

parative case study mode, but at the sacrifice of more systematic monitoring of program outcomes or national trends.[8] Most other studies of the effects of federal programs on local processes have been of single communities and have focused on the dynamics of program functioning in a way that suggests a generalizable model but leaves unclear the universe of program contexts to which it might be applicable.[9] For example, in their study of the process for deciding the location of public housing projects in Chicago, Meyerson and Banfield observed:

> The reader should be cautioned . . . against inferring that the political history of public housing in other cities has been identical with that of Chicago. Generally speaking, the interests which came in conflict in other cities were very much like those which came in conflict in Chicago. The rhetoric of the conflict was also very much the same. But there were nevertheless differences of great importance from city to city [San Francisco is briefly contrasted with Chicago]. . . . How far, then, can the facts of the Chicago case be taken as descriptive of the situation in other cities? The best answer to such a question is probably that the Chicago experiences should sensitize the reader to certain influences and relationships which are likely to be found, although not exactly in the same form, in most other cities. In short, acquaintance with what happened in Chicago may give the student of the public housing issue some indication of what to look for in other cities.[10]

In that sense every case study is a very tentative exploration of a universe the single case itself cannot fully describe. Nor can it comprehend its own "position" in the universe—the degree of similarity or difference with other places.

The Field Network Evaluation Study

The field network evaluation study (FNES) method, developed at the Brookings Institution in the 1970s to study grant-in-aid programs is an

8. For a discussion of the community action program, see Peter Marris and Martin Rein, *Dilemmas of Social Reform* (Atherton, 1969). For the model cities program, see U.S. Department of Housing and Urban Development, *The Model Cities Program: A Comparative Analysis of the Planning Process in Eleven Cities* (U.S. Department of Housing and Urban Development, 1970); and Lawrence D. Brown, "Condition of Federal Urban Policy: Organizational Politics in Three Model Cities" (Ph.D. dissertation, Harvard University, 1973).

9. See Langley C. Keyes, *The Rehabilitation Planning Game* (MIT Press, 1969); Martin Meyerson and Edward Banfield, *Politics, Planning and the Public Interest* (Free Press, 1955); Robert Dahl, *Who Governs?* (Yale University Press, 1961); Jeffrey Pressman and Aaron Wildavsky, *Implementation* (University of California Press, 1973); Martha Derthick, *New Towns In-Town* (Urban Institute, 1972); and Fred Powledge, *Model City* (Simon and Schuster, 1970).

10. Meyerson and Banfield, *Politics, Planning and the Public Interest,* p. 12.

attempt to respond to these methodological dilemmas.[11] An FNES uses a middle-range sample—usually forty to sixty jurisdictions—making it possible to gauge dominant national trends while maintaining the ability to differentiate and compare diverse jurisdictions. The field research approach relies on a national network of experienced researchers in the social sciences who apply a common analytical framework over time to the study of an agreed upon set of procedural and programmatic issues in their localities or in nearby communities with which they are familiar. A central analytical staff then aggregates the data and narrative information from the field reports to determine national patterns and trends. The method provides a number of advantages in coming to understand the effects of federal programs on recipient communities, but it is not a substitute for the case study as a way of comprehending local effects in detail. While the responses of field associates are reasonably detailed, the field analysis is based on a series of specific questions that limit the range and detail of the responses. The responses must then be further simplified by the central staff analysts to be aggregated with others. For example, field reports and subsequent analyses are useful in determining the relative influence of various actors in decisions. They are less helpful in fully understanding how a program works in specific localities to produce those relationships and how in turn these relationships influence specific pro-

11. The CDBG research, which is the basis for this study of the transitional years of the CDBG program, is one of three FNES projects carried out at Brookings. The first, initiated in 1972 and supported by the Ford Foundation, was a five-year study of the general revenue sharing program enacted that year. Two revenue sharing volumes have appeared to date: Richard P. Nathan, Allen D. Manvel, and Susannah E. Calkins, *Monitoring Revenue Sharing* (Brookings Institution, 1975); and Richard P. Nathan, Charles F. Adams, Jr., and Associates, *Revenue Sharing: The Second Round* (Brookings Institution, 1977). A third volume dealing with revenue sharing and the broader context of federal grants is in preparation. The CDBG study was begun in 1975 under contract with HUD. Three reports have been published: Richard P. Nathan and others, *Block Grants for Community Development* (HUD, January 1977); Paul R. Dommel and others, *Decentralizing Community Development* (HUD, June 1978); and Paul R. Dommel and others, *Targeting Community Development* (HUD, January 1980). A fourth and final report, "Implementing Community Development," is expected to be published in 1982. The third FNES project, initiated in 1977 under contract with the National Commission on Employment Policy to study the public service employment program, resulted in three reports: Richard P. Nathan and others, *Monitoring the Public Service Employment Program* (NCMP, March 1978); Richard P. Nathan and others, *Monitoring the Public Service Employment Program: The Second Round* (NCMP, March 1979); and Richard P. Nathan and others, *Public Service Employment: A Field Evaluation* (Brookings Institution, 1981).

gram decisions. The FNES method is not intended to produce this level of detail.

In 1975, soon after the CDBG legislation was enacted, a central staff at the Brookings Institution in collaboration with field associates in sixty-one jurisdictions began to study the program. This research extended for six years, focusing on HUD-local relations, the local decisionmaking process, program choices, and the distribution of program benefits.[12]

The case studies in this book supplement the first two years of the field research and are integrated into the broader FNES findings to achieve the advantages of both approaches—to obtain the depth and explanatory power of the case approach (chapters 3–7) while maintaining sight of the broader context of the field study findings (chapter 8).

The authors of the case studies were members of the Brookings field research network and closely followed and reported on the CDBG program in their jurisdictions from the inception of the study in 1975. The case studies are of Chicago, Phoenix, Houston, Allegheny County (Pennsylvania), and Carbondale (Illinois). The jurisdictions were selected to provide a diverse range of program settings (see table 1-1).

Houston and Phoenix share the strongest surface similarities among the five jurisdictions. Both are growth cities conforming to the sun belt stereotype. The three northern jurisdictions—Carbondale, Chicago, and Allegheny County—are characterized by stable-to-declining populations and economic bases, as well as by increasing fiscal pressures.

Regional differences among the five jurisdictions are further emphasized in that the three northern jurisdictions were all intensive and experienced users of the federal programs consolidated into the block grant. Carbondale, a city of 27,000 residents, was exceptional among jurisdictions of this size in having been extensively involved in both model cities and urban renewal programs. Since Carbondale's population was too small to qualify the city as an entitlement jurisdiction under the CDBG program, Carbondale is the only jurisdiction among the five that faced a drastic loss of funds once the three-year hold-harmless period established to protect communities against the sudden loss of funds expired (see chapter 7).[13] Houston and Phoenix are at the lower end of the experience

12. The published reports of this research are cited in note 11.

13. The hold-harmless provisions of the CDBG law specify that for the first three years of the program, communities would receive the same amount as their average grants between the years 1968–72. In the fourth year entitlement cities would be phased down by one-third of the differences between the formula and hold-

Table 1-1. *Key Characteristics of the Five Case Jurisdictions*

Item	*Houston*	*Phoenix*	*Chicago*	*Carbondale*	*Allegheny County*
Type of jurisdiction	Central city	Central city	Central city	Nonmetropolitan	Urban county
Population in 1975	1.3 million	664,000	3.1 million	27,000	897,000
Form of government	Strong mayor, at-large council	City manager, at-large council	Strong mayor, aldermanic, ward-based council	City manager, at-large council	At-large commission, combined executive-legislative
Urban conditions index[a]	40	21	255	122	121
Level of experience under HUD categorical grants[b]	Moderate	Low	Moderate	High	High
Urban renewal	No	Yes (small)	Yes	Yes	Yes
Model cities	Yes	No	Yes	Yes	Yes

a. The mean urban conditions index for the monitoring sample was 100. Higher values are associated with higher levels of local distress. The urban conditions index is computed as follows:

$$\frac{\left(\frac{\text{Percent poverty}}{\text{Mean percent poverty}}\right)\left(\frac{\text{Percent pre-1940 housing}}{\text{Mean percent pre-1940 housing}}\right)}{\left(\frac{100 + \text{percent population change}}{100 + \text{median percent population change}}\right)}$$

For a full discussion of this index see Paul R. Dommel and others, *Decentralizing Community Development* (U.S. Department of Housing and Urban Development, June 1978), chap. 2.

b. Based on the ratio of each recipient unit of its per capita amount received under the previous programs to the national per capita mean. "High" is over 150 percent of the national mean of $17.63 per capita (annual average 1968–72); "moderate" is 50–150 percent of this amount; and "low" is 50 percent or less.

scale. Houston had only model cities experience and Phoenix only an embryonic neighborhood development project before the advent of the block grant.

Politically and institutionally, the sample jurisdictions also show important differences. Despite other regional similarities, the two southern cities have strikingly different institutional and political settings. Phoenix has a reform government (the weak mayor-council-manager model), and local politics is dominated by an economic elite. City management has achieved a reputation for bureaucratic professionalism, and citizen activity in local public affairs is low. Houston, however, has a strong mayor form of government, and a large role is played by liberal-conservative and racial or ethnic cleavages; there are highly politicized, well-organized minority communities.

Politically, Chicago would stand out in any sample. Despite a nonpartisan, aldermanic form of government, it has been dominated by one of the most potent party machines in the country, the Cook County Democrats. At the inception of the CDBG Mayor Richard J. Daley was the chief administrative officer of the city as well as the head of the Cook County machine. By contrast, Carbondale is a university town that has what the author of chapter 7 describes as a "public regarding" civic culture with a strong and active liberal enclave. Allegheny County is the only urban county among the five cases and thus has unusual institutional features as the grant recipient for a broad range of suburban municipalities and townships in the Pittsburgh metropolitan area.

To facilitate comparing the case studies and to integrate them with the national FNES findings, the cases were developed within a common framework.

1. *Background.* Each author presents a general profile of his jurisdiction that covers socioeconomic characteristics, governmental structure, and the extent of experience with the categorical programs.

2. *Decision process.* Because of the decentralizing objective of the block grant, the case studies give considerable attention to the establishment of the local decisionmaking process and how the process operated.

---

harmless amounts; in the fifth year, by another one-third reduction; and in the sixth year a city would receive its formula amount. If not an entitlement jurisdiction, the community in the sixth year would be eligible for only a HUD discretionary grant. When the program began, 751 nonentitlement communities were eligible for hold-harmless funds, averaging about $590,000 per community; Carbondale's hold-harmless amount in the first year was nearly $3 million.

Here, the reader should be alert to how the five communities with their great diversity in size, experience, and political culture came to deal with issues found in all communities—the role of the executive and legislature and what to do about citizen participation.

3. *Plans, allocations, and benefits.* The immediate product of the decision process is the application for the block grant funds. It is in the application that one first detects a local development strategy, or the lack of one, and begins to see the relationship between the decisionmaking process and the specific program choices. In the applications of the transitional years one also sees the legacy of the categorical programs and the constraints that past program experience put on the range of choices, even with the much greater flexibility of the block grant. The authors also discuss the distribution of program benefits among income groups.

4. *Conclusion.* What's different under CDBG? The authors analyze this question in terms of both process and programs, summarizing their views about how decentralization worked at the local level in the transitional years and taking a look at what lay ahead in their communities as both local and federal officials gained more experience.

CHAPTER TWO

Legislating and Implementing a Block Grant

This bill climaxes years of efforts to replace the rigid programs of the past with a more flexible approach by sweeping away seven categorical grant programs such as urban renewal and model cities and replacing them with a single "block grant" program for community development. . . . [T]his bill will help to return power from the banks of the Potomac to people in their own communities. Decisions will be made at the local level. Action will come at the local level. And responsibility for results will be placed squarely where it belongs—at the local level.

—President Gerald R. Ford, August 22, 1974

THE STATEMENTS ABOVE, made by President Ford when he signed the Housing and Community Development Act of 1974 capsulized two major complaints.[1] The first statement focused on the growing disenchantment with the ability of the federal government to contribute to the solution of urban problems through multiple, discrete, and narrowly focused grants that were expanding in both number and complexity. The second was aimed at the federal aid system in general and the growing complaint that the increase in federal aid dollars and the number of programs had brought the federal government into more and more decisions that had previously been left to state and local officials. The evolution of the federal aid system in the 1960s and 1970s provides an important backdrop to the decentralization of decisionmaking in community development.

The Coming of the New Federalism

In the post–World War II period the most notable feature of federal grants to state and local governments was their growth in volume.[2] Along

1. "Statement on the Housing and Community Development Act of 1974, August 22, 1974," *Public Papers of the Presidents: Gerald R. Ford, 1974* (Government Printing Office, 1975), pp. 43, 44. (Hereinafter, *Public Papers.*)

2. By the end of the 1970s the rate of growth began to slow as the outlays for

Table 2-1. *Growth of Federal Aid, 1959–80*

Period	*Dollar growth (billions)*	*Percent of state and local expenditures at end of period*
1959–60	4,767	14.7
1960–70	16,994	19.4
1965–70	13,110	
1970–80[a]	64,931	25.3
1972–76	35,079	
1977–80[a]	20,731	

Source: Derived from *Special Analyses: Budget of the United States Government, Fiscal Year 1981,* table H-7, p. 254.
a. Estimate.

with this dollar growth came an increase in the relative importance of such aid to state and local governments. In 1950 federal grants represented 10.4 percent of state and local expenditures; by 1980 the proportion had risen to an estimated 26.3 percent. The greatest increases have come since 1965, when aid totaled $10.9 billion. Between 1965 and 1970, as the Great Society programs of Lyndon B. Johnson went into operation, aid increased by more than $13 billion (table 2-1), largely in the form of categorical grants with an urban emphasis. In 1970–76 during the Nixon-Ford administrations, general revenue sharing, greatly expanded environmental protection aid, and some antirecession programs went into effect, along with large increases in medicaid costs. In 1977–80 the antirecession programs were significantly expanded; this had the important effect of raising the amount of federal aid going directly to local governments, particularly distressed cities.

The years 1965–70 were important in the evolution of federal grants-in-aid, for besides being a time of great expansion in federal assistance, this was also a time of rising discontent with the aid system. During the 1960s the number of individual grant programs rose from 161 to about

major countercyclical aid programs began to drop and as efforts were made to reduce the budget deficit. As a result, federal aid became a shrinking part of the national budget after 1978. Between 1950 and 1978 federal grants increased from 5.3 percent to 17.3 percent of the total budget and from 8.8 to 22.9 percent of the domestic portion of the budget. In 1980 these proportions declined to 15.8 percent of the total budget and 21.1 percent of domestic spending. In proposing changes in the 1982 budget, President Reagan contemplated reversing the pattern of growth by reducing federal aid substantially.

400.[3] (By 1980 there were some 500 grants, although about 420 of these accounted for only 10 percent of all grant funds.)[4] Alone, this increase may not have been disturbing, but it was associated with increased fragmentation and overlapping of the programs themselves that frequently required local officials to negotiate with several bureaucracies for a single project. Thus many state and local officials began to complain about the lack of coordination among federal agencies administering similar programs, the red tape involved in getting project proposals approved, and the insensitivity of federal bureaucrats and of rigidly conceived programs to the diversity of local conditions. The growing array of programs and the increased complexity of the application requirements were particularly troublesome for small or inexperienced communities lacking the expertise to navigate the grants maze. This gave rise to a new public figure, the grantsman, typically an in-house expert at an agency or a hired consultant who was expert in comprehending program requirements and completing the necessary applications. Valued by his employers for his skill in raising money, he was deplored by others as a symbol of the growing pathology of public management. The cumulative result of these diverse complaints was a demand to simplify the system and devolve decisionmaking authority "from the banks of the Potomac" to the state and local levels.

Another source of increasing tension in the federal aid system concerned citizen participation in decisionmaking. The federal government has required citizen participation in various programs since the 1930s, when farmers were brought into decisionmaking about crop allotments.[5] During the late 1960s the primary beneficiaries of this participation came to be the lower-income groups living in neighborhoods affected by new federal programs, a development that made many local officials unhappy. They believed that the federal government was sponsoring a threatening rearrangement of local power relations.

Paralleling the growth in grants and the accompanying expressions of discontent was a growing interest in providing fiscal relief for state and

3. Advisory Commission on Intergovernmental Relations, *Urban America and the Federal System* (GPO, October 1969), p. 15.

4. Advisory Commission on Intergovernmental Relations, *In Brief, The Federal Role in the Federal System: The Dynamics of Growth* (GPO, December 1980), pp. 4, 29.

5. For a history of citizen participation, see Advisory Commission on Intergovernmental Relations, *Citizen Participation in the American Federal System* (GPO, 1980).

local governments in the form of revenue sharing, with no strings, or very few, attached to the use of the money. The idea of revenue sharing had been around for a number of years but gained new visibility in 1964, when Walter W. Heller, chairman of President Johnson's Council of Economic Advisers, endorsed it as a means of plowing back into the economic system some revenue surpluses expected by the federal government from the economic stimulus of a major tax cut. President Johnson initially appeared to endorse the idea but ultimately abandoned the proposal when it ran into opposition from bureaucratic, labor, and congressional sources. Although the federal government continued to rely primarily on the narrow-purpose, categorical approach to federal aid during the 1960s, President Johnson made some gestures toward grant simplification. In 1966 he proposed and Congress adopted the consolidation of eighteen separate health programs in the Partnership for Health Act. (It should be noted, however, that this same proposal had been made eleven years earlier by a federal commission headed by Meyer Kestnbaum, established in 1953 to find a means of delineating federal and state responsibilities.)[6] The model cities program, likewise enacted in 1966, represented another recognition of the need to make federal aid more flexible. The model cities program provided broad grants to selected cities so as to give flexibility to local program designers to fund specific activities in impoverished areas, subject to federal approval.

Although revenue sharing proposals were abandoned by the Johnson administration, the idea did not die; along with block grant proposals, revenue sharing was put forth by congressional Republicans in the late 1960s as a means to reduce federal controls in intergovernmental aid. Block grants are funds given in a general functional area, such as education or manpower training, leaving the choice of specific activities and projects to state or local officials. The Republican position on grant reform was stated clearly in 1967 by Congressman Melvin R. Laird, chairman of the House Republican Conference, who said that Republican members would "continue to press vigorously for early enactment of a general revenue-sharing measure to replace the existing grant-in-aid programs. If the Democratic Members of this body fail to see the wisdom of our proposal, however, we will advocate block grants in place of specifically tied grant-in-aid funds."[7] Congressional Republicans had some

6. See U.S. Commission on Intergovernmental Relations, *A Report to the President for Transmittal to the Congress* (GPO, 1955).

7. *Congressional Record,* daily ed. (February 15, 1967), pp. 3450–51.

successes in their block grant strategy during Johnson's last two years in office. In 1967 House Republicans, joined by southern Democrats, succeeded through floor votes in converting administration proposals for categorical grants to local governments for law enforcement and juvenile delinquency programs into block grants to state governments, the Safe Streets and Crime Control Act, and the Juvenile Delinquency Prevention and Control Act. The Senate accepted the block grant approach when it approved the legislation the following year. But the major push for more decentralized decisionmaking through revenue sharing and additional block grants came following the election in 1968 of Richard M. Nixon, who altered the politics of decentralization and grant reform by giving strong presidential support to the new types of aid.

Development of the Urban Block Grant

On August 9, 1969, in a nationwide television broadcast President Nixon stated: "After a third of a century of power flowing from the people and the States to Washington it is time for a New Federalism in which power, funds, and responsibility will flow from Washington to the States and to the people."[8] Nixon's New Federalism proposed to shift the emphasis of intergovernmental aid policy from eliciting local compliance to encouraging local discretion.

The centerpiece of Nixon's New Federalism was revenue sharing, a plan to distribute a portion of the federal income tax to about 39,000 state and local governments with no strings attached.[9] The New Federalism got off to a slow start, however. The revenue sharing plan initially foundered on congressional opposition, particularly that of Chairman Wilbur D. Mills of the House Ways and Means Committee, who objected to distributing federal revenues without federal controls. It also aroused objections from some congressional liberals who feared that revenue sharing would be financed by taking funds from some of the older categorical

8. "Address to the Nation on Domestic Programs, August 8, 1969," *Public Papers: Richard M. Nixon, 1969* (GPO, 1971), p. 638.

9. For a history of general revenue sharing, see Paul R. Dommel, *The Politics of Revenue Sharing* (Indiana University, 1974); Richard P. Nathan and others, *Monitoring Revenue Sharing* (Brookings Institution, 1975), app. C; and Richard E. Thompson, *Revenue Sharing: A New Era in Federalism* (Washington, D.C.: Revenue Sharing Advisory Service, 1973).

programs they supported. The proposal died in Congress without a hearing.

In 1971 the Nixon administration reworked its revenue sharing plan into a $16 billion package made up of a $5 billion general revenue sharing program and $11 billion for six special revenue sharing programs. The latter—urban development, rural development, education, transportation, job training, and law enforcement—were to be funded by consolidating $10 billion from existing grants in these areas and adding $1 billion in new federal money. In keeping with the goal of increasing local discretion, these special revenue sharing funds were to be distributed automatically by a formula to state and local governments without the need of prior federal approval of applications or plans. The Urban Community Development Revenue Sharing proposal of 1971 was part of this package, and though it failed to pass, it became the legislative precursor of the community development block grant (CDBG).

Despite their suspicions of general revenue sharing, congressional liberals reluctantly voted for it after repeated administration assurances that it would provide new funds rather than be used as a substitute for older programs. A well-organized coalition of state, city, and county officials also put strong pressure on lawmakers to go along with the revenue sharing plan, which was enacted in October 1972, just before the elections.

The special revenue sharing proposals were of even greater concern to many members of Congress. Unlike general revenue sharing, which was only a potential threat to established aid programs, special revenue sharing was a frank substitute for them. Special revenue sharing proposed to eliminate many federal policy controls, including the right to say yes or no to specific projects, and to provide grants for very broad purposes to state and local officials as entitlements, leaving altogether to them the decisions about what projects or activities would actually be funded. If local officials decided to continue a particular activity previously funded through a federal categorical grant, they could do so; if they wished to end a program or cut it back, they could do that also. The congressional supporters of programs marked for consolidation into the special revenue sharing grants feared that there would be cutbacks. Many also did not like either automatically distributing money without federal approval of how the money would be used or giving funds to communities, many of them well-off, that had never participated in the categorical grant programs. The special revenue sharing proposals were also suspect because they threatened to disrupt relationships of influence that had grown up over the years between congressional committees with jurisdiction over the programs, the federal and local bureaucracies administering them, and the local program beneficiaries. Of the six special revenue sharing proposals, only two were enacted, and those in greatly modified form. Manpower training and public employment programs were consolidated in 1973 into the Comprehensive Employment and Training Act. Urban development programs were consolidated in 1974 under the Housing and Community Development Act.

The urban development proposal of 1971 called for merging urban renewal, the neighborhood development program, model cities, water and sewer grants, and housing rehabilitation loans that together provided about $2 billion annually in federal assistance to communities. The administration later expanded the list of programs to be consolidated to include neighborhood facilities and open space grants, and public facility loans. Urban renewal, neighborhood development, and model cities together represented about 90 percent of the funds of the programs intended for consolidation (urban renewal and neighborhood development 65 percent and model cities 25 percent). Urban renewal and model cities also represented contrasting approaches to urban development and reflected the evolution of efforts to introduce more local discretion into urban assistance programs.

Urban Renewal

The urban renewal program, originally called urban redevelopment, was part of the Housing Act of 1949. Initially it emphasized slum clearance and new construction, but beginning with amendments in 1954, it provided as well for renewal and rehabilitation. At the beginning it had the support of businesses and construction unions because both benefited from the downtown revitalization and jobs generated by redevelopment. It was also supported by housing advocates who thought urban redevelopment would increase or improve the housing stock. And local officials liked it because it promised to enlarge the tax base and revitalize declining downtown areas. Very early, however, urban redevelopment drew criticism for destroying the dwellings of lower-income groups, often minorities, to make way for other kinds of projects that yielded them few or no benefits. Projects also started to lose support among local officials and business interests in some cities as development encountered prolonged delays and as citizen participation complicated the planning and development process. Although the urban renewal program began to shift toward revitalization of residential neighborhoods in the mid-1960s, it continued to experience local resistance; homeowners were frequently reluctant to spend savings or borrow funds to bring their property up to required building, health, and safety code standards that were often an integral part of the revitalization project.

An important issue associated with urban renewal concerned the locus of program control. In our view the degree of federal control over urban renewal is no more clear in retrospect than it was during the twenty-five-year active life of the program. The principal federal policy concerns were related to the mix of slum clearance and rehabilitation and to the conflict between developing housing for low-income groups and improving the tax base by developing upper-income housing and retail and commercial uses.[10] Federal policy on how much of a renewal project to allocate to lower-income housing or to tax base improvement was never so firmly and consistently established that the policies imposed rigorous constraints on local officials designing projects. The substance of a community's urban renewal program was guided more by local factors, such as the need to build local political support and the anticipated willingness of developers to buy and develop land, than by explicit federal directives.[11]

If the question of control shifts from project planning to implementation, however, the federal role appears to be greater. Detailed federal

10. For a general history of urban renewal, see Ashley A. Foard and Hilbert Fefferman, "Federal Urban Renewal Legislation," in James Q. Wilson, ed., *Urban Renewal: The Record and the Controversy* (MIT Press, 1966), p. 71; *Building the American City,* Report of the National Commission on Urban Problems (GPO, 1968), chap. 6; and *The Central City Problem and Urban Renewal Policy,* Study by the Congressional Research Service for the Subcommittee on Housing and Urban Affairs of the Senate Committee on Banking, Housing and Urban Affairs, 93 Cong. 1 sess. (GPO, 1973).

11. The patterns of influence and control could vary from place to place. Early case studies of Chicago, Boston, and New Haven—cities with forceful mayors who had great interest in renewal—indicated that local views dominated project planning. A case study of Newark, N.J., however, shows a major federal role in project planning. See Harold Kaplan, "Urban Renewal in Newark," in Wilson, *Urban Renewal;* Peter H. Rossi and Robert A. Dentler, *The Politics of Urban Renewal: The Chicago Findings* (Free Press, 1961); Walter McQuade, "Urban Renewal in Boston," in Wilson, *Urban Renewal;* and Robert A. Dahl, *Who Governs?* (Yale University Press, 1961).

standards were established for many actions such as land acquisition procedures, relocation of residents and businesses, site clearance, construction of site improvements and supporting facilities, and disposition of land. The urban renewal administrative process drew considerable criticism because it was so long and encumbered with red tape. A national commission referred to the "unconscionable" amount of time involved, generally five to ten years to complete a project, and in some cases more than fifteen years.[12] With such long time lapses, city demographics frequently changed, altering the prospects for certain kinds of development; development costs also changed, and prospective developers lost interest. A result in some cities was that the project proceeded through the land-clearance stage, but the planned development did not take place, frequently leaving large amounts of vacant land. In a study of urban renewal in San Francisco in 1973 Richard LeGates concluded that hardly anyone was really in charge, and that urban renewal projects were the products of an excruciatingly slow process of excessive scrutiny by a multitude of federal technical experts, each responsible for a narrow portion of the overall project.[13] LeGates judged that the Department of Housing and Urban Development (HUD) had overregulated matters of detail and underregulated matters of importance.

Nor is the degree of control of urban renewal by semiautonomous, "specialist" agencies clear in retrospect. The urban renewal program provided grants and loans to "local public agencies" that were authorized to undertake renewal projects; the statutes did not mandate, however, how such agencies must be structured. The structural form of the agencies and the powers given to them were determined by state law; the most important power was the right to take private property for a public purpose (including private reuse). In many cities these agencies were established as semiautonomous bodies with substantial authority for planning and executing a renewal project. Usually the mayor or city manager had the authority to appoint the head of the agency or some of the members of a governing board and thus presumably could influence decisions. In some cities the renewal agency was established as a regular department of the local government directly under the control of the mayor or manager.

12. *Building the American City,* p. 165.

13. Richard T. LeGates, "Can the Federal Welfare Bureaucracies Control Their Programs: The Case of HUD and Urban Renewal," *Urban Lawyer,* vol. 5 (Spring 1973), p. 260.

Mayors were often the prime movers and dominant figures in urban renewal programs, as case studies demonstrated.[14]

Yet the perception of specialist dominance became widespread, just as did the perception of federal control, and these perceptions, perhaps as much as the realities, influenced the philosophy, design, and implementation of the block grant.

In 1968 the neighborhood development program was initiated by Congress, providing an alternative approach to large-scale urban renewal. The objectives of the program were to speed up renewal activities and to give communities more flexibility in renewal planning and implementation. The neighborhood development program permitted communities to undertake various smaller-scale renewal activities in several areas simultaneously rather than to concentrate their efforts on a comprehensive, large-scale project. Communities could stage various activities, as needed, in different renewal areas. For example, new areas could be opened up for renewal, beginning with infrastructure development, while other areas might begin at a more advanced stage of housing rehabilitation. In this sense community development planning and implementation were intended to become more oriented toward process and less toward projects.

To support this approach, a major change was adopted in the funding arrangements for renewal. Under the original urban renewal program, when a project was approved a sum of money was reserved to complete the project over a specified period of time. Because of increasing costs and project changes, the reserved funds were often insufficient, and additional money had had to be set aside. This tied up large sums of money for extended periods of time and limited the number of new projects that could be approved.

The neighborhood development program changed the funding of renewal projects from a reserve system to annual funding. In the case of a neighborhood development project with several planned activities, a portion was funded each year on the basis of how much money was

14. Robert Dahl makes clear that urban renewal in New Haven was very much under the control of the mayor. Peter Rossi and Robert Dentler came to a similar conclusion in a case study of Chicago. A case study of Boston's urban renewal program revealed the key roles of Mayor John Collins and Development Administrator Edward Logue. Newark, N.J., may be a case of bypassing elected officials. A study of that city pointed to the secrecy maintained between officials of the city renewal authority and potential developers. See Dahl, *Who Governs?* pp. 117–22; Rossi and Dentler, *The Politics of Urban Renewal,* p. 240; McQuade, "Urban Renewal in Boston," pp. 259–77; and Kaplan, "Urban Renewal in Newark," pp. 250–51.

needed to complete a given amount of work within the year. This arrangement for annual funding of specific renewal activities eliminated the need for the comprehensive plan required for conventional urban renewal projects before they could be approved and funded. While providing greater flexibility to development planning, neighborhood development had some disadvantages. Since communities could not be assured in advance of how much money they would receive, annual funding introduced a stop-and-start character to development planning.[15] There were also delays in HUD approval of funding increments. As a result, the anticipated advantages of fostering a local development process generally did not occur, and a project orientation continued.

Model Cities

In 1966, before the neighborhood development program, a broader conceptualization of urban development led to the model cities program, a five-year demonstration project to show how neighborhoods could be revitalized. It departed from urban renewal in encompassing the social and economic, as well as the physical, revitalization of low-income neighborhoods, while avoiding the displacement of residents that so frequently occurred under urban renewal. Model cities stressed local planning flexibility and the coordination of federal grant programs. From the outset federal officials under the Johnson administration viewed model cities as a "mayor's program."[16] As one observer noted:

> The powers of Washington HUD officials over Model Cities were limited, specific, and exhausted early in the program. . . . [T]he department issued planning grant application guidelines (which in essence merely told cities to include "everything" in the document), reviewed the applications, chose winning cities, reviewed and allocated supplemental grants. Once these tasks were completed the control of HUD officials in Washington over the program effectively ended. . . . At no time did Model Cities officials in Washington (whether under Presidents Johnson or Nixon) attempt to guide the cities' choice of general or operational goals.[17]

However, while flexibility in the content was an important feature of model cities, program implementation was hindered by excessive federal

15. *The Central City Problem and Urban Renewal Policy,* pp. 245–46.

16. See Bernard J. Frieden and Marshall Kaplan, *The Politics of Neglect: Urban Aid from Model Cities to Revenue Sharing* (MIT Press, 1975), pp. 73–79.

17. Lawrence D. Brown, "Condition of Federal Urban Policy: Organizational Politics in Three Model Cities" (Ph.D. dissertation, Harvard University, 1973), pp. 447, 448.

review of local plans and by the complexities of trying to link the model cities grant with other federal aid programs.[18]

To avoid the problems that could occur with semiautonomous agencies and that were often found in the urban renewal program, and to avoid the bypassing of elected officials, as had happened in the antipoverty program, the model cities law required a participating community to establish a "city demonstration agency" as part of the general-purpose city or county government. The model cities arrangement was an explicit effort to strengthen the capacity of local general-purpose governments to carry out development programs.[19] As such, it escaped the criticism of "specialist dominance," yet it did not succeed as an experiment in generalist control.

The model cities program fell on hard times soon after it began. Its designers anticipated being able to coordinate a variety of existing federal categorical programs to inject large sums of money into the model neighborhoods. The model cities funds themselves were intended to serve primarily as a supplemental source to pay for innovative, locally designed programs that could not be funded out of categorical grants. Coordination of multiple federal programs failed, and with it went the critical mass of money presumably needed to make the program work. The cost of the Vietnam War limited the growth of domestic programs at this time, but just as important, the categorical programs had their own set of constituents and demands, and as a result, funds could not be redirected into the model neighborhoods. Because the funds that designers expected to get from the established categorical grants failed to materialize, the model cities program remained relatively small compared with the original legislative aspirations and local expectations. In many cities the program became heavily oriented toward social services that were paid for from the supplemental grants, and local residents outside the model neighborhoods began to complain about being left out.

Early in the administration of President Nixon, model cities began to lose White House support. One plan considered by the White House would have diverted a large share of model cities money to a fund to assist school desegregation in the South; another plan called for a complete termination of model cities at the end of 1971.[20] Both plans were dropped because of the strong opposition of mayors, congressmen, and urban lobbying groups. At the same time, HUD was developing other plans to

18. Frieden and Kaplan, *The Politics of Neglect,* pp. 228–31.
19. Ibid., pp. 69–72.
20. Ibid., pp. 207–14.

use model cities as a vehicle to smooth the transition to a major consolidation of various urban aid programs. In the summer of 1971 a "planned variations" experiment was initiated. This permitted twenty selected local governments to expand model cities into a citywide program, gave the local chief executive a coordinating role for review of all applications for federal funds affecting the model cities area, and eliminated most federal program and project reviews. In a statement on July 29 President Nixon said that planned variations would "convert a portion of present Model Cities grants into a test of what can be accomplished under the revenue sharing approach to intergovernmental relations."[21]

Legislative Issues

Despite the initial congressional coolness toward the urban development special revenue sharing plan proposed by President Nixon in 1971, the central question that emerged was not whether there should be a consolidation of the categorical programs—substantial sentiment developed both inside and outside Congress for grant reform—but how far to go in increasing local discretion. Agreement on grant consolidation was hastened in early 1973 when President Nixon froze the major federal housing subsidy programs and the urban grants chosen for consolidation. The freeze forced some opponents of grant merger to back the change in order to restart the flow of housing and development funds to the cities.

Throughout 1971–74 the Nixon administration, as could be expected, strongly supported decentralization. In his message to Congress in 1971 the President said: "Decisions about the development of a local community should reflect local preferences and meet local needs. No group of remote Federal officials—however talented and sincere—can effectively tailor each local program to the wide variety of local conditions which exists in this highly diversified land."[22] Decisions about which activities to support and what proportion of available funds to give each activity would be made locally. "*No federal approval would be required* [emphasis added]. Cities would simply be asked to indicate how they plan to use their funds and to report periodically on how the money was expended."[23]

21. Nixon quoted in ibid., p. 212.

22. "Special Message to the Congress on Special Revenue Sharing for Urban Community Development, March 5, 1971," *Public Papers, Nixon, 1971* (GPO, 1972), p. 398.

23. Ibid., pp. 401–02.

The Senate was far more cautious and throughout the three years of legislative consideration of the urban block grant sought to preserve some federal control over how communities spent the money. Senator John J. Sparkman, chairman of the Committee on Banking, Housing and Urban Affairs, complained in 1973 that "the principle of special revenue sharing . . . carries with it a transfer of responsibility for meeting national objectives from the federal government to local governments with no built-in means for directing or evaluating how the federal funds are spent other than a post-audit for accounting purposes."[24] Republican Senator Robert Taft, Jr., of Ohio went further:

> With the advent of general revenue sharing to supplement local tax efforts and improvement in the budget predicament of many localities, there is no reason to create another fund transfer program which simply provides localities with more federal money to use virtually as they see fit. . . .
>
> Furthermore, the essence of any community development program—housing and physical development and redevelopment—probably deals more fundamentally with the problems of racial integration, which have proved so difficult for localities to tackle even with strong federal directives, than any other federal program. Because of such problems, I feel that community development is one of the least suitable types of program areas for a totally "hands-off" revenue sharing approach.[25]

The House took a middle position, favoring decentralization but with some controls.

These relative positions on the issue of centralization versus decentralization were evident throughout congressional consideration, which between 1971 and 1974 dealt with two separate administration proposals and several congressional plans. The first administration bill was the special revenue sharing plan, introduced in 1971 and then substantially modified by Congress. The Senate passed one version of the legislation in March 1972, but the House failed to concur. The second administration bill, introduced in 1973 soon after the Nixon freeze on the categorical grants, was called the Better Communities Act (referred to by some opponents representing minority groups as the Bitter Communities Act). This version, modified by Congress, eventually became the Housing and Community Development Act of 1974, the CDBG charter. There were three central issues: (1) determining the degree of local discretion, mani-

24. *1973 Housing and Urban Development Legislation,* Hearings before the Subcommittee on Housing and Urban Development of the Senate Committee on Banking, Housing and Urban Affairs, 93 Cong. 1 sess. (GPO, 1973), pt. 1, p. 3.

25. *Housing and Community Development Act of 1974,* S. Rept. 93-693, 93 Cong. 2 sess. (GPO, 1974), pp. 175–76.

fested specifically in defining national objectives and application procedures; (2) reshaping the decisionmaking process, including the roles of federal administrators, local officials, and citizens; and (3) deciding how to allocate the block grant.

National Objectives

In both the 1971 and 1973 administration bills the central purposes of the proposals were grant consolidation and decentralization. The administration's 1973 Better Communities Act proposal referred to the "ineffective use" of the narrow-purpose categorical grants and stated that the purpose of the new approach was

> to help States and units of general local government to deal more effectively with the broad range of community development concerns by replacing inflexible and fragmented categorical programs of Federal assistance with a simpler, more certain, and more expeditious system of Federal revenue sharing assistance which will encourage the exercise of State and local responsibility.[26]

The Senate Committee on Banking, Housing and Urban Affairs, reporting its version of the bill in February 1974, countered the charge of ineffectiveness by citing the "major achievements" of the categorical grants.[27] Where the administration bill defined the major purpose of the legislation as decentralization, the Senate bill, borrowing in part from the urban renewal statute, said the purpose was "the development of viable urban communities through the provision of decent housing, suitable living environments and expansion of economic opportunities, principally for persons of low and moderate income."[28]

To achieve this objective, communities could choose from a long list of eligible activities specified in the legislation. In general the list included all activities eligible under the programs to be consolidated and several new activities, among them the construction of solid waste, flood, and drainage facilities, and certain planning and management activities; funds could also be used for the payment of the local share of other federal grants related to community development. Recipients would select the kinds and mix of development activities they preferred. However, the bill of the Senate Committee on Banking, Housing and Urban Affairs set four

26. H.R. 7277, *Better Communities Act,* April 19, 1973, sec. 2(b).
27. *Housing and Community Development Act of 1974,* S. Rept. 93-693, p. 48.
28. Ibid.

specific limits to local discretion: (1) activities had to be geographically concentrated; (2) physical development was to be emphasized by limiting social service expenditures to 20 percent of the total and requiring that they be related to areas where concentrated development was taking place; (3) 80 percent of the funds had to go for activities benefiting low- and moderate-income residents, or to areas that were blighted or deteriorating, or to meet an urgent community need; and (4) certain types of projects, such as the construction of schools, libraries, hospitals, and city halls, were prohibited.[29] Three Republican members of the committee—John G. Tower of Texas, Robert W. Packwood of Oregon, and William E. Brock III of Tennessee—opposed these limits on local discretion. The bill passed the Senate on March 11, 1974, by a vote of 76 to 11.

The House version, passed 351 to 25 on June 21, also included national objectives concerning the "achievement of the national housing goal of a decent home and a suitable living environment for every American family" and coordination between housing and community development activities.[30] It did not, however, establish a set of constraints on local decisionmaking as the Senate had done.

In the compromise, which received final congressional approval in early August 1974, the national objectives section of the legislation was virtually a stapling together of the separate House and Senate versions. Two separate objectives found in different places of the final legislation carried the same phrase, "a decent home and a suitable living environment." In the Senate language, which became section 101(c)(3), the phrase ended with "for all persons, but principally those of low and moderate income."[31] The House version, borrowed from the 1949 urban renewal legislation, ended with "for every American family";[32] this became section 101(d)(3). This illustrates a difference that was to persist between the two houses as the program evolved. The Senate continued to emphasize the concentration of CDBG benefits on low- and moderate-income groups, whereas the House argued that such specificity ran contrary to decentralization and made one national objective more important

29. Ibid., p. 52.

30. *The Housing and Urban Development Act of 1974,* H. Rept. 93-1114, 93 Cong. 2 sess. (GPO, 1974), p. 47.

31. *Housing and Community Development Act of 1974, Conference Report,* H. Rept. 93-1279, 93 Cong. 2 sess. (GPO, 1974), sec. 101(c)(3), p. 2.

32. Ibid., sec. 101(d)(3), p. 3.

than others. The final revision dropped the four constraints included in the Senate proposal, thus protecting the flexibility of the block grant.

Applications and Funding

How the funds would be made available to localities was as important to the issue of federal versus local control as the definition of national objectives. Should funding be automatic with few or no questions asked, or should recipients be required to submit a formal application subject to approval by federal officials?

Both the administration and Congress generally agreed that the funds should be provided in such a way that recipients of grants would have some certainty about the amount and continuity of the money they would receive and could expect minimum delays in getting it. Nixon proposed automatic funding; that is, an amount determined by a statutory formula would go to the jurisdiction without any need to apply for the funds and thus without any federal approval of an application. An entitlement would have been created. Neither the House nor the Senate was willing to agree to automatic funding. The Senate proposed an application and approval process whereby the application "should be brief rather than elaborate" and review "should be limited in its scope"; approval or disapproval must be within ninety days of submission.[33] The Senate plan thus anticipated simplifying the review process characteristic of the categorical grants. But the Senate preserved the authority of federal officials to say no to an applicant if the proposed program did not meet federal objectives. The House proposed a "veto only" whereby HUD had sixty days to consider an application, which if not disapproved within that time was automatically approved. The final congressional version required an application and gave HUD a seventy-five-day veto period, following the House approach.

The House-Senate compromise and resolution of the important differences between Congress and the administration were facilitated by earlier behind-the-scenes negotiations between key members of the House Subcommittee on Housing and administration officials.[34] These negotiations had begun shortly after the start of subcommittee hearings in October 1973 and continued throughout House consideration of the bill. The

33. *Housing and Community Development Act of 1974,* S. Rept. 93-693, p. 55.

34. Richard P. Nathan and others, *Block Grants for Community Development* (U.S. Department of Housing and Urban Development, January 1977), pp. 43–46.

principal House negotiators were Democrat Thomas L. Ashley of Ohio and Republicans William B. Widnall of New Jersey and Garry Brown of Michigan; the principal spokesman for the administration was HUD Secretary James T. Lynn. The general result of this negotiation process was that when the bill later went to a House-Senate conference for resolution of differences, the Senate was at a bargaining disadvantage and most major disputes were resolved in favor of the House version.

House subcommittee members, like those in the Senate, insisted on an application process that would permit some federal control; the veto device represented a compromise between the House and administration negotiators. The House-administration negotiations also led to a resolution of differences over the housing provisions of the legislation. A community development bill sponsored by Democrats William A. Barrett, subcommittee chairman, and Ashley had included as well a new low-income housing program, whose funds were to be distributed by formula. The plan provided for large-scale modernization and renovation of public housing and the continuation of some housing subsidies for new construction. Barrett and Ashley dropped this proposal in favor of an administration plan for a single housing program to replace several existing ones, but at Ashley's urging the House version of the community development bill linked housing subsidies to the block grant by requiring that a housing assistance plan be prepared by each block grant applicant and be submitted to HUD as part of its application.[35]

Resolution of congressional-administration differences was also made easier by the Watergate affair, an increasing threat to the survival of the Nixon presidency. House members saw a need to move quickly to avoid having the legislation bottled up by possible impeachment proceedings. Moreover, as White House officials became more preoccupied with Watergate, Lynn became freer to negotiate independently, with the result that he abandoned the administration's initial inflexibility and adopted a more compromising attitude. Both sides, particularly the administration, were urged to take more flexible positions by groups lobbying for passage,

35. The housing assistance plan seeks to link local housing needs and community development activities by requiring jurisdictions to (1) survey the condition of their housing stock; (2) determine the extent and character of present housing needs and establish the housing needs of those people expected to reside in the jurisdiction; and (3) establish a realistic annual goal of the amount and type of housing assistance to be provided. The plan is prepared annually as part of a community's CDBG application.

particularly the National League of Cities and the U.S. Conference of Mayors.

The Decision Process

Supporters of the block grant argued that categorical grants had fragmented local decision processes at the expense of elected officials by encouraging special-purpose agencies to deal directly with counterparts in the federal administration. President Nixon made this point in his message to Congress in 1971:

> Some of these Federal programs require local communities to work through semi-autonomous local officials—often bypassing the elected local leaders. Thus, even if one leader, a mayor, for example, *does* manage to create a comprehensive development plan for the money he controls, he is often unable to include in his plan that Federal assistance which goes directly to an urban renewal agency or a local sanitary district.[36]

A similar note was sounded in the 1974 House report on the legislation: "Grants are awarded, by and large, on a competitive, rather than need, basis. And, most important, local elected officials are often bypassed, their authority weakened by semi-autonomous special-purpose agencies not directly responsible to them."[37]

As indicated earlier, the validity of such statements was likely to vary among cities. Whatever the case, the CDBG program avoided any requirements on local structural arrangements. The law specified only that the grants were to go to general-purpose local government, thus implicitly strengthening the position of elected officials.[38] This permitted communities to organize administration of their block grant programs as they chose, such as placing the CDBG program in an existing urban renewal authority or model cities agency, or creating new program offices and leaving the older ones in place to compete for a share of the local CDBG funds.

Citizen participation was another important factor in Congress's con-

36. "Special Message to the Congress," p. 397.

37. *The Housing and Urban Development Act of 1974,* H. Rept. 93-1114, p. 3.

38. In a bill proposed in 1971 by Senator Sparkman as a counterproposal to the administration's plan, the National Association of Housing and Redevelopment Officials succeeded in having urban renewal authorities included as possible grant recipients, but this was dropped from the bill that passed the Senate in early 1972. A new bill introduced by Sparkman in 1973 provided that grants would go only to general-purpose governments.

sideration of the CDBG process. Congress wanted to continue federal requirements for citizen participation, which had been an important part of the urban renewal and model cities programs, whereas the Nixon administration wanted to leave local decisionmaking alone. Soon after taking over, HUD officials in the Nixon administration had moved to make citizen participation in model cities more clearly advisory than substantive, thus protecting the authority of the local elected officials.[39]

Consistent with this, the administration's 1973 better communities proposal provided only that local officials must publish their development plan sixty days before making it final, giving an opportunity for comments to be submitted by interested groups and persons. Both the House and Senate bills, however, provided for public hearings on the block grant application before its submission to HUD and an opportunity for citizens to participate in developing the application itself. The Senate would even have required citizen participation in the execution of the program. In response to such proposals, Lynn told the House subcommittee: "[W]e only seek to require that citizens be informed of community development plans and to insure that citizen views are considered; we do not believe that there is any national purpose to be served in requiring such views to be expressed or considered in any given manner."[40] The final version required a public hearing before local submission of the application but did not establish any additional structural or procedural requirements. It also specified that an opportunity to participate in the development of the application must be provided but did not specify what that meant.

In extending the principle of citizen participation into the block grant, Congress also transformed the nature of this participation, perhaps unwittingly. Citizen participation, as it evolved in the 1960s in the antipoverty and model cities programs, sought to assure access to the decision process by lower-income and minority residents in target neighborhoods. But the CDBG program was not legislatively confined to operating in such neighborhoods, and thus citizen participation potentially meant involving a broader range of income groups and expanding the number and range of local demands. This in turn meant a potential for increased local conflict as local officials came under pressure to spend some of the money in better-off areas of a community.

39. Frieden and Kaplan, *The Politics of Neglect*, pp. 88–89.

40. *Housing and Community Development Legislation: 1973*, Hearings before the Subcommittee on Housing of the House Committee on Banking and Currency, 93 Cong. 1 sess. (GPO, 1973), pt. 1, p. 310.

Program Performance

Although the national objectives and the grant applications were the primary focal points for retaining some federal controls, they were not the only places in the block grant process where HUD would have the opportunity to get involved in the substance of local programs. The CDBG legislation required each jurisdiction to submit an annual performance report to HUD describing the relationship of the grant activities to national objectives. It also provided for the following:

> The Secretary shall, at least on an annual basis, make such reviews and audits as may be necessary or appropriate to determine whether the grantee has carried out a program substantially as described in its application, whether that program conformed to the requirements of this title and other applicable laws, and whether the applicant has a continuing capacity to carry out in a timely manner the approved Community Development Program.[41]

The House Committee on Banking and Currency stated in its report:

> Since Federal application review requirements are being simplified to such a great extent, the post-audit and review requirements will serve as the basic assurance that block grant funds are being used properly to achieve the bill's objectives. . . . [T]he Committee expects the secretary to exercise his responsibilities in this respect with great diligence.[42]

The legislation thus gave HUD opportunities to be involved in substantive decisions from the application through the performance stages.

One aspect of the block grant other than program decisions and performance audits would require HUD-local interaction. This concerned federal requirements that cut across various aid programs, such as environmental review, nondiscrimination and affirmative action, construction wage standards on federally funded projects, historic preservation, facilities for the handicapped, and assistance for relocating persons displaced by federally funded construction.

Under the predecessor programs, detailed plans for local compliance with several of these requirements had to be submitted as part of the application for project funding. There were differences, however, in the assignment of responsibility for providing such assurances. In the case of environmental protection, HUD officials themselves made the impact study before approving a project. In the case of the relocation of persons and businesses displaced by a project, local officials had to submit a detailed relocation plan as part of the application. As part of decentraliza-

41. P.L. 93-383, sec. 104(d).

42. *The Housing and Urban Development Act of 1974,* H. Rept. 93-1114, p. 10.

tion under CDBG, and to speed the application and approval process, the new law initially permitted local governments to show compliance in all these various areas by certifying in their annual grant applications that they were complying with the federal requirements. HUD had the authority to check on the local certification as projects progressed, but the local government was given the initial responsibility for achieving compliance. There was also an important shift of responsibility for assuring compliance with the National Environmental Policy Act of 1969. Responsibility for assessing the environmental impact of an activity was transferred from HUD to local officials, although HUD would not release the funds for a particular project until local officials certified that the assessment had been completed and that the public had had an opportunity to comment on the review.

The process of certifying compliance with these many federal requirements had several implications for local administration of the CDBG program. It would force many local governments to enter technical and legal areas in which they had little or no prior experience. Especially in the case of environmental review, this would mean new paperwork for local officials. Second, while the complicated tasks of detailed project planning and application characteristic of the categorical process were eliminated, site monitoring to assure compliance under the CDBG process was potentially enlarged and could produce some sticky conflicts between HUD and local officials as the program progressed. But perhaps more important, in communities that had little or no prior experience with federal aid programs, the CDBG money opened up the possibility of new and significant federal intervention in local decisionmaking that could have the effect of constraining rather than restoring local discretion. Thus how much decentralization would really come with the CDBG depended very much on a community's previous experience with federal grants.

Targeting

Who gets the money is a key question in analyzing the effects of a federal aid program, and this issue became more contentious in the late 1970s as intergovernmental policy discussions focused increasingly on the concept of targeting. The term refers to the idea that federal grants should be concentrated on areas or groups presumed to have the greatest need. In the CDBG program two types of targeting issues developed.

The first issue involved interjurisdictional targeting, the allocation of federal funds among places. The second involved intrajurisdictional targeting—the extent to which a jurisdiction should concentrate its development resources in a relatively small area (geographic targeting) or on the most needy neighborhoods or individuals (social targeting).

Interjurisdictional Targeting

The CDBG allocation system adopted in 1974 resulted in two significant shifts of urban aid funds: (1) a regional shift, with the South and West increasing their share of money at the expense of the Northeast and Midwest; and (2) a shift in shares from the older, declining central cities to the suburbs and nonmetropolitan areas. Two factors accounted for these shifts: the eligibility criteria, which had the effect of spreading the money among more places, and the formula factors that were used.

ELIGIBILITY. In the 1971 special revenue sharing legislation, the Nixon administration proposed a formula that would have awarded entitlements to metropolitan cities, defined as every central city of a metropolitan area and suburban cities with a population of more than 50,000 persons. A total of 445 jurisdictions would have received entitlements—313 central cities and 132 suburban cities. But over the three years that Congress considered the program, the number of entitlement jurisdictions increased substantially.

In 1972, under pressure from the National Association of Counties, the House added urban counties to the entitlement list.[43] When the administration resubmitted its bill in 1973 as the Better Communities Act, it also included urban counties. Inclusion of the urban counties illustrated the politics of fund-spreading that accompanied the shift from the categorical programs to the block grant; it also demonstrated the influence in Congress of suburban jurisdictions. The chief advocates for including the urban counties were Republican Congressman Widnall, whose constituency included Bergen County, New Jersey; and Democrats Richard T. Hanna of Orange County, California, and William S. Moor-

43. Generally an urban county is defined in the CDBG legislation as a county having a population of 200,000, excluding its central city or cities; suburban cities with populations of 50,000 or more; and any other municipalities that choose not to participate in the CDBG program. The county must also have the powers to perform "essential community development and housing assistance activities." The eligibility standards for urban counties are more fully discussed in chapter 6.

head of Allegheny County, Pennsylvania.[44] All were members of the House Subcommittee on Housing. Opposition came from the National League of Cities, which was concerned about the diversion of funds from the central cities to suburbs. Congressman Ashley from Toledo, Ohio, originally opposed including the counties but eventually shifted his position to get the bill passed. During the hearings he said: ". . . because of the political realities involved . . . we are looking forward . . . to running the Better Communities Act with very limited resources, and we are looking forward to doing so in a way that will accommodate suburban America, so that the legislation will have a chance of passing."[45] Moorhead, a backer of urban counties, made the same point to the National League of Cities: "Unless the bill carries a broad appeal for governments other than metropolitan cities, we don't have a chance of winning on the floor. Reflecting new demographic patterns, more and more Congressmen find themselves representing suburban constituencies."[46] HUD estimated initially that about seventy-five counties would qualify but that only about ten or twelve would actually participate, an estimate that proved to be quite wrong: seventy-three counties subsequently qualified and participated in the first year.

Another factor adding to the number of entitlement areas was a redefinition in 1973 by the Office of Management and Budget (OMB) of standards for designating metropolitan areas, the effect of which was to lower the population threshold for designation.[47] This opened the door to a sizable number of new designations and qualified the central cities of these areas for CDBG entitlements. Between 1970, the year used by the administration in determining the original set of entitlements, and 1975 the OMB designated forty-four new metropolitan areas, some having more than one central city. By the time the CDBG program went into effect on January 1, 1975, the number of entitlement jurisdictions, including metropolitan cities and urban counties, had increased to nearly 600; during 1975 seven more metropolitan areas with eight central cities were established.

Of the nearly 600 entitlement jurisdictions, about a third had received

44. Nathan and others, *Block Grants for Community Development*, pp. 46–49.

45. *Housing and Community Development Legislation, 1973,* Hearings before the Subcommittee on Housing of the House Committee on Banking and Currency, 93 Cong. 1 sess. (GPO, 1973), p. 416.

46. Quoted in John L. Moore, "Outlook Improves for Passage of Community Development Bill," *National Journal,* vol. 6 (April 13, 1974), p. 561.

47. For a discussion of the designation process, see Nathan and others, *Block Grants for Community Development,* pp. 222–26.

little or no funding under the categorical programs that were consolidated into the block grant. Most of these new "winners" were in the suburbs—suburban cities or urban counties,[48] of which many were in the South and West. California alone contained forty entitlement jurisdictions that had received on the average less than $100,000 a year between 1968 and 1972 from the categorical programs. Under the CDBG allocation system, the smallest grant to any of the forty was about $500,000 a year. The creation of entitlements for a large number of jurisdictions that had received little or no money from the categorical programs added to the political attractiveness of the program.

The formula entitlements were the centerpiece of the CDBG allocation system, but there also were substantial discretionary funds. Of the money provided, 80 percent was earmarked for use in metropolitan areas and 20 percent for nonmetropolitan communities.[49] After this basic division was made, the funds were further subdivided for formula, hold-harmless, and discretionary allocations. The first distribution of funds from the metropolitan share was for the formula entitlements to the eligible cities and urban counties. There were no formula shares for communities outside metropolitan areas.

The second distribution was for hold-harmless grants to protect users of the categorical grants from a sudden loss of this money. The CDBG legislation provided that for the first three years of the new program, communities that had urban renewal, neighborhood development, model cities, or code enforcement programs (a category of urban renewal) would continue to receive the annual average of what they had received under all the earlier programs between the years 1968 and 1972. The hold-harmless provision applied to both metropolitan and nonmetropolitan communities. Full protection was to last for the first three years; if the hold-harmless amount was greater than the formula entitlement, the protection would be phased down over the fourth and fifth years of the program.[50] In the sixth year, recipients with a formula entitlement would

48. Ibid., table 4-6, p. 114.

49. Before making the 80–20 split, 2 percent of the funds were set aside for a discretionary fund that the HUD secretary could use for a variety of purposes.

50. Special procedures were established for phasing down the hold-harmless credit for model cities. A community was entitled to the average annual amount for five years in the model cities program. At the end of these five years, the city's hold-harmless credit for model cities declined in three yearly steps, to 80, 60, and 40 percent. In some cases this meant the total hold-harmless amount began to decline before the third year of the block grant. This is illustrated in chapter 6 in the Allegheny county case study.

receive funding entirely on the basis of the formula. Those without a formula entitlement, both inside and outside metropolitan areas, would have to rely on discretionary grants.

There were two separate discretionary funds—one for communities outside metropolitan areas and one for those within. The nonmetropolitan discretionary funds were allocated by formula among states on the basis of population, overcrowded housing, and poverty in the nonmetropolitan area of the states, the same elements used in the entitlement formula. The metropolitan discretionary funds were allocated among the metropolitan areas, after taking out the entitlement jurisdictions, on the basis of the formula factors. To secure funds, a nonentitlement community must apply directly to HUD for a discretionary grant from its state or metropolitan allocation. At the outset of the program the actual amount in each fund depended on the distributions made first for formula and hold-harmless grants, but as the hold-harmless grants were phased down, the released money went into the appropriate discretionary fund. For the nonmetropolitan fund, this meant that in the sixth year all funds would be distributed on a discretionary basis. In metropolitan areas, at the end of the sixth year the discretionary fund would account for an estimated 30 percent of the metropolitan money. Thus by the sixth year about half of all the block grant money would be distributed on a discretionary basis.

It cannot be known how well cities that were successful in getting categorical money in the past would have done in the future if the categorical programs had been continued, but the CDBG allocation system created a class of "losers" whose new formula entitlements fell below their categorical grant level. A number of older, declining central cities, particularly in the Northeast, fell into this group. There were many other communities both inside and outside metropolitan areas that had received categorical funding yet faced the possibility of a complete loss of funds after the hold-harmless period expired because they would not qualify for an entitlement. In the sixth year they would have to seek discretionary grants. Among our cases, Carbondale fell into this group.

The CDBG system of formula and discretionary grants, with hold-harmless provisions in effect for five years, significantly and immediately expanded the number of communities receiving federal development assistance. In the first year nearly 2,900 grants were made. By comparison, 147 communities had received model cities funds, and 1,200 communities (some of which were also model cities grant recipients) had received urban renewal–neighborhood development assistance between 1949, when the program was created, and 1974, when it was merged into the CDBG program. As of 1973, 723 communities had active renewal projects.

THE FORMULA. The second factor accounting for the regional and central city–suburban shifts was the character of the entitlement formula. The formula proposed by the Nixon administration in April 1971 would have based distributions on population, overcrowded housing, housing with plumbing deficiencies, and poverty. A few months later Chairman Sparkman of the Senate Committee on Banking, Housing and Urban Affairs introduced a consolidation bill of his own. Reflecting the pressures of urban lobbyists, this bill would have distributed 75 percent of the funds on the basis of prior program experience rather than a formula, thus keeping a large share of the money going to places that had been heavily involved in the categorical programs. Twenty-five percent of the funds would go for discretionary grants, with the protected communities also having access to this money. In the bill reported to the Senate floor in early 1972, however, committee Republicans succeeded in having a formula allocation system substituted for Sparkman's provisions. Sparkman had some success in protecting the experienced cities by including past grants as a formula factor, substituting it for plumbing deficiencies, and by including a permanent hold-harmless provision. The administration bill had not contained any hold-harmless provision, although the administration said it would use funds remaining after the formula distributions for this purpose. The bill, with the formula, passed the Senate by a vote of 80 to 1. The House Committee on Banking and Currency adopted the Senate-passed formula and hold-harmless provisions, but the bill failed to reach the House floor before adjournment.

The following year the administration submitted its Better Communities Act, retaining the formula approach but including only the population, overcrowded housing, and poverty factors; the plumbing deficiency factor was dropped. The administration also included a hold-harmless provision, but unlike the Senate-passed bill of the previous year, which used hold-harmless as a permanent minimum guarantee, the administration's act proposed to end the guarantee after four years. With HUD's assistance, the Senate Committee on Banking, Housing and Urban Affairs tried various formula alternatives, but none were satisfactory, partly because data on urban counties were not available and partly because the data were inadequate for seeing how various formula combinations would work. The committee then returned to Sparkman's position of 1971, dropping the formula system, and provided a hold-harmless allocation system to protect localities already receiving community development funds and discretionary funding for other communities. This reversal surprised urban lobbyists who had come to accept a formula system as inevitable after the enactment of general revenue sharing in October 1972.

In its report, the committee concluded: "The formula approach, while having certain benefits, was rejected because it failed to include a number of important measures of community need; it imposed a too rigid system of allocation; and it made necessary limiting entitlement to certain types of jurisdictions."[51] Senator Taft added his view:

> I find it difficult to argue in principal [sic] against the concept of fund distribution based upon a formula which reflects an "objective" indication of community needs. . . . Unfortunately, no formula which was presented to the Committee seemed to match my sense of relative community needs any better than the funding distribution under the past programs.[52]

In a supplemental statement to the committee report Senators Tower, Packwood, and Brock objected to dropping the formula system, saying: "All depends upon grantsmanship and, over time, the Secretary's discretion. This, we submit, is substantially the system which we have had in the past. It is the system which we should be trying to replace with something better."[53]

The Senate bill reflected the committee's ambivalence about the appropriate allocation system by requiring HUD to study the system. The committee report said the study should contain "recommendations for improving the program by changing the method of allocating and distributing federal funds and stressed that "the Committee clearly intends that the matter be reconsidered after some experience has been gained under the new program."[54]

The House Committee on Banking and Currency had been negotiating for some time with the administration about various aspects of the bill and sided with it on the formula issue. The committee adopted the administration's three-factor formula and the principle of phasing out hold-harmless grants but extended the hold-harmless protection to five years.

51. *Housing and Community Development Act of 1974,* S. Rept. 93-693, p. 59.

52. Ibid., p. 176.

53. Ibid., p. 169.

54. Ibid., pp. 58, 59.

The House version prevailed in conference. As enacted in 1974, the formula allocated funds on the basis of three elements—population, overcrowded housing, and poverty.

The poverty factor had a double weighting in the formula and particularly benefited cities in the South, which often have disproportionately large numbers of persons below the poverty level. An analysis done at the Brookings Institution soon after the program started revealed that the poverty and overcrowded housing factors were highly correlated, thus weighting distributions further toward poverty and adding to the shift toward the South.[55] The population factor worked to the advantage of growing cities, many of which were in the South and West, and to the disadvantage of declining cities, concentrated primarily in the Northeast and Midwest. As population grew, a recipient got more money; cities losing population received less.

The study's projections showed that as a result of the entitlement system and the formula elements, the combined share of the Northeast and Midwest would decline from 56.2 percent of the categorical money distributed between 1968 and 1972 to 46 percent of the CDBG funds by 1980, the sixth program year, when the allocation system would be fully implemented. The southern and western share would increase from 43.8 to 54 percent. An even greater shift was evident in the projected decline in the share of funds going to central cities, a drop from almost 72 percent to just over 42 percent. The suburban share would more than double from 15.6 to 37.8 percent by the sixth year. The nonmetropolitan share was already up from 12.6 to 20 percent, the level prescribed by the CDBG legislation.[56]

These shifts in allocation were important to the political controversy that emerged in 1977 over changing the CDBG formula. The last chapter returns to the formula issue and the major changes proposed in the Brookings study.

Intrajurisdictional Targeting

Model cities and urban renewal required the community to define geographic project boundaries—geographic targeting; the neighborhood development program loosened the requirement on the geographic con-

55. This analysis is presented in Nathan and others, *Block Grants for Community Development,* chaps. 3–6.

56. Data in this paragraph are from ibid., pp. 139, 150.

centration of activities but retained the area approach. The CDBG law, however, did not require any delineation of target areas, thus making it possible at least in principle for communities to expand federally assisted development activities across their whole area. The model cities program also included social targeting; that is, the model neighborhood was to be made up of lower-income groups who were to benefit from the activities funded. The CDBG law included provisions concerning social targeting that were the source of a major policy dispute.[57]

The Nixon proposals of 1971 and 1973, with their emphasis on decentralized decisionmaking, included no provisions on social targeting. The provisions were developed in the Senate committee. Two phrases of the Housing and Community Development Act of 1974 were the basis of the social targeting objective: (1) the requirement (section 104) to give "maximum feasible priority" to activities benefiting low- and moderate-income families; and (2) the requirement (section 101) that benefits go to "principally persons of low and moderate income." To give effect to this objective, the Senate Committee on Banking, Housing and Urban Affairs proposed to set a limit of 20 percent on program expenditures "which are not intended to be of direct and significant benefit to families of low or moderate income, or to areas which are blighted or deteriorating, unless the Secretary finds modification of this limitation necessary to meet urgent community needs."[58]

The House bill reported out on June 17, 1974, included no language on social targeting, but in conference the Senate prevailed in making social targeting a national objective. The 20 percent limit was removed from the bill, however. Thus at the outset of the program the Ford administration and the House accepted targeting as an objective but emphasized decentralized decisionmaking, while the Senate pressed for more federal oversight of local programming to maximize benefits for those with lower incomes.

In addition to social targeting two other major goals were stated in the statute: (1) the prevention and elimination of slums or blight; and (2) meeting other needs of a particular urgency in a community. But the law set no priority, in case objectives conflicted. For example, a community

57. For a detailed discussion of this issue and its implementation by HUD, see Raymond A. Rosenfeld, "Who Benefits and Who Decides? The Uses of Community Development Block Grants," in Donald B. Rosenthal, ed., *Urban Revitalization* (Sage Publications, 1980), chap. 9.

58. *Housing and Community Development Act of 1974,* S. Rept. 93-693, p. 52.

might choose to emphasize the elimination of slums and blight in a way that displaced lower-income residents. A growing community might use its funds to install infrastructure in an expanding residential area and ignore lower-income areas in the city's core, arguing that the infrastructure needs were particularly urgent. Thus the statutory problem of multiple and potentially conflicting goals arose. A further complicating factor was the statutory objective of decentralization. The intent of the CDBG program was to transfer more decisionmaking authority from federal to local officials. As the last chapter explains, the issue of which of these national objectives should have priority subsequently became linked to the question of who should decide the priorities.

Implementation: A Hands-Off Policy

As the program got under way, in August 1974 HUD adopted a permissive hands-off policy toward local recipients of aid. David Meeker, the assistant secretary for planning and community development in the Ford administration, said in an interview:

> In the past, there has been a very large temptation to insert ourselves [HUD] into the decisionmaking process of local elected officials. We had to say whether you could or could not do anything. We are now trying to limit HUD's role to those [cases and problems] that are constitutional in nature.[59]

This policy of limited involvement was conveyed to local officials at conferences held shortly after enactment of the program and to the HUD field staff in a series of training sessions held in Washington and several other cities during the summer of 1974.[60] This led to an initial expectation that HUD would not give much scrutiny to decisions made at the local level. HUD declined even to publish a handbook on the CDBG program; the handbook for urban renewal, however, was a detailed manual guiding local officials on matters ranging from the size of pipe to be used for storm drains to financial accounting procedures. While the decision not to have a CDBG project handbook was of symbolic significance initially, it also responded to practical realities. The urban renewal handbook was a specialists' tool for use in a special-purpose agency, whereas under CDBG a variety of local bureaucracies with local as well

59. Quoted in Arthur J. Magida, "Housing Report: Major Programs Revised to Stress Community Control," *National Journal,* vol. 6 (September 14, 1974), p. 1374.

60. Nathan and others, *Block Grants for Community Development,* p. 68.

as CDBG responsibilities would be involved in carrying out projects. Under these circumstances standardized and detailed federal guidance laid on top of long-standing local procedures would not be welcome and probably would not work. The absence of such guidance, however, resulted in a flood of questions from local officials about the eligibility of certain kinds of activities, especially social services. In response, different interpretations were sometimes given by the HUD area offices responsible for approving applications.

The hands-off policy was extended to the structure of citizen participation and the social targeting provisions. In issuing regulations governing citizen participation, HUD said that it had received suggestions to "prescribe more fully the procedures, process, and local structure for citizen participation,"[61] but declined to do so, thus leaving it to local officials to decide whether there was to be a formal committee for citizen participation, how such a committee would be composed, and what its powers would be. HUD also chose not to define the legislative term "maximum feasible priority" or the requirement that benefits go "principally" to lower-income groups, which were the basis of the social targeting objective. The department set no floor or ceiling to guide a community nor any objective measure against which to evaluate a community's social targeting results. At the beginning of the program local officials were required only to send with their application a certification that they had complied with the citizen participation and national objectives provisions of the statute, including social targeting.

Limited involvement in program decisions was probably a practical position for HUD to adopt in the first year as well as an explicit policy preference. The schedule for submission of the first applications gave communities only five months to establish the application process and develop a program. Meeker adopted as a slogan "No second-guessing of local officials and a minimum of red tape."[62] Local applications in the first year received speedy HUD approval, thus giving early confirmation to local expectations about decentralization.

But HUD's hands-off policy did not go unchallenged during the transition period, particularly in the Senate, which had been more aggressive in seeking continued federal policy controls. In hearings held in 1976 Senator William Proxmire, chairman of the committee with jurisdiction

61. *Federal Register,* vol. 39 (November 13, 1974), p. 40136.

62. Quoted in Nathan and others, *Block Grants for Community Development,* p. 68.

over the program, took issue with Meeker over HUD's administration of the program: "What isn't clear is whether the program that you have been administering is the program Congress passed. . . . Some critics say HUD has been implementing until relatively recently the administration's [special] revenue sharing bill."[63] The House, in keeping with its preference for decentralization, generally took a more sympathetic view of the dilemma HUD faced in accommodating both the national policy objectives of the law and the goal of greater local discretion. A House committee staff report noted: "An issue here is how can HUD satisfy its administrative responsibilities and at the same time meet the mandate for decentralized decisionmaking."[64] Moreover, court cases and administrative complaints to HUD about its administration of the program and local spending decisions were filed soon after the program started.[65]

Partly because of these factors, HUD began as early as the second program year to give closer scrutiny to local applications, as can be seen in the case studies.

Conclusion

Overall, the 1974 legislation represented a major victory for the Nixon administration, which nonetheless was forced to go along with some congressionally imposed federal controls on how the CDBG money could be spent. These controls, however, were defined so generally in terms of broad national objectives and a long list of eligible activities that at the outset of the program recipient communities enjoyed considerable latitude in deciding on the specific kinds and mix of activities they would fund. With the exception of model cities, the grants consolidated into the CDBG had been more specific about what activities would be federally funded. In addition, the two major consolidated programs, urban renewal–neighborhood development and model cities, implied that some

63. *Oversight on the Administration of the Housing and Community Development Act of 1974,* Hearings before the Subcommittee on Housing and Urban Development of the Senate Committee on Banking, Housing and Urban Affairs, 94 Cong. 2 sess. (GPO, August 1976), p. 505.

64. *Community Development Block Grant Programs,* Committee Print, Subcommittee on Housing and Community Development of the House Committee on Banking, Finance and Urban Affairs, 95 Cong. 1 sess. (GPO, February 1977), p. 9.

65. Paul R. Dommel and others, *Decentralizing Community Development* (Department of Housing and Urban Development, June 1978), app. 4.

parts of the city were to be excluded from the programs. Such geographic constraints were initially absent from the block grant program. Thus in two important areas, what to do and where to do it, local governments had considerably more discretion under the block grant. A community could carry out housing rehabilitation if it wished; it could give rehabilitation assistance in the form it chose—loans, grants, interest subsidies, loan guarantees or combinations of these; it could set the income eligibility standards for assistance. Alternatively, it could put all its entitlement into a flood control project if that were an urgent community need, and the project could be planned and engineered without step-by-step federal control.

This greater discretion was also evident in the establishment of the administrative and decisionmaking process. The urban renewal legislation had provided for the administration of the program through a "local public agency," which was frequently established as a semiautonomous renewal or redevelopment authority. The model cities legislation provided for a "city demonstration agency," which was to be a part of the city or county government. The CDBG legislation carried no similar provisions, leaving it up to local governments whether to use existing agencies, reorganize them, or create new ones. Similarly, in providing for citizen participation in the decisionmaking process, the CDBG legislation was less specific than the urban renewal and model cities programs on who the citizens would be and how this participation would be organized.

In short, in the important areas of project choices, project location, and organizational arrangements, local governments enjoyed considerable freedom of choice. But while the CDBG provided greater scope for local program preferences than the predecessor programs, it also included opportunities for federal program administrators to exercise their preferences to achieve broad national objectives. The potentially conflicting preferences created the likelihood of continued tension between federal and local officials as the program proceeded.

CHAPTER THREE

Phoenix, Arizona

JOHN STUART HALL

From the ashes of the past shall arise a new civilization. The Phoenix bird of ancient mythology means resurrection and I suggest this new settlement be named Phoenix.

—*Darrell Duppa, credited with naming Phoenix in 1881.*

BY ANY STANDARDS Phoenix is one of America's newest cities. More than 80 percent of its current housing stock has been constructed since 1950 to accommodate a dramatic increase in population from about 107,000 in 1950 to 669,000 in 1975. This growth has paralleled the city's phenomenal areal expansion from 17.1 square miles to 276 square miles.[1] More than $100 million of commercial home loan activity took place in the city in 1976, and local contractors complained of inadequate material and supplies to meet the current housing demand.[2] The city's spectacular growth accounts for the tendency of local realtors and prospective home buyers to categorize houses as "new-used" and "old-used." All are becoming harder to acquire. In more than one case entire housing subdivisions have been sold before the first unit was constructed.

There is substantial room for growth within city limits and good reason to expect continued economic development. The city's population density of 2,423 per square mile in 1975 was low compared not only with such per-square-mile extremes as Manhattan (67,808) and Philadelphia (15,164), but also with the most well-known example of urban

1. Valley National Bank, *Arizona Statistical Review* (Phoenix: The Bank, 1976), p. 10. These data are used to reflect the city's characteristics at the time the community development block grant program started.

2. This is a minimum estimate based on home loan disclosure data obtained from local lending institutions. Data are incomplete or unavailable from three major lending institutions. For a discussion, see John S. Hall and Richard A. Eribes, "Politics of Housing Finance: Patterns of Investment and Hardship in Phoenix," paper presented at the Annual Conference of the Western Political Science Association, Los Angeles, March 16–18, 1978.

sprawl, Los Angeles (6,073 per square mile).[3] Local planners and economists project that the city's population will continue to grow over the next two decades at a rate that will require increasing attention to the development of currently unused land.[4]

In Phoenix the community development block grant was implemented within this context of rapid development. The story that follows is about the application of CDBG objectives and dollars to local problems and projects. Since a major goal of the Housing and Community Development Act of 1974 (which established the CDBG program) was to improve the nation's housing stock, neighborhoods, and living conditions for the poor, it is important to examine the act's impact in an area of relative growth and affluence. Because of Phoenix's growth-related development needs, one might expect that only a small proportion of CDBG resources would be used for redevelopment activity. But more than the physical setting needs to be considered to understand the CDBG decisionmaking calculus in Phoenix. Equally important are the local political culture, form of government, development needs, and past experience with federal aid and related federal programs. Taken together, these elements constitute the setting of decisionmaking surrounding the first two years of experience with the CDBG program.

Patterns of Growth

The direction of the Phoenix population growth since 1950 has been heavily influenced by the private housing market. Developers, realtors, and others profiting from the local housing industry promoted the aggressive annexation policy that accounted for the city's large population growth. Annexation has continued because of the strong voice of local economic interests and the political ease of expansion and because the city could afford to grow. As other analysts have noted, many older urban areas were forced to conform to their physical boundaries, but the flat "pool table" topography of Phoenix provided the freedom to expand "outward, upward or in whichever direction technology allowed.

3. Valley National Bank, *Arizona Statistical Review,* p. 5.

4. Several reports from the Arizona State Office of Economic Planning and Development and from the City of Phoenix Planning Department project large increases in city population to the year 2000.

[Phoenix] chose low density residential construction and the automobile encouraged an outward, even remote, expansion."[5]

Aesthetic, economic, and sociopsychological costs accompany this particular form of development, which has resulted in urban sprawl. For many, the haphazard dispersal of people, businesses, services, and shopping centers over this wide area causes problems. Poor public transportation combined with mounting energy costs means that increasing numbers of the city's elderly and disadvantaged populations are isolated from needed services and competitive markets. As noted by other critics, the Phoenix type of development "consumes an enormous amount of energy, a result of inefficiencies designed into cities when energy was cheap and population levels low."[6] City officials are becoming increasingly concerned not only about these general costs of urban sprawl but also about costs associated with spreading city services to newly annexed areas.

But the rapid leapfrogging residential development of Phoenix has resulted in benefits for some. The city's low population per square mile is appreciated by those who seek refuge from urban overcrowding. Many would argue that the city's low density and openness contribute to the overall high quality of life in Phoenix. This kind of reasoning certainly dominates the city's Planning Commission hearings over proposed zoning changes that would increase densities. Residents of the more affluent areas of North Phoenix and adjacent suburbs have a stake in the style of life that accompanies parcels of one acre per dwelling unit.

Despite recent concern over the costs of annexation, most city officials contend that past decisions to annex have resulted in net benefit to the city. City expansion has increased local property tax revenues and has thwarted some flight to suburbia. City officials are wary of population loss to suburbs and point with pride to the overall population gain that has accompanied annexation.

Phoenix's population increase, like that of other boom areas of the Southwest, has a number of causes, of course. One major factor is the city's diversified and healthy economy. In earlier times the economic

5. R. James Becker, Richard A. Eribes, and Jeannette Goodstein, "The Policy Challenge," in Nicholas Henry, ed., *Of, By and For the People* (Tempe, Ariz.: Arizona Academy and the Center for Public Affairs, Arizona State University), p. 152. The author has benefited from discussions with Professor Eribes concerning many of the points made in this section.

6. Ibid.

base of Phoenix was said to depend heavily on the "four Cs"—citrus, cotton, copper, and cattle. Although these remain important segments of the state's economy, other industries make larger contributions to current employment in Phoenix. Wholesale and retail trade accounts for over one-quarter of the jobs in the metropolitan area. Almost 20 percent of metropolitan area employment in 1976 was in government, a fact reflecting Phoenix's position as the capital of the state, the county seat, a regional office center, and the hub of a metropolitan area.[7] The large white-collar work force in Phoenix is attributable to development in the direction of light industry rather than heavy industry. As Goodall has observed:

> In Phoenix the major manufacturing firms are electronics and space age industries of which Motorola, General Electric, Sperry, and AiResearch would be among the largest. Consequently, the main opportunities for employment in manufacturing are for engineers, computer experts and other technically trained personnel of a white collar rather than blue collar nature.[8]

Arizona and Phoenix are also noted for their tourist industry, which yielded an estimated $2.25 billion for the state in 1976. The retirement industry also provides an important stimulus to the local economy, although some argue that the effect of this industry can easily be overstated, particularly after public service costs are subtracted. In contrast to the stereotype, population profiles for Arizona and metropolitan Phoenix suggest very little difference among national, state, and local proportions of elderly people. In all three cases the proportion of the population exceeding age sixty-five is roughly 10 percent.[9] But within the context of rapid population growth in Phoenix, this trend also suggests a major influx of elderly citizens.

It is common to assert that the area's conservative political stance is partially attributable to the in-migration of predominantly white-collar, elderly people. In addition many contend that the midwestern origins of

7. Valley National Bank, *Arizona Statistical Review,* p. 18. The area's 85,000 government jobs in June 1976 accounted for 19.5 percent of the total employment of 437,400. Wholesale and retail trade accounted for 115,200 jobs. In contrast, the statewide employment total in agriculture was only 23,600 and in copper mining, 21,600.

8. Leonard E. Goodall, "Phoenix: Reformers At Work," in Leonard E. Goodall, ed., *Urban Politics in the Southwest* (Tempe, Ariz.: Institute of Public Administration, 1967), p. 113.

9. Valley National Bank, *Arizona Statistical Review,* p. 13; and *Inside Phoenix: 1976* (Phoenix Newspapers, Inc., 1976), p. 8.

new residents reinforce conservative patterns.[10] The area's dramatic population increase in the 1960s was the result of one of the nation's highest levels of in-migration during that decade.[11] Newcomers are more likely than residents who have lived in the city five or more years to be white, have white-collar occupations and high incomes, and be well educated.[12] According to one survey, 29 percent of the area's new residents in 1975 gave employment as a reason for moving to Phoenix. The remaining 71 percent listed education, health, climate, retirement, and other reasons.[13] It is important that among the 29 percent who responded that they had moved to the area for reasons of employment, only 6 percent were looking for a job upon arrival. The remaining 23 percent arrived to accept waiting jobs.[14]

The population increase in Phoenix and its underlying social and economic dynamics have many ramifications. Two direct effects are particularly important for this story.

First, politically, this growth creates occasional contradiction, and the realities of rapid population change sometimes conflict with the predominant local philosophy of political conservatism. To some, recent history and future forecasts suggest immense pressure to "manage growth." Other local interests are less concerned by these changes and are likely to advocate more growth and less regulation. Many would agree that in the past the latter have tended to dominate policymaking in Phoenix and in Arizona generally. As one observer put it:

> Public policies are hard to promote in a part of the country where rugged individualism is the old religion and growth is the new one. Arizona, after all, passed a law two years ago requiring all high school students to take a course called "The Benefits of Free Enterprise." Its former Governor has proclaimed an annual "John Birch Day." Affirmation of property rights and deprecations of public spending are echoed daily in the two Phoenix papers. . . . There is no inheritance tax and it is commonly said that Arizona is "a good place to die."[15]

10. It is true that between 1960 and 1965, 31.9 percent of all new Phoenix residents came from Michigan, Ohio, Indiana, Illinois, and Iowa; during 1976, 25 percent of the new residents came from these states. For 1960–65 data, see Goodall, "Phoenix: Reformers at Work," p. 111. For 1976 data, see Valley National Bank, *Arizona Statistical Review,* p. 16.

11. U.S. Bureau of the Census, *Statistics for Federal Regions, States, Metropolitan Areas* (Government Printing Office, 1974), p. 906.

12. *Inside Phoenix: 1976,* p. 17.

13. Valley National Bank, *Arizona Statistical Review,* p. 16.

14. Ibid.

15. Michael T. Kaufman, *New York Times,* April 5, 1975.

In issues ranging from implementing medicaid at the state level to adopting a housing code for the city, public policy has often lagged behind other states and communities. Another political reality is the ascendancy of the Republican Party. The GOP has benefited most by the in-migrations, as demonstrated by the increasing Republican proportion of political party registration in the state and in the Phoenix metropolitan area over the past twenty-nine years. Republican registration increased from 18 percent of total registered voters in 1948 to 50 percent in 1977; Democratic registration decreased from 80 percent in 1948 to 44 percent in 1977.[16]

Second, economic expansion and diversification have provided a solid fiscal base for local government. A 150 percent increase in total city budget expenditures (from $144 million in fiscal year 1972 to $358 million in fiscal 1977) was partially financed by an 88 percent increase in local tax revenues and state-shared taxes. At the same time, bond revenues increased by 166 percent and federal grant revenue increased a dramatic 875 percent from $4.5 million in fiscal 1972 to almost $45 million in 1977. During the five-year period between 1972 and 1977 local tax revenues increased in dollars but declined as a share of total expenditures from 45 percent to 33.9 percent. This decline was partially offset by a proportionate increase in federal aid as a percentage of total city expenditures from 3.2 percent in 1972 to 12.5 percent in 1977.

It is critical to understand that a major share of the overall revenue increase of this period was automatic. Large federal aid increases can be traced to general revenue sharing and block grants, including the CDBG, that are formula based. The city's earlier experiences with federal aid were almost solely categorical. Although some special projects like the city's Sky Harbor Airport had received substantial federal subsidy, revenues for expanding general government services were generated at the state and local level.

Increased local-and-state-shared tax revenues during this period were largely the result of economic expansion rather than tax rate increases. The city's 1 percent sales tax remained constant throughout the 1970s.[17]

16. Dickinson McGaw, "The 1968 Election in Arizona and the Emerging Republican Majority," *Public Affairs Bulletin* (Arizona State University), vol. 9, no. 1 (1970); and unpublished data as of July 1977 from the Maricopa County Elections Office.

17. All budget data for these comparisons are taken from the *Phoenix Annual Budget,* 1971–72 through 1976–77, schedule 1. The city attempted to raise its 1 per-

The local property tax rate has increased only once, from $1.75 to $1.89 per $100 of assessed valuation, during the past twenty years. The residential property tax assessment is based on a valuation set at 15 percent of fair market value. This means that the owner of a $30,000 home pays only $75 in city property tax. It is important to note, however, that the city does not provide health, education, and welfare services on the scale of its eastern counterparts. Special districts provide these services. When school, county, state, and other special district assessments are added to the bill for a $30,000 home, property taxes total approximately $600.[18] Although this amount is deemed excessive by the local media, most political candidates, and many residents, it probably would seem quite palatable to residents of cities who must rely on the property tax to fund much greater service needs. Boston, for example, assesses residential property at a rate of $252.90 per $1,000 of assessed valuation, with that figure set at 35 percent of fair market value. This means that the Boston homeowner would pay $2,600 in local property taxes for a $30,000 home.[19]

Even with the relatively low property tax rate, growth nearly doubled the city's property tax yield during the 1970s (from $16.5 million in fiscal 1973 to an estimated $30.2 million in fiscal 1978). Other major sources of revenue also benefited from the region's economic growth, and growth has enhanced the city's ability to sell bonds. Thus Phoenix's fiscal condition is good relative to that of many other large cities. Nevertheless, analysis of the city's finances during the 1970s suggests two potential perils.

One peril involves reliance on a local-and-state-shared sales tax, which is a good source of revenue during growth but is extremely sensitive to economic downturns. During the recession of 1975 city revenues from this source decreased drastically, resulting in the city's smallest budget surplus and largest vocal concern over finances in recent years.

The second peril is the city's greater reliance on federal aid to fund city services. In 1975 Mayor Margaret Hance's campaign oratory con-

cent sales tax to 2 percent in the 1976–77 fiscal year. This additional 1 percent tax, which carried an exemption for certain food items, was rescinded by voters in a special election in February 1977. Thus the tax was only in effect for six months.

18. This varies somewhat, depending on a taxpayer's particular location, because of special district levies. Service fragmentation has many consequences, not the least of which is complication of the tax burden formula for the taxpayer and policy analyst.

19. Jana Bommersbach, *Arizona Republic,* June 19, 1977.

cerning "over-reliance on federal aid" was based on this trend. As noted above, federal aid represented an increasingly large share of total city operating expenditures during the 1970s, while local revenues decreased as a proportion of total expenditures.

Forging a Municipal Government

Phoenix is the capital of the last of the contiguous forty-eight states to be admitted to the union.[20] The history of the city's government dates to 1881. From then until 1948 different forms of government were tried in attempts to take the turbulent capital city out of the "last frontier." The strong mayor system employed from 1881 to 1914 was strong in name only. During that time, there were twenty-seven changes of administration.[21] Things did not improve following the charter reform of 1913, which established a commissioner-manager or commission forms of municipal government. Phoenix experimented with a hybrid in which each of four commissioners was responsible for certain departments, with certain administrative functions delegated to the appointed city manager. During this period annual elections brought multiple shifts in power resulting in thirty-one city managers for the thirty-five years following 1914.[22]

Municipal reform finally came to Phoenix in 1948. Eugene Pulliam, the new owner of the city's two daily newspapers, the *Arizona Republic* and the *Phoenix Gazette,* led the battle for reform. Other civic groups and leaders joined in the effort to find a form of government that would help reduce the city's high rates of crime and corruption. Because of widespread prostitution and venereal disease, Phoenix had been declared off-limits to servicemen during World War II. It was not difficult to find support for change.

In 1948 voters approved a council-manager form of government. Under this system policy is made by six council members and a mayor who are elected simultaneously for two-year terms. Council members

20. Arizona became a state on February 14, 1912. For a good discussion of the conflicts and barriers encountered in the move toward statehood, see Ray Everett, *Arizona History and Government* (Center for Public Affairs, Arizona State University, 1977), chap. 4. The history of Phoenix is currently the subject of an ambitious research project under the direction of Wesley Johnson, who provided some insights used in this section.

21. Goodall, "Phoenix: Reformers At Work," pp. 110–26.

22. Ibid., p. 116.

are elected at large in nonpartisan elections held in November of odd-numbered years. The city manager is the city's top administrator and is hired by the council. The manager in turn appoints heads of the city's major departments. Most city employees are now part of the city's merit system. In making policy city officials rely on over fifty citizen advisory boards and commissions for citizen input.

The government reform of 1948 allowed for the development of a large cadre of professionals and city workers. Vocal critics of the costs of government would be quick to point to the great increase in the size of local government under the reform. A city staff of approximately 2,556 in 1960 expanded to over 8,000 by the end of fiscal year 1977. That growth, however, must be seen against the backdrop of the city's overall economic expansion and complexity of development. Not surprisingly, personnel increases have exceeded the norm in city departments concerned with community enrichment, urban development, housing, and economic development.

Some would argue that the development of a strong city administration has had its costs. Since the 1948 reform, the city council and mayor have been elected from a slate nominated by a local elite group called the Charter Committee. This group traditionally has been heavily representative of business, development, and banking interests. In a pattern familiar to many civic elite associations, new members are recruited by invitation from insiders. From the inception of the committee, its intent has been to find persons committed to the philosophy of reform and "good government" contained in the 1948 revisions. The group has traditionally advocated a business approach to city government and has established an informal two-term (four years total) tradition for council members. Thus the normally difficult task of creating citizen interest in local government and politics has been compounded in Phoenix by elitist nomination and election procedures, an increasingly powerful administration, and increasing ambivalence over the Charter Committee's objectives. Critics of the committee and its views contend that politics has not been taken out of city government but has been monopolized by the local social and economic elite and "professionalized" by their hired functionaries. But the contention that staff will dominate policy in weak mayor-council arrangements has often been suspect in Phoenix and became more dubious following the dismissal in August 1976 of City Manager John Wentz for his alleged inability to communicate with the city council. The council has also taken an active role in policymaking and implementation of many of the city's new programs.

Perhaps most important, the committee nominating system now appears vulnerable. Until 1975 only two candidates had successfully challenged the committee slate. In the 1975 election, however, voters chose four independent candidates for the council and elected independent Margaret Hance as mayor. For the first time, potential candidates for the next election clearly appeared more concerned about their constituencies than about committee endorsement. A prominent explanation for the emergence of successful independents in 1975 was lack of voter trust in anything connected with the establishment. In partial deference to that potential backlash, current incumbents did not actively seek committee endorsement. These developments, accompanied by reports of factional disputes within the committee, have led to inevitable speculation about the "demise of Charter" unless the organization is made more "open."

Poverty in the Midst of Sun Belt Affluence

In its first year under the CDBG Phoenix was entitled to \$2.75 million; in its second year, \$5.77 million; and in its third year, \$9.66 million. These amounts represented substantial increases over the city's previous experience with the programs "folded into" the CDBG. For the five years (1968–72) preceding the CDBG, previous categorical grants from HUD averaged \$1.31 million and were largely used for the city's open space program expenditures, which averaged \$639,000 for the base years 1968–72. These funds were used to acquire and develop neighborhood parks, to provide modest development in existing recreation areas, to acquire a new large recreation area called Cave Creek Park, and to purchase mountain areas encircling the city in response to environmentalists' pressure to limit development.

The city had no model cities experience, and federally supported urban renewal activity was limited to one neighborhood development project, the Booker T. Washington neighborhood development program. Earlier, the Department of Housing and Urban Development (HUD) had rejected overtures to fund urban renewal programs because the city lacked a housing code. The Booker T. Washington project was established in 1971 and had average annual expenditures of \$450,000 before the CDBG. The development neighborhood encompassed 121 acres adjacent to downtown Phoenix and was dedicated to what became a neighborhood slogan: "community renewal and not just community removal." Many dwellings in this mixed commercial-residential area were dilapidated and in need of substantial rehabilitation or replacement. Over 50 percent of the area's residents were low-income minorities according to 1970 census classifications.

Many considered the Booker T. Washington area hopelessly blighted. Located in the corridor between the city's Sky Harbor International Airport and downtown, the area was a local embarrassment. This core of poverty and decay provided a poignant counter to the Chamber-of-Commerce-type introduction to "modern Southwestern living." Local business interests and public officials agreed that "something had to be done," but there was less agreement about what that something was. As a result, the neighborhood development program was begun without an overall downtown development plan and with multiple and sometimes conflicting objectives. Most people agreed that a certain amount of clearance and demolition provided a necessary condition for renewal. Thus neighborhood development activity concentrated on the specification of clearance and demolition needs, stimulation of citizen involvement, acquisition of property, and initial clearance. Although the city was committed from the outset to a general land use plan and to a project that would stabilize and revitalize the area for both residential and commercial purposes, specific plans affecting the eventual shape of the neighborhood were not actually agreed upon until after the four years of project experience that led to the first-year CDBG allocations.

Descriptions of the city's economic and fiscal health, coupled with its image of sun belt affluence, might lead one to conclude that with the exception of the neighborhood development program, Phoenix did not need to participate in HUD programs designed to cope with urban ills. Residents of almost one-quarter of the city's census tracts endured severe urban hardship, however. According to an analysis by the city's own staff, as well as HUD officials, between twenty-five and thirty of the city's more than one hundred census tracts were characterized by large concentrations of poor people living in poor housing conditions. The tracts in question contained the largest proportion of city households that are "housing-deprived."[23] These same tracts had median family in-

23. City of Phoenix, Commission on Housing, *Housing in Phoenix* (City of Phoenix, 1974), vol. 3, p. 17. This report contains data on the following factors that provide an index of housing deprivation in Phoenix: (1) lack of complete kitchen or plumbing facilities; (2) one or more structural mechanical defects; (3) more than 1.51 persons per room; and (4) residents pay more than 25 percent of gross income for rent.

comes below the poverty level in 1970, high proportions of large households and female-headed households, and high concentrations of poorly educated, unemployed, and minority persons. In Phoenix, minorities clearly shared disproportionately in low incomes and poor housing.

Blacks comprised 5% of the Phoenix population in 1970 and Mexican-Americans 14%. However, Blacks comprised 12% of all families with incomes under $4,000 and 8% of all under $7,000. Mexican-Americans comprised 19% of all families with incomes under $4,000 and 17% of all families under $7,000. While 27% of all "other" families had incomes under $7,000, the share for Blacks and Mexican-Americans was 64% and 45%, respectively.[24]

Minority households represented 42 percent of the city's "moderately overcrowded" housing (1.01 or more persons per room) and 56 percent of severely overcrowded housing (1.51 or more persons per room). The city's own assessment was that "it is clear that low income households and minorities are a majority of those with housing problems."[25]

These tracts of greatest housing need and highest minority and low-income concentration occupy most of the area known as South Phoenix. Until 1939 Phoenix schools were segregated, and minority children were required to attend schools south of the Salt River and the railroad tracks that divide Phoenix.[26] In Phoenix as elsewhere, segregation was supported by other forms of discrimination encountered by minorities who crossed the boundaries. Today one can tour the large South Phoenix area and find ample evidence of the residual effects of discrimination and consequent racial and low-income concentration. Many streets remain unpaved, vacant lots are common, and dilapidated, often unoccupied, residential and commercial buildings abound. The condition and prevailing attitude of many minority residents are summarized in their nickname for the state—"Aribama."

Thus by classic indicators of urban hardship, such as unemployment, dependency, education, income, crowded housing, and poverty,[27] the South Phoenix area is clearly distinguished from the rest of the city.

24. City of Phoenix, "Community Development Program 1976: Annual Performance Report," submitted to HUD, February 22, 1973, p. 87. Additional detail documenting the interrelationship of low income, large minority population, and poor housing in Phoenix may be found in City of Phoenix, *Housing in Phoenix,* vol. 3, pp. 138, 148.

25. Ibid., p. 148.

26. Interview with historian Wesley Johnson.

27. The hardship index derived from these factors is relatively low for Phoenix, resulting in a central city hardship index rank of forty-nine out of fifty-five of the nation's sixty-six standard metropolitan statistical areas. Richard P. Nathan and Charles Adams, "Understanding Central City Hardship," *Political Science Quarterly,* vol. 91 (Spring 1976), pp. 49, 52.

Timothy Barrow, former Phoenix mayor, correctly contends "that the problem outlined by the Kerner Commission report—the emergence of two nations, one rich and white and the other poor and black—is very much a part of Phoenix."[28] The "South Phoenix problem" is obvious and points to a long-standing area of community development need. The city's overall affluence partially masks these physical and human needs, but they are severe. Population deconcentration has taken place in Phoenix in the form of annexation and leapfrogging development, but the city's sprawl left in its wake a concentrated population in great need.

The benefits of constant expansion of city boundaries to keep pace with a growing population created large future costs and long-range community development concerns that go beyond the needs of the city's isolated poor population. Human problems associated with sprawl are less easily targeted but are clearly identifiable in Phoenix and other sun belt boom areas because of the complaints of increasingly vocal groups of elderly citizens and others who feel the impact of the form of isolation generated by urban sprawl. Those who can afford it drive private automobiles to the city's many shopping centers, schools, and government and business offices distributed throughout the sprawling city. Because of this decentralization of services and businesses, few convenient residential areas exist for those who lack transportation. Public transportation is inadequate for most of the city. In addition, as a result of this pattern of development and the relatively late arrival of zoning, there is little definition of "neighborhoods" or any real center of community activity.

It is clear, therefore, that the city's lack of participation in earlier HUD renewal and redevelopment programs could not be explained by a lack of urban problems. While the city is relatively young, age alone provides insufficient explanation. The state's only other metropolitan city, Tucson, developed similarly but had acquired substantial urban renewal experience before the CDBG program. The low level of HUD programs in Phoenix was a product of local political culture and administration.

Slow Acceptance of Federal Aid

Phoenix traditionally considered federal aid a last resort in dealing with local problems. For the most part, elected local policymakers were

28. As reported in Michael T. Kaufman, *New York Times,* April 5, 1975.

conditioned by neither belief nor demand to look for such solutions and were skeptical of them. The statement of one elected official who contended simply that "the federal government is evil" may not be representative, but it was likely to receive substantial support in Phoenix. The lack of visible demand for the improvement of neighborhood and group conditions in the city could be explained partially by the absence of neighborhoods and the lack of supporting political infrastructure—such as a ward system—that might foster better communication between city council members and identifiable groups of constituents.

For whatever reason, elected policymakers and key staff officials avoided consideration of federal aid for urban problem-solving until 1963. The mayor elected that year, Milton Graham, was a member of the community elite, had been nominated by the Charter Committee, and on many issues shared the conservative views of his predecessors. But Graham was more pragmatic than earlier mayors and council members and brought new life to the role of mayor and the place of the council in local policy formulation.[29] Known to the committee's inner circle as "Uncle Milty," Graham personally got in touch with federal officials, made trips to Washington, D.C., and generally increased the awareness of local officials about the new revenue sources represented by categorical grants. Without abandoning the philosophy and rhetoric of "local control," succeeding mayors—particularly John Driggs (1969–73) and Timothy Barrow (1973–75)—also advocated using federal dollars to attack urban problems.

Thus a more active and receptive official approach to federal aid for urban problems did not begin until the late 1960s and early 1970s. The establishment of several urban problems commissions to deal with crime, the environment, housing, and so forth did not take place until after the election of Mayor Driggs in 1969. Similarly, the interest in urban renewal and neighborhood development that was generated among some staff and elected officials in the late 1960s was stymied by the absence of a housing code. Not until 1971 did the city receive from HUD a Workable Program Certification, permitting the city to receive urban renewal and some other forms of aid. From the municipal election of 1961 (in which fundamentalist Reverend Aubrey Moore railed against the housing code as a tool

29. This description is drawn from Goodall, "Phoenix: Reformers At Work," p. 123, and from interviews with participants and observers of local government at that time. The recollections of David Berman, professor of political science at Arizona State University, were most helpful in making this assessment.

of the international communist conspiracy) to the present,[30] a housing code for the city of Phoenix appeared politically unfeasible. The Workable Program Certification, which removed the final technical barrier to the city's first participation in a HUD-sponsored urban program—the Booker T. Washington neighborhood development program—was issued only after the 1970 council amended the construction code to provide for systematic housing inspections, the minimum requirement for certification. A more detailed review of the city's more recent and relatively unsuccessful attempts to implement these inspections on anything other than a voluntary basis would be out of place here; it is enough to note the remark of one local official that federal officials "fail to appreciate the political climate that makes housing inspections difficult here."

Administrative organization is another factor that impeded attempts to acquire federal aid. The municipal government structure described earlier continues to undergo formal and informal change. One constant, however, is apparent when recent organization charts and lists of significant actors in community development activities are compared: organizations that implement federal programs are traditionally within the formal municipal government. The city's antipoverty agency—Leadership and Education for the Advancement of Phoenix (LEAP)—is a regular department of city government, as are the public housing and neighborhood development departments. Unlike most cities, Phoenix has not set up the public housing agency as an independent authority. The current arrangement that centralizes municipal services and thus produces some economic efficiencies, funnels public demand and professional recommendations through the city government. It also solidifies the status quo and impedes change. In many cities public housing, urban renewal, and antipoverty agencies were quasi-independent and aggressive in seeking federal aid to meet constituency demands. In Phoenix any aggressive tendencies were dampened by the location of these agencies within a government structure that frowned on federal aid.

While changes in attitude were important in the city's pursuit of federal funds, more than any other single factor the automatic nature of formula grant distributions to cities accounted for the emergence of federal aid as a significant source of revenue for Phoenix. In the 1971–72 fiscal year, before the enactment of the CDBG, federal aid accounted for only 3.2 percent of expenditures and 21.7 percent of operating revenues. Although

30. Ibid., p. 119.

a recent city report of federal aid lists 109 "active" federal grants, a very large proportion of total federal funds is derived from a few formula entitlements.[31] In 1976–77 the CDBG, manpower programs, social services (title 20 of the Social Security Act),[32] antirecession fiscal assistance, and urban mass transit accounted for almost 72.2 percent of the city's federal grant activity. The CDBG program alone represented 9.1 percent of the city's total federal aid for this period. The sheer magnitude of the grant guaranteed its impact on processes and institutions.

For many cities these sources of funds represented an expanded intergovernmental fiscal relationship. In Phoenix the programs marked a new era and thus raised several questions. How would lack of experience with categorical programs, and lack of organizational forms for dealing with them, affect the planning, allocation, and implementation of new block grant programs, including the CDBG? Would the city's lack of previous experience in HUD programs foster innovation in such a way that it would serve as a model for those who plead for greater decentralization? Or would it produce delay and dissipation of resources?

The Decision Process: Year One

The enactment of the CDBG introduced a new player and a new resource to Phoenix government. HUD's previous marginal involvement in local affairs, through the Booker T. Washington neighborhood development categorical grant, was now destined to expand. The new CDBG entitlement would yield over $17 million in the first three years. This was a far cry from the neighborhood development program, which averaged $450,000 in annual expenditures.

In the summer of 1974 City Manager John Wentz and his staff were uncertain of the total implications of this shift in revenue and intergovernmental relations. Nevertheless, Wentz and Deputy City Manager Glenwood Wilson were convinced that the block grant could have many effects

31. The unpublished report was produced by the city's Office of Federal Aid Coordination.

32. Title 20, enacted in 1974, is an addition to the Social Security Act. It provides grants to cover 90 percent of the cost for family planning services and 75 percent for other social services, such as helping certain persons achieve self-sufficiency, protecting them from neglect or abuse, and securing appropriate institutional care for them when necessary. Grants are made to state governments on the basis of population, and the state in turn may fund local programs.

on local politics and programs. The new resource represented welcome revenue for a local government feeling a financial pinch owing to a temporary local economic downturn. At the same time, the CDBG was seen by city management as harboring the potential for interdepartmental conflict. The utility of the new revenue as well as its potential for conflict hinged on the strings attached to its use. What were the objectives of the act? What activities would be eligible for funding? How much discretion would Phoenix city government have in program operations? It was clear to Wentz that answers to these and other basic questions would have to precede detailed planning and allocation. Accordingly, two key decisions were made in the summer of 1974. First, the first-year application would not be delegated to a line department but would be prepared in the city manager's office. Second, preparation of the application would be the responsibility of the city's federal aid coordinator, James Rhone.

Gaining Approval of the Council

At this early stage the city manager and his staff needed information that linked HUD requirements to city needs; Rhone was the logical choice for gathering this information and preparing the application. Unhampered by line department allegiance, experienced in federal aid, equipped with legal training and a masters degree in public administration, experienced as an employee of the city of Phoenix, and given full authority by Wentz, Rhone would be comfortable sorting out and transmitting messages from HUD and responding to questions from city elected officials, departments, and constituents. Moreover, as federal aid coordinator, Rhone had kept abreast of national legislative proposals that preceded the CDBG. In January 1973 he accompanied the city manager and the mayor to a HUD-sponsored meeting in San Francisco to discuss provisions of the Better Communities Act, President Nixon's legislative proposal that eventually became the basis of the CDBG program. Rhone then prepared a discussion paper on the implications of the Better Communities Act for Phoenix. In retrospect city officials remember these early discussions as being very speculative and initiated primarily by general information from Rhone and a city representative stationed in Washington.

The pace of discussion and level of information increased rapidly following the enactment of the CDBG in August 1974. Rhone and Deputy City Manager Wilson spent approximately two weeks discussing strategy before going to the city council in early September to explain the act. At that early meeting the city staff supplemented its own presentation with a National League of Cities slide show that was greatly oversimplified, according to both staff and some council members. According to one council member, this presentation told the council little more than "this is merely another way of doing business with the federal government." What was clearly conveyed at the meeting was the need for council approval of the staff's plan and a timetable for preparing the first-year application. At the time, HUD told Rhone that funding for the Booker T. Washington project would be interrupted at the end of the categorical grant period—January 1975—unless the new CDBG application was approved or a new categorical grant application was submitted. Confusion over the substitution of a portion of the new block grant to continue the neighborhood development project was one of the results of the lack of knowledge of the CDBG program on the part of both HUD and city officials.

Local policymakers were virtually unanimous in favoring completion of Booker T. Washington, the city's only development project. This concern that the project continue provided a basis for council acquiescence to the very compressed first-year schedule. According to this schedule, public announcements, staff meetings with various citizen groups, public hearings, city council subcommittee sessions, and final city council action would all take place in little more than one month (from mid-October to the November 18 council session). The council accepted this proposal and in keeping with past practice created a subcommittee of three council members to monitor the application process. At this stage, council members knew little more than that they were responsible for a final decision on November 18 that would be partially pro forma—the portion needed to continue the development project—and would partially involve new allocations to be defined later in city dealings with HUD and local groups.

Citizen Input

Having gained the approval of the council for its overall application plan, the city manager's staff, particularly Rhone, then had the task of quickly learning and merging HUD program objectives with somewhat vague citizen participation requirements and local needs. The city chose existing citizen advisory boards and commissions as its vehicle for citizen participation. Approximately thirty-seven such organizations existed in

Phoenix at this time, composed of volunteers who were usually appointed by the city council with some suggestions from the city manager's office. These boards and commissions had varying amounts of autonomy from city departments and the public officials who appointed them. They also varied in composition from "civic elite" to more representative groups.

Rhone's communication with the HUD area office in Los Angeles convinced him that the compressed time schedule for citizen participation was required if the development project was to continue without interruption in January 1975. The council had little choice but to acquiesce to both the urgency of the process and the use of the citizen advisory boards. As a result, Rhone prepared a memorandum that outlined the legislative provisions of the CDBG, the local timetable for preparing the application, eligible activities from HUD regulations, and citizen participation plans. This memorandum was sent on October 11 to city boards and commissions "interested or affected" by the general provisions of the program. Aside from brief news announcements of public hearings, the memorandum represented the city's sole attempt to stimulate citizen participation in first-year CDBG planning.

The decision to use existing citizen's groups to meet citizen participation requirements obviously made life easier for city officials. Rhone and his staff were able to direct their efforts during the last two weeks of October toward explaining provisions of the act and answering questions from members of commissions and city departments concerned with social services, planning, housing, parks, environmental quality, library, streets, and the Booker T. Washington project. Presentations were made at regular and special meetings of these groups, and substantial informal communication took place between the Federal Aid Office and interested city departments.

Public hearing participation was clearly limited by the timetable and invitation list adopted by city staff. Over one hundred citizens attended the November 4 meeting of the council subcommittee, most representing or sympathizing with the Neighborhood Development Board, the Housing Commission, and LEAP. Some who attended that hearing were not on the city's invitation list and were accordingly critical of the process. The executive director of Chicanos por La Causa stated this position at the meeting:

> One thing, just sitting down with my staff and with some people from the community that were there, *they were not aware . . . of these monies.* Of course, we had signed the Community Housing or the Development Act and,

as a matter of fact, just recently went on a trip to San Francisco to gather information on it. Mr. Rhone went to that same meeting. It surprises me *that all these things are happening*. [Emphasis added.][33]

The process favored boards, commissions, and departments that already had plans for eligible projects. By the end of the public hearing the council subcommittee had heard requests totaling $5.2 million, primarily from LEAP, the Housing Commission, the Neighborhood Development Board, and the Streets Commission. Requests from group spokesmen illustrated varying degrees of preparation and political acumen. Clearly, the most articulate, well-planned, and comprehensive proposal came from the Housing Commission.

The Housing Commission

The Housing Commission emerged in 1972 as one of several urban problems commissions created to advise the city council at the recommendation of Phoenix Forward, an elite citizen's planning group. The group's chairman, appointed by the city council in 1969, was John Driggs, who subsequently was elected mayor on a platform that included the promise to implement some of the ideas that emerged from Phoenix Forward planning sessions. Driggs's appointments to the Housing Commission included prominent bankers, builders, and developers; the housing industry was well represented. But the mayor also appointed representatives of minority organizations and the city's antipoverty agency to the original seventeen-member commission. From the inception of the commission, some members have addressed the needs of the disadvantaged housing consumer.

Unlike some of its counterpart urban problems commissions, the Housing Commission was active—meeting monthly—and influential almost from the beginning. This was due in large part to the personalities and skills of several commission members, particularly the original vice chairperson, Joy Carter, a dynamic, intelligent, and consumer-oriented social worker who was later elected to the city council, and Chairperson Robert Bulla, an influential newspaper executive. Both were well-schooled in local politics and economics. As one of its major accomplishments, the Housing Commission after one year of activity was able to persuade the city to appoint a full-time staff administrator to the commission. Wayne Putnam, a professional planner who had served as a city

33. Transcript, Community Development Public Hearing, November 4, 1974.

planner and administrator, was appointed in 1973 and served as an active advocate for Housing Commission interests through the first two years of CDBG activity.

The major product of the Housing Commission's deliberations during the first two years was the city's Housing Element of the Comprehensive Plan. Stimulated by HUD, the Workable Program Certification, and key members of the city's Planning Department, the Housing Element was the result of two years of continuous deliberation by the Housing Commission, the Planning Commission (a citizen advisory group), the city planning staff, and interested public officials and staff. City officials estimate that the three-volume, 1,000-page analysis of Phoenix housing problems and needs required 20,000 man-hours to complete. The Housing Commission battled for months over the more than seventy programs that were initially recommended in a first-phase report prepared under the direction of City Planner Joy Mee. The result was the final Housing Element, which listed twenty-four objectives and thirty-nine specific programs designed to alleviate housing problems.

The ink was hardly dry on this report in the fall of 1974 when the Housing Commission became aware of the potential for CDBG funding. It was clear to commission chairpersons that CDBG funds represented a momentous opportunity to implement their proposed attack on housing deterioration and red-lining in the city's most disadvantaged neighborhoods, primarily those of high minority concentration in South Phoenix.

The commission appeared at the November 4 public hearing armed with data and testimony to support (1) continuation of the Booker T. Washington project; (2) a Residential Restoration and Preservation Program (RRPP) to operate in deteriorated areas; (3) a Neighborhood Housing Services rehabilitation loan program for a moderate income tract;[34] (4) a Federal Housing Administration (FHA) repossession-rehabilitation program for two other low-income tracts; (5) an Emergency Home Repair Program to focus on low-income households throughout the city; and (6) a study of housing rehabilitation needs in the high-noise area adjacent to the airport. The package was justified by commission members and city planning staff as a first pilot step toward a

34. Neighborhood Housing Services are independent, nonprofit, state-chartered corporations that bring together residents, lending institutions, and the local government to focus reinvestment efforts in a small neighborhood. The program is sponsored by the National Neighborhood Reinvestment Corporation, which usually provides a grant to start a revolving fund for subsidized loans for housing rehabilitation to residents unable to obtain a loan from private lending institutions.

series of housing and neighborhood improvement needs described in depth by the Housing Element. Proponents contended that these programs best met the objectives of the federal legislation, the desires of HUD, and the needs and hopes of the residents of South Phoenix. Commission spokesmen contended that the Housing Element provided a far better map of local housing needs and projection of housing trends than would be given in the minimum information required by the housing assistance plan.

The logic and data in support of the Housing Commission's request, coupled with apparent unity and the strength of their coalition, made competition from other interests for CDBG funds difficult. Requests for street improvements, a new social service center, park acquisition, and a center for the mentally retarded were all presented with some justification but lacked the data and political support that accompanied the housing request.

The council's subcommittee met with commission staff in the week following the public hearing and presented five different alternatives for budgeting the first-year CDBG allocation. Significantly, each of the five alternatives assumed continuation of the Booker T. Washington project at $1.6 million, equivalent to more than half of the first-year entitlement. The evidence was strong that the council subcommittee was persuaded before the public hearing that the Housing Commission should take priority. The commission staff had met several times with the subcommittee before the public hearings and had emphasized that parks, streets, and social services all had recourse to local bonds and other sources of federal aid. In addition the Housing Commission's strong political showing reinforced the inclination of both the city staff and the council subcommittee to support these projects.

Accordingly, the subcommittee chose the city staff's alternative A, which was simply everything the Housing Commission had asked for with the exception of the noise study (the lowest priority item). The subcommittee presented its recommendation to the full council on November 18, two weeks after the first public hearing. It was clear during the subcommittee deliberations and the council session that the Housing Commission had been successful in selling the CDBG as a *housing act*. The only significant discussion centered on criteria used by the commission to choose sites for the initial housing programs. In the end the council accepted the Housing Commission's rationale for site selection, program selection, and approximate funding levels. Only two small grants for parks and streets—$50,000 and $80,000, respectively—were approved in addition to the Housing Commission program. Both grants represented pet projects of two council subcommittee members. Housing Commission leaders had hoped to convince other local decisionmakers that the CDBG was housing. Apparently they had succeeded.

By funding only a limited number of activities Phoenix limited the scope of conflict that some members of the staff as well as the city council believed would occur if more widespread participation was encouraged. As one council member said, with only the established boards and commissions participating, "the shopping list was already too long."

Inexperience Leads to Dissension and Delays

After HUD approved the city's first-year application in March 1975, attention turned to organization and implementation strategies. Aside from the neighborhood development program, the city lacked experience in the kinds of programs called for by the Housing Commission. As the first program year began, all the administrative, legal, and organizational details associated with rehabilitation, Neighborhood Housing Services, and other home loan programs remained to be straightened out. There was substantial confusion. As one staff member noted while describing the first few months of CDBG activity: "We didn't know what the hell we were doing. It's that simple." In these early days key staff members lacked a consensus regarding how to go about implementing a housing program. Indeed, the first project coordinator for the RRPP was not hired until the second program year (July 1976). Until then the RRPP and other new housing activities were placed in the hands of the city's Housing Service Division, which was experienced as the city's housing inspection agency but had not been responsible for any rehabilitation.

The unanimity surrounding the first-year CDBG allocation was destined not to survive the rigors of implementation. A major dispute surfaced in April 1975 over where the RRPP project should operate in the city. The staff of the Housing Services Division had been critical of the proposed site (census tract 1161) from the outset. Some initial survey work reinforced their contention that this neighborhood, with its heavy concentrations of the poor, old, and black, was too far gone for rehabilitation and would instead require extensive and costly redevelopment. Rhone and Deputy City Manager Wilson were convinced that only 40 of over 700 dwellings in the area could be feasibly rehabilitated at the level of funding that they had recommended and that had been adopted by the council. Accordingly, they proposed a second site to the Housing Commission as more feasible and more likely to result in efficient use of CDBG funds by "showing the impact of rehabilitation." The neighborhood recommended by the city manager's staff was almost 50 percent white and had higher housing values than the commission's choice. The city manager's staff was making a plea for triage; the Housing Commission's retort was to save the drowning man. The commissioners responded by noting that they had selected the site because it would fulfill a need and because rehabilitation appeared feasible in that neighborhood. Most important, the Housing Commission contended that residents of the neighborhood were already alienated and would become more disaffected if the promised benefits were withdrawn. In 1970 the average house value for tract 1161 was $6,700, and the residents were 80 percent black.

The debate increased in intensity as the issues of race and general city finance were mixed in with the agreed upon objective of housing rehabilitation. It was not resolved until late April, when the full council followed the recommendation of its subcommittee and elected to stay with the original choice of the Housing Commission. This response on the part of a majority of the city council was to be tested several times in the future. The council coalition was eventually disrupted by reelection and realignment, but the decision to stay has survived largely under the auspices of council member Joy Carter. Carter, the former Housing Commission vice-chairperson, saw the issue as symbolically critical and was able to rally support from other council members each time the question of the viability of the selected tract was raised.

Delays caused by the political and administrative struggle over the RRPP, communication snags with HUD over such matters as environmental review, and administrative and organizational problems associated with lack of experience in housing rehabilitation delayed implementation of the rehabilitation program. This led to a major reallocation of resources at the end of the first program year. By the end of the first year (January 1976), it was calculated that $704,000 would be carried over from the first-year housing programs. This represented 27.4 percent of the total allocation and most of the amount ($880,000) budgeted in the first year for housing programs. But property acquisition, demolition, and relocation activities were progressing well in the Booker T. Washington project. As a result, the staff revised that budget by adding $323,281 of unused rehabilitation funds to the first-year neighborhood development allocation.

Year Two

The decision process in the second year paralleled that of the first year in both form and substantive outcomes. The city manager's office retained control of the application process. Federal Aid Coordinator Rhone prepared a memorandum almost identical to the first-year announcement and distributed it in early July 1975 to the same citizens' groups that had received the first-year version. This announcement said that public hearings would be held September 2 and 9 and that the council would make final allocation decisions at its September 11 meeting. Potential applicants for funds were given a little more time than in the first year, almost two months, to "contact Mr. Rhone for assistance in your presentation." Because of this additional time, Rhone was able to see more groups and to observe the intensity of some demands. It was clear from some of these encounters that the RRPP site dispute and associated delays would continue to affect the city's credibility with residents of the area. In an attempt to allay these concerns, Rhone and other staff members met with citizens from the rehabilitation area several times. One staff member described the audience of one such presentation as "old blacks, not your radicals, yet very distrustful. They felt that the city was out to somehow rip them off."

The issue of the site of the RRPP program was raised again at the opening public hearing of September 2 and during council subcommittee–staff deliberations the week of September 17. By this time city staff members were even more convinced that the area was unsuitable for rehabilitation. Although the findings from the city's structural and sociological surveys of the neighborhood were not fully analyzed by this time, the staff contended that the council should look to other neighborhoods that could be saved with the type of rehabilitation program envisioned.

Residents of the tract were represented at both public hearings and found strong spokesmen in their Housing Commission and neighborhood development program allies. Most important, two of three subcommittee members defended the original choice throughout budget deliberations in September. The council coalition remained solid and in the end supported the Housing Commission's second-year request to allocate over $600,000 to tract 1161.

The Housing Commission's plea to continue other activities begun in the first year as well as to initiate a new counseling program and purchase sites for a housing project for the elderly and a central office for public housing were all approved with little debate or controversy. As in the first-year hearings, the Housing Commission defended these programs as logical extensions of first-year activities and important components in an overall plan.

A principal difference between the first- and second-year application process was that this time over twice as much money was involved. The city's second-year entitlement was over $6 million; the first-year total was $2.6 million. This allowed the council the luxury of entertaining expected incremental demands of the housing coalition *and* hearing requests from emerging groups and interests. The Housing Commission and its friends were aware of the need for more costly relocation and replacement benefits for this area. The original recommendation by the Housing Commission, however, was not fully funded by the council. Expanded second-year funds also allowed the city council to respond to requests from the Parks Commission ($732,000) and from the Library Board ($70,000). Essentially, council subcommittee recommendations formulated the week of September 17 were accepted without question by the full council five days later.

It was in this atmosphere of relative tranquillity that Rhone was advised by the HUD area office that the completed application should be held up pending revision of the total entitlement. This delayed the submission of the second-year application until January 1976 and reinforced the local contention that changes in signals and misinformation from HUD were responsible for many program frustrations and inefficiencies. In this case the council was required to meet again in January to subtract $382,000 from the CDBG budget agreed on earlier. This was accomplished by removing the library allocation and reducing the parks budget.

Focusing on Objectives

Most communities have encountered goal conflicts emanating from the CDBG legislation itself, from HUD, and from local attempts to implement the legislation. As explained earlier, most Phoenix officials initially acquiesced in the local housing coalition's emphasis on the legislative objectives of eliminating slums and blight, conserving housing, and expanding economic opportunity for low- and moderate-income people. Most local officials considered the first-year allocations for South Phoenix projects in keeping with these objectives, which were loosely translated into "doing something for those people." HUD officials also recognized the primacy of these objectives and were accordingly very pleased with first-year plans.

Second-year allocations, however, were not made under conditions of comparable agreement. In the second year HUD area office officials suggested that in certain areas in South Phoenix not enough was being done to promote deconcentration of minority and lower-income residents.

Increased segregation could well be a side effect of the city's proposed CDBG housing projects and related attempts to stimulate new construction and "substantial rehabilitation" through section 8 housing assistance and section 312 rehabilitation loan programs in South Phoenix.[35] Yet the demographic and geographic maps of the community strongly suggest that a housing program designed to produce the opposite effect—deconcentration—would result in many abandoned and blighted inner-city areas. City officials argued that this is precisely what architects of the legislation intended to prevent and that the legislators' position was reinforced by HUD comments to the effect that Phoenix had an acceptable plan in terms of the act's stipulation that slums and blight must be eliminated. City officials also provided the familiar argument that relocation should be a matter of choice, and that many minority residents prefer to remain in areas where people like themselves are concentrated. "Free choice" is very popular in this political culture. The local high school district has practiced a "free choice" program for several years as its method of dealing with segregation.

Many minority leaders as well as public officials in Phoenix give neighborhood development in minority neighborhoods priority over neighborhood integration. In the Phoenix case, and from the perspective of local officials, the federal program contains conflicting objectives. City officials have chosen to pursue the elimination of slums and blight as a first priority unless HUD forces deconcentration at the expense of that objective. From the perspective of many local officials deconcentration would counter both the overall goal of decentralization and the specific objective of neighborhood preservation. This position was made clear by the mayor in her protest against HUD restrictions on the use of section 8 rental assistance money in census tracts with concentrations of lower-income resi-

35. Section 8 of title 2 of the Housing and Community Development Act of 1974 authorizes HUD to make rent subsidy payments for qualified lower-income renters in new, rehabilitated, or existing housing provided by developers or public housing authorities. Section 312 is explained in note 5, chapter 1.

dents: "Such designation is both contrary to the spirit of the community development program and an infringement on the City's local decision-making authority."[36]

It should also be clear, however, that HUD was not the only, or even the prime, source of CDBG goal conflicts among local officials. Apparent unanimity among key local officials in the first year was never as strong as the allocation decisions suggested. By the second program year local politics forced key actors to examine the program in the light of broader constituencies. However, as a result of multiple political pressures, including a mayoralty race between the incumbent and the chairperson of the council subcommittee, programs that expanded benefits to wider segments of the community had to be defended and justified.

Accent on Housing

A starting point for the assessment of "winners" and "losers" centers on program choices. The Booker T. Washington neighborhood development program, for example, benefited from a commitment and a coalition established before the CDBG program. The Booker T. Washington grant was received three years before the CDBG, enough lead time to establish a sunk cost of resources and expectations and to build neighborhood and political support for the project. The project was aimed at the comprehensive residential and commercial redevelopment of a low-income, minority-dominated neighborhood between the heart of downtown Phoenix and the airport. Because of the neighborhood development program's comprehensive goal and its early start, the program staff was able to spend CDBG allotments plus some budget transfers from programs that were late getting under way.

The major changes from earlier spending patterns were in housing and in neighborhood conservation. The housing coalition emerged just in time for the CDBG, and the first victory was the neighborhood development grant. The major accomplishment involved selling the council and some of the staff on several new housing rehabilitation and repair programs. The major projects included:

1. The Residential Restoration and Preservation Program in census tract 1161, intended to upgrade this poor neighborhood by providing

36. Letter, Mayor Margaret T. Hance to Roland E. Camfield, HUD area director, August 31, 1976.

housing rehabilitation for owner-occupied dwellings through some combination of low-interest loans and grants. In addition, the original plan called for the demolition of structures found beyond repair and the relocation of displaced homeowners. Certain public improvements, such as streets, sewers, and parks, would be provided eventually, although one reason for selecting this site was that, unlike some impoverished areas of the city, the tract had already received many of these improvements.

2. Neighborhood Housing Services, a rehabilitation loan program targeted for a basically residential neighborhood where a high percentage of owners could qualify for their own home improvement loan. The area had begun to show signs of deterioration and was a moderate-income area by HUD definition. City funds were used to match an Urban Task Force Grant of $100,000 to provide a high-risk loan pool.

3. FHA repossession-rehabilitation in tracts 1159 and 1163, a program to acquire vacant and vandalized repossessed units. After being rehabilitated, these units would be refinanced and leased to the Phoenix Public Housing Department, which in turn would sublease to a low-income tenant and provide maintenance and management service until the tenant was financially qualified to buy and had demonstrated home-ownership capability. The target areas were both moderate-income tracts of South Phoenix.

4. Housing services and home improvements in various tracts, a program to provide emergency repairs to bring houses into compliance with codes when the owner is unable to pay the costs.

A major selling point that partially accounted for the concentration of allocations for housing and related inner-city neighborhood activities stemmed from the Housing Commission's ability to label the federal program a "low-income housing act." Members of the housing coalition, including sympathetic planning staff, were happy to supply this definition for council members who were uncertain of the meaning of "community development." City policymakers found this definition easy to accept for several reasons. First, they were constantly reminded by planning staff and Housing Commission members that neighborhood preservation and improvement of low-income and minority housing conditions were important national objectives. Second, local housing needs were apparent.

The housing coalition's first-year victory provided a solid incremental base for continued allocations. As table 4-1 suggests, however, the strength of that coalition was tested in the second year. Some "spreading" was indicated by the allocation of approximately 13 percent of second-

Table 3-1. *Allocation of the Community Development Block Grant in Phoenix, by Functional Program*

Program	First year: Amount (thousands of dollars)	First year: Percent of total	Second year: Amount (thousands of dollars)	Second year: Percent of total
Completion of urban renewal programs begun before the grant	1,560	60.7	3,960	68.6
Housing and neighborhood conservation	960[a]	37.4	963[a]	16.7
New economic development	0	0	0	0
Social services and facilities	0	0	100	1.7
General development	50	1.9	749	13.0
Total	2,570	100.00	5,773	100.00

Source: "City of Phoenix Budget Allocations for the Community Development Block Grant, Fiscal Year 1975," and ibid., fiscal year 1976.
a. Includes $80,900 for street repair in specific low-income target areas.

year resources to general development. Most of these allocations were for parks and recreation projects. The spreading of CDBG dollars to a broader area and constituency was significant. While some of these funds were earmarked for South Phoenix, others were allocated to more affluent areas of the city.

Judging by the increase in general development activity and by the nature and amount of council debate over these allocations, the spreading of CDBG activity in Phoenix appeared to be accompanied by a broadening of the definition of community development. The pressure that this competition for other kinds of activities placed on the housing coalition was magnified by strain within the coalition caused by debate over program implementation (discussed in the next section). Overall, the expectation was fostered that general development activities would expand in future allocations in part because of problems in implementing the housing programs and in part because of the area office's continuing interpretation that social service activities were generally not eligible. Thus as the city council became more deeply involved in distributing this large and growing resource, it was very likely that wider distribution of benefits would follow.[37] Indeed, if the grant was really the model of decentralization that some of its advocates envisioned, reallocation of benefits to a wider range of income groups seemed inevitable.

In sum, in the transitional years of the CDBG Phoenix made substantial plans and allocations for a housing rehabilitation and urban development program for a large and blighted area of the city. Increasingly, however, city officials tended to speak of the grant as a source of general fund revenue. And as the program became a more visible and important political resource, the housing interests that enjoyed early successes faced increasing challenges to their monopoly on its use.

Wider Distribution of Benefits

The moderate spreading of activities observed in the second-year application was accompanied by the dispersion of benefits to higher-income neighborhoods and groups. Funds budgeted in the first-year application were devoted almost entirely to programs for low- and moderate-income areas of South Phoenix.[38] Over 70 percent of funds that could be identified as intended to produce an effect in low- and moderate-income areas were designated for low-income areas. In the second year the addition of parks and recreation and other "general development" activities redistributed approximately 20 percent of program benefits to neighborhoods whose residents had incomes that exceeded low or moderate standards. Nevertheless, the CDBG did provide a major new influx of funds into low-income sections of Phoenix in the initial program years,

37. The assumption is that public budget benefits increase and spread as a normal function of democratic process, however imperfect. For an expanded discussion, see John Stuart Hall, "Who Benefits: Washington and Arizona Communities," in Henry, ed., *Of, By, and For the People,* pp. 99–108. The link between democratic process and budget growth is a subject of substantial importance. For two divergent but equally incisive perspectives, see William A. Niskanen, Jr., *Bureaucracy and Representative Government* (Chicago: Aldine-Atherton, 1971); and Anthony Downs, "Why the Government Budget is Too Small in Any Democracy," *World Politics,* vol. 12 (July 1960), pp. 541–63.

38. For this analysis "low" income refers to households with 0–50 percent of the standard metropolitan statistical area median income, and "moderate" income refers to households with 51–80 percent of the SMSA median income. Census tract median-income data for 1970 are used to make these classifications, which present obvious problems. On the basis of more recent local surveys (such as *Inside Phoenix: 1976*) the relative position of these areas on an income scale appears to have remained very stable.

and the primary beneficiary of the total grant was some of the city's poorest areas.

The Booker T. Washington project, which accounted for over 60 percent of the allocations, is located in one of the city's poorest areas (1970 median family income of less than $5,000). As noted before, the major activities in the neighborhood development program included demolition, property acquisition, relocation, and some land sales—activities centered on preparing the area for redevelopment. Objectives of this redevelopment were in some ways as broad as the 121-acre site of the project, which attempted to combine economic development, neighborhood renewal, and downtown business district redevelopment by creating an industrial park on the southern boundary of the project, aiding commercial revitalization of businesses in the area, and providing new and rehabilitated housing for local residents. During the first two years of program activity, more than half of the sixty-three homeowners, churches, and businesses initially identified as in need elected to cooperate with the project. Many were able to use relocation aid and section 8 housing assistance payments to purchase new structures and remain in the neighborhood. Completed activities included several of the fifty-two scheduled units of new single family housing, 110 units of new section 8 housing for the elderly, and rehabilitation and replacement of several small businesses in the area. In addition historical preservation was well under way with several units. The city also reached agreement with a major development firm to market the industrial park area.

If the project is completed according to plans, the neighborhood will also have a twenty-four-unit publicly owned apartment, a twenty-unit privately owned apartment for lower-income persons, and an estimated 270 units of multifamily, higher-density housing.[39] Those who staff the project felt that, when completed, it would make a difference in people's lives and in the environment.

Allocations for the other housing programs were also expected to directly benefit low-income families and individuals. Although slightly different standards were applied, the Emergency Home Repair, Neighborhood Housing Services, RRPP, and FHA repossession-rehabilitation programs limited eligibility to low-income families. The net long-term effects may vary among the different programs, however. Under the Emergency Home Repair Program, eligibility is determined on a case-

39. These data are from an undated staff-prepared summary of the Booker T. Washington project.

by-case basis and most recipients are on some form of public assistance. The program was essential for humanitarian reasons but probably will make no long-term difference in the lives of the recipients or the appearance of the neighborhoods. Housing and redevelopment activities are often justified by theories asserting the beneficial long-run effects of improved residential environment on individual and group behavior. According to such theories, peoples' feelings about themselves should be improved along with the environment, resulting in multiplier effects that will eventually pay social, psychological, and economic benefits to the community. Even if the theory is strongly supported and even if housing intervention of this type produces significant social and economic benefits, long-range community improvement objectives may prove difficult to reach owing to the insufficient size of the treatment relative to the scale of the problem. Substantial concentrations of poverty and poor housing exist in Phoenix. It is apparent from indicators such as overcrowding, excessive rent payments, and structural defects that between 17,000 and 25,000 households suffer from multiple problems of poverty, including inadequate housing. Even if the RRPP and neighborhood development program were completed and functioning perfectly, they would be directly treating fewer than 1,000 households in small corners of two census tracts.

Conclusion

Community development goals in Phoenix, indeed the definition of community development, shifted as the program progressed. There was no community development program, per se, in the first two years. The activities described on the CDBG applications were coordinated only at the application stage. After the applications were approved, the funds and implementation responsibility were distributed among the city's Housing Services Division, the Parks Department, the Booker T. Washington project, and the Streets and Engineering departments. Community development activity was centralized only for budget and reporting purposes. Except for informal communication among affected employees, different departments had little way of knowing about progress or lack of it toward the vague overall community development goals stated in the application.

The city's relative youth and inexperience with urban development programs as well as internal political conflicts and external communications difficulties with HUD can be said to have limited the city's ability to utilize aid in a productive manner.[40] It was little comfort to those whose expectations were at times thwarted by lack of progress to note that it probably required substantial investments of time and resources to build such capacity.

With the slow rate of implementation in a number of the city's programs, the more immediate and evident effects of the CDBG were on the local decision process and the Phoenix city government. Phoenix officials not only had limited experience with HUD categorical grants but also had spent little time considering housing problems and policies before the block grant. Given these conditions, the CDBG had major agenda-setting, information-generating, and organizational effects in Phoenix.

Implementation Becomes a Learning Process

The block grant and the related requirement for a housing assistance plan forced city council members and high-ranking city staff to listen to new information developed by the city's Housing Commission and Planning Department.[41] The block grant placed housing and redevelopment on the agenda, and these activities benefited from the new sense of urgency and legitimacy attached to them. "Reliance on federal aid" was another new agenda item in Phoenix as a result of the CDBG and the arrival of other major grants such as general revenue sharing and manpower funds.

Giving increased attention to the problems of housing and urban renewal and to methods of financing solutions was a learning experience for most local officials. Council members actively began to seek information about the mechanics of housing rehabilitation programs in other cities. Largely because of the CDBG and other new federal block grant programs, the council also began to pay much more attention to establishing overall city goals and identifying major public problems.

Similarly, a new learning process began for the city's professional staff.

40. Jeffrey L. Pressman, *Federal Programs and City Politics* (University of California Press, 1975), p. 115. For more on this concept, Pressman cites Albert Waterston, *Development Planning: Lessons of Experience* (Johns Hopkins Press, 1965), pp. 30 ff.

41. See note 35, chap. 2, for an explanation of the housing assistance plan.

In the exchange between staff generalists and specialists that took place because of the CDBG, each learned something about the plight of the other. Housing advocates became more aware of overall budget considerations, while the city manager's staff gained more information and ideas about housing and development needs and proposals. At the end of two years some generalist staffers appeared to know almost as much about housing rehabilitation strategies and options as the housing specialists most directly concerned with the issue. This was not the case before the CDBG program began.

Substantively, the coming of the CDBG program made it possible for the city's housing coalition to press new housing demands they viewed as being reinforced by the new federal policy. More important, new resources were available to help meet those demands. In some communities with extensive experience with HUD programs, a large share of the CDBG funds had to be earmarked for the continuation of old programs. This was not the case in Phoenix where the block grant really took the form of new money, although the city's downtown neighborhood development program did initially affect the distribution of these new funds. But even this program continuation effect was in the direction desired by the housing coalition. The main consequence was that the CDBG, in conjunction with mounting local government and political pressures, served to focus policymakers' attention on previously unarticulated and unmet needs of South Phoenix. This almost fortuitous convergence of federal and local policy resulted in large allocations for redevelopment and housing rehabilitation in low- and moderate-income areas outside the neighborhood development site. Low-income housing and redevelopment programs were the big winners in Phoenix, receiving 100 percent of the first-year entitlement ($2.57 million) and over 75 percent of the second-year allocation ($5.77 million).

Although subsequent allocations proceeded incrementally from the housing coalition's initial success, the local political system soon felt the pressure of other interests, including the need to expand participation, and reacted by spreading a portion of CDBG benefits to other areas of the community. Advocates of other programs, such as parks and recreation, became active and promoted the view that the CDBG funds be treated as a general fund. The strategy of this group was to stress potential matching of CDBG funds with other grant sources for parks projects and to present data documenting their version of "need" and treatment for urban ills. The strategy proved at least partially successful, as evidenced by the increase from approximately 2 percent of the first-year allocation to 13 percent of the third-year application for such activities.

New Emphases in the Third Year

As the program progressed beyond the transition years, HUD's interpretation of national legislative objectives affected the local allocation process. Particularly important in this regard was the HUD area office concern in the third year about the concentration of minorities and low-income families in census tracts slated to receive most of the CDBG benefits and HUD decisions on the ineligibility of new general development activities. Local officials were receptive to the housing coalition's interpretation of the neighborhood preservation and renewal objectives of the federal program, but in Phoenix such program concentration eventually came to be seen by HUD as conflicting with "spatial deconcentration" of lower-income groups, another objective of the act. Initially this conflict was not perceived by local policymakers because the spatial deconcentration objective was unarticulated. In the third year, however, HUD emphasized this objective because of its concern over relocation within the target areas. But HUD ruled against some proposed parks and general development activities in the third-year application, an act that served both to check local demands for the spreading of benefits and to provide important support for the housing coalition's neighborhood programs that concentrated spending in the low-income areas.

The HUD policies seemed to have one lasting effect: they united local officials who had been former adversaries and made them allies in the intergovernmental struggle with HUD. Phoenix in the third year continued to allocate large portions of its CDBG budget for activities that were in accord with the city's view of the intent of the act and its own needs.

At the implementation level, in the third year the initial delays, largely attributable to a lack of program experience within the city and in HUD, appeared to be partially overcome. Organizational capacity was becoming stronger, with increased resources and experiences in community development. Direct benefits in the form of visible improvements had already been delivered to some areas and residents of the city. Through active and professional management, the city was able to use most of its first two years of entitlement for continued redevelopment of the neighborhood area while building organizational resources for new housing programs. Given the predominant political culture and consequent late entry of the city into federal urban programs, not much more could have been expected.

This city's relative success with the CDBG program prompts at least two conclusions concerning the block grant experiment. The optimistic one is that if decentralization partially works in Phoenix, it can work anywhere. From the federal perspective, generally acceptable activities were being planned and carried out, largely on local initiative. Local officials sometimes complained about adverse decisions and strings attached to the grant but generally seemed satisfied. But close observation, particularly in the third-year application process, suggests the need to add a note of caution to such optimism. Decentralization allows much to happen by chance. This city's decision process and governmental structure responded to the CDBG as they did because of the almost simultaneous coming of the block grant and the articulation of urban housing and development needs by a new but powerful coalition. But it is a process and a set of decisions that could change in major ways. Indeed, it could be argued that a one-vote change on the council or any significant change by HUD on program eligibility issues could redirect the program. Community development by definition is constant change. In its decentralized and block form, federally supported community development can take many directions.

As the program proceeds, prominent members of the local housing coalition perceive and are concerned about local political pressure to spread benefits. HUD has served as a partial ally in this issue but has also aligned itself with interests advocating new economic development activity such as a new industrial park in the neighborhood development program and the development of a Mexican-American marketplace (the Mercado) in a blighted downtown area. These and other economic development proposals have emphasized targeting and leveraging to get maximum use of the federal dollars. The ability to leverage private capital has also come to be increasingly expressed in defense of sorely needed downtown redevelopment activity. With the increases in CDBG allocations over the first three years, and the future increments, the current winners obtained, and are likely to continue to get, large shares of the allocations for the near future. It is also likely that planned economic development and rehabilitation programs will grow.

CHAPTER FOUR

Houston, Texas

VICTOR E. BACH

HOUSTON, with its lack of zoning regulation, is considered a favorite deviant case by those who study municipal governance and development. Furthermore, it is the only major city in Texas that has a strong mayor form of government rather than the prevailing city manager structure, a fact that has given it the reputation of being a "very political city."

The City's Profile

Houston began in the 1830s as a land speculation scheme of the Allen brothers of New York, who attempted to carve out of the wilderness a major new settlement and port at the head of the bayous connecting with the Gulf of Mexico in the emergent Texas territory. Despite an unfavorably humid climate, which rapidly prompted the republic's legislature to shift its seat to Austin in 1839, and despite the unreliable navigability of the bayous and rivers, from the vantage point of the 1980s Houston has far exceeded its developers' strongest expectations.[1]

Growth Patterns

Now the fifth most populous city in the country, with a population of 1.6 million, Houston is the central core of a metropolitan area of about 2.6 million residents.[2] Its spectacular growth and development have been the result of location, entrepreneurship, and a serendipitous abundance of natural resources.

1. For a historical account of the development of the city, see David G. McComb, *Houston: The Bayou City* (University of Texas Press, 1969), pp. 10–18.

2. Population estimates for 1978 are from U.S. Bureau of the Census, *Statistical Abstract of the United States, 1980* (Government Printing Office, 1980), tables 27 and 28, pp. 27–28. The population and subsequent descriptive data are used to reflect the city's characteristics at the time the community development block grant program started.

The city's early commercial success had its roots in the pre–Civil War expansion of cotton plantations onto the rich, black soil of East Texas; raw cotton was sent to Houston for compression into rock-hard bales, then shipped on to the textile mills of the Northeast and Europe. The dominance of cotton in Houston's economy shifted after 1901, when an oil gusher was brought in on a salt dome formation known as Spindletop, followed quickly by a succession of other gushers. The resulting need for a deep-water port that could accommodate large tankers led to the dredging of a fifty-mile channel along the Buffalo Bayou to the gulf, a venture that was completed in 1914. By the late 1960s Houston ranked third in tonnage among the nation's ports; regional petroleum products constituted nearly half of this tonnage. Together with its natural gas processing plants, the port complex was estimated to supply about 75 percent of the country's energy, and hence Houston became known as "the petroleum capital" of the country.[3] And the city's Chamber of Commerce proudly reported in 1976 that since 1970 over 180 major businesses, many from New York City, had transferred corporate headquarters or divisions to Houston.[4] By 1976 a dozen of the Forbes 500 top-sales U.S. companies were headquartered in Houston, nearly all energy-related.

But the quadrupling of Houston's population since the 1930s has also been partly the result of federal investment. During the Johnson-Rayburn era of influence in Congress the Houston area and the state as a whole were favored as the location of military and defense-related establishments. This trend was capped during Lyndon Johnson's vice presidency by the decision to locate the National Aeronautics and Space Administration's Mission Control Center in the Houston area.

Houston's population is fairly heterogeneous. In addition to a 60 percent Anglo majority, it has a sizable black population (26 percent, or about 400,000 residents) and a substantial Mexican-American population (14 percent, or about 200,000 residents).[5] The city's population growth and relative prosperity continued in the face of the national recession of the mid-1970s and perhaps because of it, Houston has increasingly come to be viewed as one of the sun belt's magnets of opportunity. The influx of migrants to the city is estimated at 1,000 a week; only a quarter of them are either black or Chicano. Most of the newcomers are middle-

3. Stuart E. Jones and William Albert Allard, "Houston, Prairie Dynamo," *National Geographic,* vol. 132 (September 1967), pp. 338–77.

4. Nene Foxhall, *Houston Chronicle,* June 27, 1976.

5. Population estimates are as of December 31, 1977, and were supplied by the Houston Chamber of Commerce.

income whites with strong professional, managerial, or technical skills, who have moved as a result of a job transfer or a job change.[6] It is said that even elite "headquarters types" from New York City rapidly become confirmed Houstonians, content with the city's urbane atmosphere and cultural offerings—good theater, a well-housed opera of good repute; a major sports dome; and a temperate climate conducive to outdoor life-styles.

Houston's striking population growth has been accompanied by a corresponding territorial expansion, from 72 square miles in 1930 to 434 square miles in 1970. Under state law, the city can exercise an annexation privilege to prevent the incorporation of any new communities within a radius of five miles from its boundaries. And Houston, like other large Texas cities, has made frequent use of that option in a conscious attempt to preserve and expand the tax base of the city. The city proper now constitutes nearly two-thirds of the metropolitan population and maintains a low density among cities of comparable population. But a serious lag in the development of infrastructure has followed rapid annexation, and many annexed areas still lack basic services. Among them are a number of poorer sections with badly paved streets and open drainage ditches that become unsanitary, encephalitic swamps during the heavy summer rainfalls.

Houston is a city of sharp contrasts. Its low median income level relative to that in other major metropolitan areas confirms that poverty as well as profit can be found in the city.[7] This is nowhere more visible than from the warping postbellum frame bungalows of the Fourth Ward black ghetto, which is adjacent to the modern skyscrapers of the downtown area, many so striking they have won the praise of noted architectural critics. An *Economist* reporter has observed that "poverty and squalor still abound in the shadow of the refineries. . . . Blacks and Mexican-Americans, while enjoying better times, still feel abused. And rightly so."[8] In 1969 roughly one out of nine Houston households had incomes below the poverty level; these included about a quarter of the city's black house-

6. This observation was generally confirmed in an analysis of immigration to Houston. See Thomas Muller, *Growing and Declining Urban Areas: A Fiscal Comparison* (Urban Institute, 1975), pp. 9–11.

7. U.S. Bureau of the Census, *Census of Population, 1970, General Social and Economic Characteristics,* Final Report PC(1)-C45, *Texas* (GPO, 1972), table 89, p. 585. Median family income for the Houston standard metropolitan statistical area was $10,174; the average median income of the nine other largest SMSAs was $11,224.

8. "The Third State: A Survey of Texas" (Supplement), *Economist,* vol. 263 (May 14, 1977), p. 16.

holds and a sixth of Mexican-American households.[9] Although the Houston area had an enviably low unemployment rate in 1976 of about 5 percent, black unemployment was substantially higher (8.7 percent), and the unemployment rate for minority teenagers was about 34 percent. The sheer magnitude of Houston's total unemployed population, numbering 58,000, was large by most cities' standards.[10] Moreover, wage levels for low-skilled workers tend to be suppressed for several reasons. The presence of a large number of illegal aliens, mostly from Mexico, increases the wage competition for low-skilled labor.[11] And the influence of unions has been weak in the state—only 13 percent of the labor force is unionized and the rate is declining; union shops are unconstitutional violations of the right to work and strikes are considered "unTexan."[12]

As in all major cities, Houston's extremes of wealth and poverty are mirrored in its residential patterns. Its most poverty-stricken and minority-dominated neighborhoods are adjacent to the central business district and include the older wards of the city; the more moderate-income and largely minority areas lie along the eastern sector of the city. The western sector contains the more affluent, established neighborhoods and the newly developed subdivisions, largely colonized by Anglo-Americans. Census data for 1970 show that only one of every ten Houston households is ill-housed, but roughly a quarter of the city's black and Hispanic households have inadequate housing.[13] And the visible preponderance of old frame structures, weakly regulated by local building and fire codes, suggests that housing conditions for the minority population are far worse than the statistics suggest.[14]

9. Bureau of the Census, *Census of Population, 1970, General Social and Economic Characteristics, Texas,* tables 95 and 101, pp. 663, 741.

10. Unemployment figures, supplied by the Texas Employment Commission, are for December 1976.

11. In 1977 R. W. Heston, district director of the U.S. Immigration and Naturalization Service, estimated there were 40,000 illegal aliens in Harris County, 80 percent from Mexico, 75 percent holding jobs. Rod Sallee, *Houston Chronicle,* February 13, 1977.

12. "The Third State: A Survey of Texas," p. 7.

13. U.S. Bureau of the Census, *1970 Census of Population and Housing, Census Tracts, Houston, Tex. Standard Metropolitan Statistical Area,* PHC(1)-89 (GPO, 1972), tables H-1, H-5. "Ill-housed" refers to lack of adequate plumbing facilities or overcrowding.

14. The extremely poor quality of housing conditions for minorities in Houston is best demonstrated by comparison. According to 1970 housing census statistics, roughly 13 percent of Detroit's black households were ill-housed; in Houston about 23 percent of black households were similarly ill-housed. See U.S. Bureau of the Census, *Census of Population, 1970, Housing Characteristics for States, Cities and Counties* (GPO, 1972), table 19, pp. 213, 215.

Political Structure

Houston's "strong mayor" has full authority over the city's score of departments, subject only to civil service regulations. But the ability of the mayor to take strong or unpopular initiatives with constituents and with established city departments is effectively weakened by a two-year term of office, which keeps the incumbent in a perennial state of seeking support for an imminent election. The eight city council members also serve a two-year term, receive nominal salaries for part-time public service,[15] and are elected at large, although five represent designated districts within which they must reside. The only other elected official (also for two years) is the city controller, who derives some power under the city charter by virtue of estimating and certifying the availability of revenues before the council makes appropriations.

Until recently the scale and sophistication of the city's governmental operations have not kept pace with its rapid growth. As of fiscal 1971 its per capita expenditures were the lowest among the ten largest cities—$157 per person, a level two-thirds that of Dallas, its nearest rival for public frugality.[16] Until 1975 the city had no formal mechanism for the advance programming of capital improvements priorities; such decisions generally had been made on an ad hoc basis by mayors in cooperation with the director of the Public Works Department. Many observers of Houston would agree with the judgment that the city had long been running a small, quasi-formal operation that more closely resembled small-town government than that of a complex, large, modern city. Although the city's expenditures more than doubled during the 1970s, Houston is still in sound fiscal health. Annual budget surpluses of from $15 million to $20 million have been common, property owners enjoy relatively low real estate taxes,[17] and the city continues to earn premium bond ratings.

Until the late 1950s Houston's local politics were controlled by a small,

15. In December 1977 the state enacted a bill enabling the city council to set its own salary. After the bill went into effect in January 1978 a council member's salary was set at $19,120 a year.

16. These are local expenditures exclusive of education. Per capita figures were derived from U.S. Bureau of the Census, *Statistical Abstract of the United States, 1973* (GPO, 1973), table 683, p. 432; 1970 central city populations are from ibid., table 23, pp. 22–24.

17. The city's property tax rate in 1977 was $1.58 per $100 valuation based on a 53 percent assessment ratio. In addition the tax rate for the independent school district was $1.70. For a comparison of property tax rates among major cities, see William G. Colman, *Cities, Suburbs, and States* (Free Press, 1975), p. 38.

conservative group of businessmen—dubbed the "8-F crowd" after the hotel suite in which they regularly met—who represented the city's energy, financial, and real estate interests.[18] Partly because of the dynamic changes in the city's population, which made the older coalitions unstable, the power structure of the city has evolved into what has been characterized as a more open system of "tripartite politics" consisting of three major blocs: Anglo conservatives, Anglo liberals, and a minority constituency dominated by a stable, cohesive black voting bloc and a less consistent but solidifying Chicano organization.[19] Despite the city's strong Republican showings in recent federal and state elections, local electoral politics are largely a result of the tripartite pluralism within the Democratic ranks and lack any overarching machine controls. As a result, mayoral elections are usually unpredictable, highly dependent on the particular appeal of personalities and the ability to form coalitions, and usually tight enough to require a run-off vote. To win, it is said to be necessary to carry one of the three blocs solidly and split the other two, while gaining credibility and support from respected business influentials. Consequently the mayoral incumbent must perform a delicate juggling act to maintain constituent support.

The Community Development Setting

Houston's traditional conservatism, its belief in small government, and its relative prosperity had long fostered aloofness and distrust toward federal programs. Lacking zoning regulations—considered an unwarranted interference with the free market and roundly defeated in periodic referenda—the city was ineligible for participation in the federal urban renewal program. But local public and private capital were sufficient to bring about the striking renewal of the city's downtown area in the 1960s without benefit of federal funds.

Houston did participate in the model cities program, however. As a condition for receiving a model cities grant from the Department of Housing and Urban Development (HUD), a local housing code was enacted by the city under pressure in 1969. During the last months of the Johnson

18. See the five-part series "Houston's Power" by Craig Smyser in the *Houston Chronicle,* June 27 through July 1, 1977.

19. This description of Houston's politics is based in part on a more expanded treatment in Clifton McCleskey, "Houston: Tripartite Politics," in Leonard E. Goodall, ed., *Urban Politics in the Southwest* (Arizona State University, Institute of Public Administration, 1967), pp. 68–87.

administration, then Mayor Welch had acceded to an influential group of local liberals and agreed to press Washington for model cities funds. It required a White House meeting with the mayor to secure his agreement to introduce a housing code in order to overcome HUD's resistance to Houston's designation as one of the last model cities.[20]

By the time the community development block grant (CDBG) was legislated in 1974, Houston's Model City Program had embarked on its third action year (out of five projected years) and constituted the lion's share (93 percent) of the city's funding involvement in HUD's categorical programs. The remaining 7 percent came from some small grants for water and sewer projects and open space development. Receiving about $12 million annually, the Model City Program was administered as a specially funded city department that functioned with a good deal of autonomy. Its target neighborhoods spanned some of the more impoverished, largely black areas of the city. Its elective citizen participatory body, the Model Neighborhood Resident Commission (MNRC) was headed by Moses Leroy, a venerable, charismatic, old-line leader in the black community and an important figure in early civil rights struggles whose power to influence black votes assured him ready access to locally elected officials.

Programmatically, the Model City Department had set itself a broad functional agenda, including physical improvements in the model neighborhoods; housing code enforcement and rehabilitation; and a range of human services programs geared to diverse needs in the community, such as day care, programs for the young and the elderly, family counseling, cultural activities, and the promotion of minority enterprise. In an otherwise service-conservative city, where the city charter is often interpreted as prohibiting the local funding of human services, the model neighborhoods were the unique beneficiaries of locally initiated human services programs not available elsewhere in the city. But by 1974 the program had garnered a reputation for inefficiency and mismanagement, characterized by a high turnover of department heads and a backlog of unspent funds.

In the elections of 1973, just before the inception of the CDBG program, Houston entered a relatively liberal period in its political history. Although blacks had provided crucial support to winning mayoral candi-

20. For an account of the early evolution of Houston's Model City Program, see Hawkins H. Menafee, *Houston Model Cities: The First Year* (Institute for Urban Studies, Southwest Center for Urban Research, n.d.).

dates since 1957 and had succeeded in eliminating open racism from Houston politics and increasing their influence with mayors, the 1973 runoff election of Fred Hofheinz represented the first instance of a successful coalition of Anglo-liberal and minority interests behind the mayoral mandate. In addition Leonel J. Castillo, a social worker by profession and a major influence in the political organization of Houston's Chicano community, was elected to replace the retiring incumbent who had long held the city controller's office. Both the presence of a local model cities program and the emergence of a new city administration, with a broad liberal and minority constituency, could be regarded as unusual occurrences, considering Houston's past. They formed the political and programmatic context within which the city's CDBG program took shape.

The First Year of CDBG Planning

The mayor played a dominant role in shaping the early CDBG planning process, and for several reasons. Hofheinz's close runoff victory in 1973 had committed him to the kinds of public investments in housing, neighborhood improvements, and community services that would be responsive to the city's minority communities. The city's prevailing budget conservatism precluded the use of local revenue for these purposes and forced the mayor to rely on federal sources of funds that could be directed at community development priorities supported by influential minority constituents. The increasing strength of minority voters, particularly blacks, in putting Houston's mayors into or out of office make it difficult for any mayor to remain passive toward federal grant programs without great political costs. As a consequence, Houston's mayor has to maintain a delicate political balance by behaving like a cautious conservative on local budget issues and like a redistributive liberal in seeking and using federal grant funds.

It came as no surprise that shortly after Hofheinz took office the city began to adopt a more aggressive and anticipatory stance toward participation in federal programs. As a consequence, Houston's rapidly increasing annual grants under the CDBG formula—from the initial hold-harmless level of $13 million to an anticipated $23 million by 1977—were of major political importance in promoting neighborhood physical improvements, housing rehabilitation, and human service programs in the city's lower-income neighborhoods. By early 1974 the mayor's new appointments to the board of the Housing Authority underlined his determination to resuscitate the institution and give it more dynamic direction.

Hofheinz's orientation and training, which included a Ph.D. in economics, led him to find ways to strengthen the city's technical and managerial capacity to cope with the complex problems of a large, rapidly growing city. Using a special HUD grant for local "capacity building" that he obtained in 1974, Hofheinz created the Policy Planning Division in the mayor's office. The division was to serve as a key executive resource in seeking and responding to new federal programs, and the preparation and planning of the anticipated CDBG program was one of its first major assignments. It was also to be the center of planning intelligence for the development of the city's first formal capital improvements program, for the consideration of an urban growth management policy, and for the consideration of local options for improved delivery of human services. George W. Strong, an analyst at the Southwest Center for Urban Research who had been instrumental in securing the HUD grant and setting up the division, was appointed an executive assistant to the mayor and became his chief adviser on CDBG-related issues.

Assigning Responsibilities

By September 1974, once CDBG became a reality, the mayor formally assigned the responsibility for preparing the first-year application to the Policy Planning Division, passing over several other city departments—City Planning, Public Works, the Model City Department—with a clear interest and role in CDBG activities. The need for coordination among the departments, both in CDBG planning and subsequent program implementation, and the sensitive nature of the decisions to be made, argued for locating the planning effort in the mayor's office, where it could be closely monitored and coordinated. The short time available for preparing a draft application from scratch—by February, within four months—made the high-powered Policy Planning Division a natural candidate for the task, but the mayor also made clear that the division's role was to be an interim one that would end with the first-year application. Which organ of city government would be charged by the mayor with the permanent responsibility for CDBG planning and implementation remained an open, sensitive issue to be deliberated and negotiated.

Under the direction of Michael V. McEnany, the division mapped out an organizational plan for the development of the application, conducted some initial data-gathering, and began to work with a newly formed interdepartmental task force consisting of representatives of the Model City, Public Works, Parks and Recreation, City Planning, and Real Estate departments, as well as the Houston Housing Authority. These efforts first gained public visibility in late October in a brief televised presentation from the mayor's press room. By early November several local groups had expressed open concern about the lack of public awareness concerning the city's planning efforts, among them the League of Women Voters, the Urban League, and a group of black professionals centered at Texas Southern University. The three groups jointly sponsored a public workshop describing the program, at which representatives of the city were present. In mid-November the mayor's office released its plan for organizing the development of the CDBG application.

The plan called for the creation of a citizen participation task force to provide advisory input to the Policy Planning Division's formulation of the CDBG application, to oversee the process of organizing neighborhood meetings, and to develop recommendations for a permanent mechanism for citizen participation to take effect once the first-year application was accepted. The composition of the task force was a delicate political issue that received the mayor's careful attention. From the inception of the CDBG program, Moses Leroy had pressed the mayor to name the MNRC the agency responsible for conducting the participation component of CDBG planning. But simultaneous pressure had been brought to bear from other quarters. Leaders in the Mexican-American community recognized their limited influence in the Model City Program; they viewed CDBG as an opportunity to expand community development activities beyond the boundaries of the predominantly black model neighborhoods and to gain a greater role in the decision process. During the fall of 1974 the mayor's office also received calls from a diverse set of local civic leaders who sought assurances that their neighborhoods would also be included among the CDBG target areas, and some had specific proposals they wanted to see implemented.

In this competitive environment a citizen participation mechanism based on representation by subarea or by neighborhood could only serve to escalate the potential conflicts already apparent and to put the mayor in a situation in which the loss of one constituency or another was inevitable. Strong cautioned the mayor to avoid "turf conflicts" by appointing a broadly based citizen task force consisting of representatives from citywide public interest organizations. The mayor heeded his advice. A list of seventeen diverse public interest organizations was drawn up by Strong in consultation with the mayor. It included, among others, the Houston Area Urban League, the League of Women Voters, the Allied Civic Clubs, the Political Association of Spanish Organizations, the Houston Council on Human Relations, the Chamber of Commerce, the local anti-poverty agency, the AFL-CIO Council, and the Community Welfare Planning Association, as well as Leroy's MNRC—the only concession to specific area interests. As a whole, the list achieved a clear ethnic balance in terms of groups that were identifiably Anglo, black or Chicano in their leadership. In addition the eight council members and the city controller each appointed a representative to the citizen task force, making a total of twenty-six members. Three consultants were hired by the Policy Planning Division to provide technical assistance to the task force in its deliberations.

Under the division's organizational scheme, the preparation of the CDBG plan was somewhat separate from that of the housing assistance plan. Though responsibility for both tasks centered in the division director, staff responsibilities were distinct with regard to each. The housing plan was to be prepared in consultation with a technical advisory group, consisting of representatives of organizations with specific interests in housing development. They included private interest groups representing realtors, builders, apartment owners, and banking interests, local chapters of relevant professional organizations (planners and architects), a nonprofit housing development corporation, the Houston-Galveston Area Council (the local council of governments), the Houston Housing Authority, the Chamber of Commerce, and others. It is clear that the housing assistance plan process was conceived as highly technical in nature; whether the citizen task force had any delegated role in the development of the plan was an open question that remained unanswered, to the frustration of many task force members.

Bargaining and Positioning

Over the fall months, the cadre of black leadership identified with the Model City Program had grown increasingly restive. The imminent shift of HUD support away from a nearly exclusive concentration on model cities efforts toward a broader yet undefined scope of community development activities posed a multiple threat: to the nucleus of human service programs that model cities funded, to those inner-city areas benefiting from the programs, and to those who controlled or had a vested interest in model cities efforts. The word from the HUD field offices was that "soft" programs, such as the human services offered by the Model City Department, were antithetical to the "hardware" (development) intent of CDBG legislation and would be strongly questioned. Attempts to persuade the mayor to transform the Model City Department into the city's CDBG agency had been tactfully resisted by Hofheinz. Despite the mayor's commitment and political debt to black leadership, his choice of the Policy Planning Division as the first-year planning body, his appointment of a citizen task force with a citywide cast of actors, and his bypassing of Leroy's MNRC had denied the leadership of the Model City Department a key role in the future CDBG program and could readily be interpreted as signs of a wavering mayoral commitment to the existing program.

Such an interpretation would have been valid. Strong had expressed serious reservations to the mayor about the Model City Department, its administrative capabilities, and its accountability for its programs. Moreover, the bitter experience of the department in failing to gain the cooperation of the established line departments pointed to the folly of continuing to vest CDBG responsibilities in a parallel department. Those factors, coupled with the sense that turf-related conflicts seemed imminent in the CDBG program, convinced the mayor to position CDBG responsibilities in a new division of his office where the entire process could be more effectively managed and coordinated under the full weight of executive authority.

Hofheinz, however, could only go so far in pursuing administrative rationality without risking the alienation of an important constituency. As the mayor's plans for the CDBG began to surface in November, an agreement was worked out with the Model City Department leadership. The department would retain its integrity as a distinct city department separate from a new Community Development Division, and 20 percent of the first-year block grant would be set aside from the start for an ongoing Model City Program. That amount, coupled with yet unexpended funds remaining in the program, would allow the department to continue for at least another year at close to the same level of effort. If economies were necessary, the mayor viewed it as an opportunity to promote greater efficiencies in model city efforts, suggesting that unsuccessful and untried programs be aborted by the department while it concentrated on those that had proved themselves.

The 20 percent figure was not an arbitrary one; it had its roots in Washington. The fate of Houston's Model City Program rested on its ability to continue to fund ongoing programs that were largely oriented to human services. In an attempt to buck the strong antiservices stance of the HUD regional office, the city executed an end run and made informal contact with HUD in Washington at the secretarial level, where it received assurances that as much as 20 percent could be expended on public services. The figure had been derived by the HUD central office from Senator William Proxmire's comments in the congressional conference report on CDBG legislation and had become an informal, not widely publicized, upper limit on CDBG service support. In effect the decision on the extent of model cities continuation funding in Houston had been made elsewhere, and the mayor could bound the local effort without jeopardizing his relations with its advocates, by claiming that his hands were tied by Washington.

Though Model City Department leadership had absorbed a number of blows, it had clearly survived any immediate threat of extinction with sufficient time to mobilize alternative initiatives for further support of its programs. Its early defeats with the mayor could also be construed as victories in that the Model City Program received favored treatment in the form of a substantial set-aside from the block grant that could not be chipped away by other emergent CDBG priorities. Since it had preempted human services funds available under the CDBG, the Model City Program also maintained its dominance as the central node of human services programs in the city.

Model City interests came to recognize that their future influence over CDBG funds depended less on organizational continuity of the Model City Department and more on lines of succession into the leadership of the new CDBG component. In December a bid was made to have the director of the Model City Department appointed to direct the newly announced Community Development Division. A group of influential black professionals, many of whom had been instrumental in Hofheinz's first election, met with the mayor to present their agenda. It included a recommendation for the appointment of Hortense W. Dixon as executive assistant to the mayor, with the proviso that she replace Strong as mayoral liaison for the CDBG. Dixon, a former vice-president of Texas Southern University in Houston, was a well-known leader in the black community and an articulate spokesperson for human services expansion in the city. Since black leaders had preferred to ascribe their frustrations with mayoral decisions concerning model cities and CDBG to the influence of George Strong rather than to the mayor himself, Dixon's appointment as Strong's replacement was viewed as necessary for the survival of Model City interests.

As a result of the confrontation, a bargain was struck in which the succession of mayoral reappointments resembled a game of musical chairs in which nearly all players got better seats than the ones they had previously occupied. The mayor agreed to the Dixon appointment if black leaders would consent to the appointment of John E. Castillo as director of the new Community Development Division. Castillo had been heading the city's Manpower Department and was considered an able administrator who could get along with everyone. In addition he had close family and political ties with the city controller, Leonel Castillo, and excellent credentials in the Mexican-American community. As part of the final agreement reached in January, the Model City Program director, Palmer Bowser, Jr., moved into the more secure directorship of the Manpower Department; a younger member of the Model City Department staff, Walter L. Jones, became its head; and Dixon was appointed as a mayoral executive assistant responsible for CDBG, Comprehensive Employment and Training Act programs, and model cities efforts. In what must have been a precarious act of juggling commitments, the mayor had achieved a more balanced ethnic visibility in the city's CDBG effort without seriously jeopardizing the support of any minority constituency or providing direct control of the CDBG to Model City Program leaders. John Castillo informally joined the CDBG planning process in the Policy Planning Division at its latter stages, and within a year after these decisions were made Strong had withdrawn from the Hofheinz administration.

Setting Program Priorities

While these deliberations were going on, the Policy Planning Division was engaged in the identification of CDBG target areas and in assessing neighborhood and program priorities. After compiling available data (largely by census tract) on income, housing conditions, the condition of public facilities, and other criteria, the division recommended twenty-three delineated subareas as target areas roughly corresponding to existing concentrations of low- and moderate-income residents in the city. The area plan was scrutinized by the citizen task force and the mayor, and minor revisions were made in boundaries. As a whole, the target areas constituted roughly a third of Houston's land area, including the model city neighborhoods as well as new target areas in outlying low- and moderate-income tracts.

At the initiative of the mayor's office, a staging plan was developed that specified eight of the new target areas for first-year funding and three additional areas for the second year, with all twenty-three areas to be phased in by the third year. The staging not only permitted a gradual expansion of the program in geographical scope as the block grant increased but also resolved some of the competing demands on the mayor by establishing a clear pecking order and ethnic balance among key constituencies to be progressively served by the program.

Between November and January a total of thirty neighborhood meetings were conducted, spanning the twenty-three target areas, at which the CDBG was described and residents had an opportunity to ask questions and discuss issues. Structured questionnaires were distributed at the meetings to canvass residents concerning community needs and priorities, and 1,000 of them were completed. Though tabulated responses differed somewhat by area, as a whole, residents stressed the need for neighborhood physical improvements—for example, street repairs, lights, parks, and recreation facilities—as well as housing improvements and various human service programs.

Although the CDBG planning process had generated much data, by mid-January few decisions had been made concerning specific proposals. The citizen task force had developed only a very generalized view of how funds should be used: the consensus was that the funds should "get out into the community" rather than be absorbed by administrative and technical planning efforts. The task force as a group favored housing rehabilitation loans and grants and human services programs, largely because they represented community needs for which city funding was unavailable.

Although the task force strongly advocated increased funding for human services activities beyond the 20 percent set aside for model cities continuation, McEnany, the policy planning director, argued that HUD would not permit any further service funding under the CDBG. In one of the few strong policy decisions made before the actual drafting of the application, it was decided that CDBG funds would not be allocated to conventional capital improvements—for example, streets, lights, parks, and recreation facilities—that the city might be expected to finance out of local revenues. This key position was formulated by McEnany and

Robert L. Moore, one of the task force consultants, and easily gained the approval of the task force. CDBG funds were to be strategically invested in those activities the city could not fund on its own. Implicit in the decision was the assumption that the city would complement CDBG efforts by investing locally generated funds in the more conventional kinds of neighborhood capital improvements that the target communities were requesting.

McEnany grew increasingly concerned about the shortness of time, the lack of specific program initiatives, and the time expended on meetings and communications with the task force, which he came to view as "an exercise in human relations." With a draft application due in early February, only weeks away, McEnany and Moore notified the task force and staff that they would retreat from the office for several days to hammer out a draft application.

Though the resulting plan reflected the key priorities that had been specified by the task force—housing rehabilitation, the construction of multiservice centers, environmental health programs—a number of task force members, resenting their exclusion from the drafting process, brought their criticisms of the plan directly to the mayor. Among the changes they demanded were an increase in human services funding in addition to the 20 percent set-aside; an increase in funds allocated to housing rehabilitation loans and grants; and the elimination of a $50,000 allocation for an automated housing market analysis, which the task force affectionately referred to as "Mike's toy." The mayor acceded to the requests with the exception of an increase in human services funding, which, he argued, was in excess of Washington guidelines and might jeopardize HUD's approval of the application.

The housing assistance plan was prepared with fewer disruptions. Available data confirmed that Houston's rental market was tight, with a 5 percent vacancy rate, and that the short supply adversely affected lower-income and elderly residents. The staff and technical advisory group agreed that new construction should play a substantial role in the first-year housing goals. But conflicting directives from the HUD field offices indicated that section 8 housing assistance was to be geared exclusively to existing housing units.[21] In further interactions, the Dallas area office requested that the city's goals in the housing assistance plan be revised to

21. Section 8 of title 2, Housing and Community Development Act of 1974, is described in note 35, chapter 3.

reflect the section 8 emphasis on existing housing. The city's planners decided to ignore these requests, however, and the plan submitted proposed to allocate most section 8 funds to the construction of new units (73 percent) and to rehabilitation (14 percent).

By February, once the citizen task force had resolved its objections to the early draft, the mayor and the council members were briefed on the draft application and requested no modifications. The task force conducted two citywide hearings in the council chambers, which 700 residents attended, and two public hearings were conducted before the council in mid-February. The hearings raised few issues that had not already emerged at the neighborhood meetings. Though many residents and neighborhood-based organizations stressed the kinds of neighborhood physical improvements that had been intentionally excluded from the application, no modifications were made to the draft application. Subsequently the application received the pro forma approval of the Houston-Galveston Area Council, the designated A-95 areawide agency,[22] and at the state level the uncritical approval of the governor's office, the endorsement of the Texas Department of Community Affairs, and a memorandum from the Department of Public Welfare urging the city to consider using future CDBG funds as a match for human services programs.

In its review of the application, the HUD area office questioned several service activities. A $188,000 allocation for housing counseling was viewed as an open-ended service not directly related to hardware activities, but the city subsequently justified the program as an information service tied to the housing rehabilitation program. A $400,000 allocation for neighborhood service centers—which were to serve as local outstations of the CDBG program in the target neighborhoods for the purpose of disseminating information, answering inquiries, and conducting local program activities—was viewed suspiciously by HUD as an attempt to set up "little city halls" or "ward heeler stations" to serve broader political and administrative purposes. Though HUD ultimately set aside its objections to the centers on the condition that they be billed as adminis-

22. Title 4 of the Intergovernmental Cooperation Act of 1968 directed the president to establish "rules and regulations governing the formulation, evaluation, and review of federal programs having a significant impact on area and community development." Circular A-95 of the Office of Management and Budget implemented this title by empowering state and areawide clearinghouses (planning bodies designated by OMB) to review and comment on proposed grant applications to the federal government, paying special attention to the consistency between the activities proposed and existing areawide plans.

trative rather than public service allocations, the issue continued to be a sore point that contributed to HUD's evolving image of Houston as a jurisdiction with a number of "questionable activities."[23]

HUD formalized its objections to the inclusion of new construction goals in the housing assistance plan and indicated it would not allocate section 8 funds for such purposes. The HUD housing management component let it be known that its approval would depend on a drop in new construction and maximum rehabilitation of Federal Housing Administration properties, indicating that HUD was encouraging the city to consider FHA's inventory of defaulted or foreclosed properties in Houston.[24] Neither of these comments convinced the city to change its housing assistance plan goals, and the matter was left at a standstill. But the jockeying between the city and the area office over eligible activities and section 8 constraints, and the city's tendency to go directly to Washington when it could not get timely or responsive decisions from the field office, had resulted in a less than optimal working rapport between the two.

A Permanent Mechanism for Citizen Participation

After the pressures of the first-year application had subsided, the interim citizen task force turned its attention to the development of a permanent citizen participation mechanism. Most of the task force was attracted to an evolving concept of target area representation through a complex, hierarchical structure of elected community councils in each of the twenty-three target areas and a central commission consisting of chosen representatives from each of the councils. It had the advantage of creating simultaneously a neighborhood-based forum for CDBG participation and a centralized areawide commission that could deal more directly with the Community Development Division and relevant city actors.

Leroy's acquiescence to the two-tiered plan was considered crucial to its passage in the task force and ultimately in the city council because of his political influence and his central role in the model cities participation mechanism. But Leroy bitterly opposed the plan as cumbersome and costly and pushed the more centralized MNRC model in which subareas

23. Information in this paragraph was obtained during interviews with HUD officials and from memorandums in HUD files on the Houston block grant.

24. HUD area office files.

directly elected representatives to serve on a central commission. His own political style was marked by central controls and direct dealings with the city rather than by more decentralized grass roots participation at the neighborhood level; the two-tiered model created uncertainties about the resulting composition and leadership of the central commission and about the fate of Leroy and the MNRC support staff. When the task force continued to press for its two-tier participation model, Leroy countered by simply walking out of the meetings, an action that was sufficient to obstruct a decision.

By June 1975 the task force had made no formal recommendations, and Leroy—in what was considered to be a brilliant political move, even by his antagonists—had quietly arranged to have his own proposal brought before the council. His plan was approved and entailed the creation of the Houston Residents Citizen Participation Commission (HRCPC), consisting of two or three elected commissioners from each of the twenty-three target neighborhoods (depending on population size). When the commission was elected in the fall of 1975, it contained a black majority, and Leroy was elected its chairman. In addition, the council had at the same time approved a refinement of the first-year CDBG application, which allocated about $400,000 of local option funds for the support of Leroy's MNRC staff as the staff resource for the new resident commission. The decision was a clear victory for Model City Program supporters: Leroy maintained his dominion over the commission and its staff; a half-million dollar burden for staff support was shifted from the Model City Program budget to the CDBG; and any further decisions concerning model cities continuation in the application process seemed destined to be approved by a majority of the commission.

The Dallas area office strongly objected to fund allocations for an independent citizen participation staff, particularly at so high a level of funding. Overall, the administrative costs of the Houston program struck HUD as excessively high; they included Community Development Division staff and neighborhood services staff as well as HRCPC staff. The city continued to pursue these funding arrangements, and the Dallas area office referred the decision to HUD in Washington, where approval was obtained directly from Assistant Secretary David Meeker.

The creation of HRCPC and, with it, a new forum for subarea interests altered the local CDBG decision process and had a strong impact on the evolving character of the program. The elected subarea commissioners were by and large committed advocates of greater program investment in their respective communities. Echoing the broad concerns for physical improvements and services articulated by residents and neighborhood groups at the first-year hearings, they had a keen sense of the city's past neglect of their areas in tending to streets, lights, drainage problems, inadequate recreation facilities, and other neighborhood irritants. Their orientation and agenda differed sharply from that of the first-year planners who had attempted to insulate CDBG funds from conventional capital projects in order to use the funds more strategically. By contrast, the subarea commissioners were less concerned with the strategic use of the CDBG to leverage local funds and simply viewed it as an opportunity to respond to a wide range of needs at the neighborhood level.

Program Amendment

There were also problems of implementation that contributed to a changing decision field and further erosion of the first-year plan. The housing rehabilitation program foundered on legal problems raised by state constitutional prohibitions that precluded Texas cities from lending or granting funds for private benefit. Other administrative obstacles further confounded attempts to implement the general provisions of the first-year plan. These problems seemed even worse in light of HUD's growing concern with the slow rate of expenditure and the uncertainties surrounding the carry-over of funds to the next year.

As a result, John Castillo decided to reprogram the first-year activities in order "to move the money." Since further investments in human service programs being requested by subarea commissioners were ruled out by HUD's 20 percent constraint, he decided instead to begin to respond to the commissioners' demands for neighborhood physical improvements.

In consultation with the various city departments, Castillo determined which unfunded capital projects were "on the books" in the first-year target areas and submitted his recommendations to the HRCPC for approval. The first reprogramming, submitted to HUD in March 1976, contained a $2 million allocation for a long-needed storm drainage project (which leveraged $200,000 from a private industrial developer and was favored by the Public Works Department) and a renewed allocation of $80,000 for the computerized housing needs analysis. A subsequent reprogramming in December included another storm drainage project, land acquisition for a neighborhood park, and the development of a branch library.

Since the city had not planned to carry out these projects during the following year, these amendments did not represent substitution effects in the technical sense, but they did substitute planned capital projects for the more innovative CDBG activities. The reprogramming decisions not only marked a clear reversal of the primary strategy of first-year planners to segregate conventional capital improvements from CDBG fund allocations, but also marked the first point at which the established city departments—particularly Public Works and Parks and Recreation—gained entry into CDBG priority-setting and funding initiatives.

The Second Year of the Block Grant

The procedure that gradually evolved under John Castillo for the development of the second-year application was designed in part "to take the fight out of the process" by resolving competing demands among the eligible target areas. Forty percent of the block grant was set aside for a system of "neighborhood pass-throughs," which represented fund allocations to each subarea on the basis of the federal allocation formula (population, poverty, and overcrowded housing). The pass-through funds were to be used for neighborhood-specific capital projects subject to the approval of the respective subarea commissioners. Another 30 percent of the block grant was reserved for areawide CDBG programs to be applied across all eligible target areas for activities such as housing code enforcement, rehabilitation loans and grants, environmental health, and neighborhood beautification programs. Ten percent was allocated to administrative costs, and the remaining 20 percent for human service programs. These basic allocations set the ground rules for decisionmaking on specific proposals.

The question of model cities under the second-year block grant hung in the balance until January 1976. Although the mayor's office had given some consideration to a transition policy for phasing out model cities and relating its programs to a more broadly conceived human services role for the city, the transition was not yet feasible in either programmatic or political terms, and the mayor proposed that the 20 percent CDBG allocation for human services be put toward the continuation of the Model City Program for yet another year. The decision was a controversial one, particularly among HRCPC commissioners from outside the model neighborhoods who had hoped that the Model City Program's preemption of

CDBG human services funds would end by the second year. The demand for various service programs—day care, health clinics, programs for the young and for the elderly—had been nearly universal among the target areas. At the subsequent HRCPC meeting the continuation proposal was hotly debated, even by several black commissioners from outside the model neighborhoods who, despite their allegiance to Leroy expressed concern about the lack of services in their communities. But when Leroy called the vote the proposal was passed by a nearly exclusive black majority who lined up behind Model City Program interests.

Apart from the model cities decision, Castillo was successful in depoliticizing the second-year planning process, while allowing both the resident commissioners and the city departments a substantial degree of initiative. Commissioners met individually with Castillo to present their proposals for neighborhood improvements to be funded under the pass-through allocations. The neighborhood service centers assisted commissioners in assessing conditions and priorities in their respective subareas and in formulating appropriate proposals. Castillo then forwarded the proposals to the relevant city departments for comment, and the departments were free to suggest alternatives and to propose other projects of high priority in the target areas. After another cycle of reviews by the commissioners and the departments—Castillo gave them "two times at bat" to reach a consensus—the final decisions on program allocations were made by Castillo himself.

Compared with the first-year planning process, which had produced a central program strategy that did not differentiate among the target neighborhoods, the second-year decision process was far more decentralized and specific in character, according priority-setting initiatives both to the subareas through their commissioners and to city departments with development interests. This was apparent in the structure of the second-year application, which listed specific capital improvements subarea by subarea.

The Policy Planning Division continued to retain formal responsibility for the preparation of the housing assistance plan but worked in close coordination with the Community Development Division. By the time the second-year application was drafted, Houston had received section 8 allocations for new construction, but HUD's increased responsiveness to the city's early housing assistance goals seemed fortuitous. At the conference of mayors in the summer of 1975, Mayor Hofheinz encountered HUD Secretary Carla Hills at a cocktail party and asked why section 8 funds were not being allocated for new construction. Her initial response was one of disbelief until another mayor, a Republican from Ohio, confirmed that his city was experiencing similar difficulties. Shortly thereafter, the Dallas office released section 8 funds for new units.

But the continuing disparity between Houston's housing assistance goals and HUD's section 8 allocations, and disputes over the proposed location of new units, led to increased tensions between the city and the housing branch of the HUD area office. HUD's insistence that section 8 construction not take place in areas of minority concentration conflicted with city development priorities for the upgrading and reconstruction of those areas. Though the second-year housing assistance plan was prepared with as much technical care as the first had been, city officials now regarded the plan with much less seriousness. One key official referred to it as "a silly joke."

City review of the second-year draft application went smoothly. The public hearings differed little from the first year, except for the emergence of clear and vocal opposition to the Model City Program's claim on human services funding. But the hearings produced no changes in the application. HUD's response to the second-year application resulted in some minor modifications and deletions. A $200,000 allocation to fund the operation of two newly constructed multiservice centers was eliminated, as was a $108,000 program to provide transportation to social services. At HUD's request neighborhood beautification and historical preservation programs were placed under the "local option" category. None of these issues were viewed by the city as of extreme importance.

Grant Allocations

Houston's first-year CDBG plan constituted a general mapping of fund allocations toward broad functional areas, such as housing rehabilitation and environmental health programs, rather than a detailed program agenda closer to the level of project specifications. The task of transforming the generalities of the plan to actionable program specifics was left to the Community Development Division during the early stages of implementation. Another distinguishing characteristic of the plan was the newness of its activities, with the exception of ongoing Model City Department service activities. The absence of any prior urban renewal commitments and the constraints on model cities continuation had left the bulk of the block grant available for local innovation. Finally, the plan registered a clear commitment to limit program benefits to the designated target areas. Although the geographic scope of CDBG activities had spread well beyond the model neighborhoods and included some upper-income areas, the attempt was to distribute benefits by and large to the city's low- and moderate-income areas. And none of the activities was targeted for citywide use.

To the extent that the plan reflected any kind of programmatic coherence, its major thrust was toward housing rehabilitation. Close to half (44 percent) of the block grant was allocated to a constellation of rehabilitation-related activities: code enforcement, loans and grants, relocation assistance, and supportive housing counseling. The plan anticipated leveraging $1.2 million in private capital from local lending institutions to supplement CDBG funds for rehabilitation loans that were to be offered at below-market interest rates. A minority-owned bank had agreed to the arrangements and several nonprofit housing sponsors were lined up to participate in the program.

The emphasis on housing rehabilitation was clearly responsive to the articulated demands of residents that program funds be used for the physical upgrading of the target communities. But the plan fell far short of the integrated approach to neighborhood conservation that was being called for. The plan was not area specific, thus loans and grants would simply be made available in all eligible first-year target areas. There were no funds to complement housing rehabilitation efforts with local public improvements in the neighborhoods.

It has already been pointed out that the exclusion of capital projects from the CDBG plan was hardly an oversight. While neighborhood conservation and upgrading had been explicit goals of the first-year planners, the intent was that CDBG funds would not substitute over the long range for projects that locally generated funds could support. Although the original plan did not specify where and how local and CDBG funds would be combined toward a concerted conservation strategy, it did indicate the intent of the administration to match at least 20 percent of the first-year community development program allocation with other funds to be used for capital improvements within the target areas. But the orchestration of local and federal funds into hard, detailed project plans at the neighborhood level had not gone beyond this general statement of intent and was contingent on further, more fine-grained planning and negotiation.

In addition to housing rehabilitation efforts, the CDBG plan launched a battery of environmental health programs aimed at improving neighborhood conditions. These included pest and rodent control efforts, cleanup of trash and rubbish, the demolition of unsafe structures, and similar activities. None of these public services had previously been provided by the city.

In terms of fund allocations, the second major priority during the first two years of CDBG was in the area of human services programs. Apart from the 20 percent set-aside for continuation of model cities efforts, new CDBG programs were geared to the construction of multiservice center facilities. The first-year plan programmed the development of three centers, allocating $570,000—4 percent of the block grant—to land acquisition and design-engineering efforts.

But the emphasis on the construction of multiservice facilities was not a new one for the city; two such centers were under construction in the model city area with categorical funds, and a third had been programmed with general revenue sharing funds. Given the low service profile of the city and the resistance to local funding of social services, those interested in expanding the scope of services in the city, including key leadership in the Model City Program, had found greater acceptance for the construction of service facilities that could house externally funded services. The question of further commitments to fund center operations remained unanswered, but the city had embarked on a strategy of using federal funds to develop a network of local multiservice centers. Although the CDBG contributed little to the expansion of services in the target areas, it served to reinforce the trend toward facility construction.

The absence of an economic development component in any of the new programs generated by the CDBG did not go fully unnoticed, but the issue was raised by only one group that testified at the public hearings. Nor had the neighborhood meetings produced any significant expression or constituency for economic development priorities.

During the reprogramming phase, when it became evident that it would take some time to overcome legal and administrative obstacles to housing rehabilitation efforts, program changes and fund shifts led to a reduction in rehabilitation funds to half the original level, less than a quarter (22 percent) of the block grant. By the time the second-year plan was drafted, there was little improvement in the prospects for housing rehabilitation and only a marginal amount of funds was added to the reprogrammed first-year allocations. What was to have been the centerpiece of the CDBG program in Houston had stumbled on implementation problems and faced an uncertain future.

The declining priority accorded to housing rehabilitation brought with it a new emphasis on CDBG funding of conventional capital improvement projects, of the kind that had been intentionally kept out of the original plan. After the reprogramming decisions roughly a quarter of the first-year block grant was allocated to capital projects—toward two storm drainage projects in target areas with persistent flooding problems, land acquisition for park development, rehabilitation of a community center in a public housing project, renovation of a branch library, and design efforts associated with future capital improvements. In the second-year application, such specific neighborhood physical improvements mushroomed under the pass-through allocations to each target area and became the dominant funding priority, representing half of the second-year block grant. Street improvements and improvements in park and recreation facilities were widespread among the neighborhoods phased in by the second-year stage. Though the plan included the acquisition of more than fifteen acres of land for parks, recreation expenditures concentrated largely on improvements to existing facilities: general renovations and refurbishing and the construction of pools, shelters, and restroom facilities; improved lighting; new equipment; and the like. Small amounts of the block grant were allocated to the construction of bus shelters and ramps and to the acquisition of a new branch library site.

The neighborhood improvement agenda progressively incorporated into CDBG plans more closely reflected the broad functional concerns residents had expressed from the start than it did the more strategic programs of the early community development planners. In that sense CDBG planning became progressively more responsive to subarea needs. But as a whole, these activities represented discrete, incremental, short-term renovation efforts rather than component parts of a concerted, long-range strategy or approach to neighborhood conservation. The city's inexperience in redevelopment planning for its lower-income areas put it at a disadvantage in attempting to establish priorities for neighborhood physical improvements with respect to longer-range conservation goals. CDBG efforts, however, represented an important step toward the physical enhancement of areas that by and large had long been neglected by the city, even if they did not reflect a fully mapped-out vision of their futures.

Target Areas

Although the CDBG target areas followed the major concentrations of low- and moderate-income residents in the city, they also reflected a good deal of diversity in income levels. Among the eighty census tracts targeted by the CDBG, eleven could be classified as low income, thirty-nine as moderate income, and thirty-two as upper income, according to 1970 median income levels obtained from census statistics.[25] By contrast, the subarea served by the model cities program was far smaller and lower in income, consisting of nineteen of the CDBG census tracts, among which seven were low income and eleven moderate income.[26] CDBG projects represented a considerable expansion of the geographical scope of federally funded community development activities in Houston and a move toward the inclusion of a larger number and proportion of subareas above the low-income level.

As a result, one would expect that the income distribution effects of the CDBG over the first two years would be regressive when compared with the earlier model cities program, which had dominated HUD's previous funding in the city. That expectation was confirmed by a rough estimate of funding allocations under the CDBG. Based on the 1970 median income levels for census tracts, between 15 and 20 percent of CDBG funds for new programs were allocated to activities benefiting low-income tracts, about 50 percent to moderate-income tracts, and over 25 percent to upper-income tracts. The model cities distribution of funds was 40 percent, 50 percent, and 10 percent, respectively. Although a number of outlying low- and moderate-income areas that were excluded from model cities were included in CDBG's target areas, there was a resultant shift in the distribution of funds by income group toward a greater investment in some of the city's moderate- and upper-income areas and a declining investment in the lowest-income areas.

This pattern was a consequence of the distributive dynamics that occurred with the shift of community development in Houston from the areally concentrated model cities efforts to a potentially citywide program, rather than a consequence of any intentional local strategy or rationale governing the income distribution of CDBG funds. It was also partly related to the staging plan for phasing in new target areas; this

25. Bureau of the Census, *1970 Census of Population and Housing, Census Tracts, Houston SMSA*, table P-4.

26. Ibid.

plan reserved some of the more impoverished inner areas served by model cities for third-year funding when the Model City Program was expected to terminate. This staging effect also resulted in an areal differentiation of program benefits; the model neighborhoods were primarily the recipients of ongoing human services programs, while the surrounding rings of moderate- and upper-income target areas received the benefit of neighborhood physical improvements at the sacrifice of scarce human services. While the geographical distribution of program benefits was likely to shift as the staging plan progressed and the Model City Program approached expiration, any major change in these observed income distribution effects was unlikely, short of a radical alteration in the original designation of CDBG target areas.

CDBG Program Shortcomings and Successes

The reach of Houston's CDBG program rapidly exceeded its grasp. By the end of its second year the program had not yet had any substantial visible impact in delivering the neighborhood renovations and the new facilities and services it had planned to make available to target area residents. The awarding of rehabilitation loans and grants still awaited council approval despite the sizable waiting lists. Legal and technical problems in the formulation of program procedures remained to be resolved, and leveraging arrangements with a potential lender were still in negotiation. Most of the conventional capital projects were still in process at the pre-execution stage. Although a portion of the funds had been expended on land acquisition and design for the development of three multiservice centers, the construction of the centers remained to be carried out in subsequent years. Those funds allocated for the support of ongoing Model City Program efforts served to continue the delivery of a variety of human service programs in the inner-city neighborhoods, but these activities did not represent an increase of what had been provided before the CDBG.

On the whole, the image of the Houston CDBG program in the target communities was that it had not delivered on its promises. Impatient and suspicious of the delays encountered in launching the housing rehabilitation program and planned neighborhood physical improvements, HRCPC commissioners continued to complain that they did not "see things in the ground," and pressed for more rapid progress. The delays in the rehabilitation program summoned the strongest bitterness, in part because of the mayoral publicity that had attended the program during the early stages of CDBG planning; one commissioner openly attacked the city administration for holding up the program. Conventional capital improvements had also been a high priority in the neighborhoods, but little progress was made because of interdepartmental snags and the long lead times involved. Although the reasons for the delays were carefully communicated by the Community Development Division to the commissioners—and through them to residents—they were not well received or fully accepted. The mayor was sensitive to these problems since the CDBG figured importantly in his campaign calculus, and its failure to materialize represented a potential burden in the coming election. He began to pressure the departments in early 1977 to step up CDBG-related activities in order to give the program greater visibility by November, but his efforts came too late. Much of what the block grant had been intended to accomplish in the target communities had not yet been realized by the end of the year.

One of the block grant's more immediate and visible effects was the development of its own institutional role within city government, with a fresh mandate to deal with community development needs and priorities across the full range of the city's less affluent residential areas. The formation of the Community Development Division in the mayor's office, the creation of a new participatory commission (HRCPC) with a broadened areal constituency, and the city's continuing role in housing planning under the housing assistance plan, all represented new institutional mechanisms and centers of activity brought about by the CDBG that had not existed before and that could begin to address the development agenda for Houston's "poorer half" as a whole. In a city formerly noted for its lack of interest and initiative in guiding the development of existing residential enclaves, these represented important institutional changes toward which the CDBG contributed.

Generally the early functioning of the CDBG manifested a simultaneous trend toward both centralization and decentralization of priority-setting initiatives in the city. The relative autonomy the Model City Department had enjoyed for better or worse through its own direct channels of funding from HUD was replaced by a more centralized operation directly under the management of the mayor. Though the mayor's concerns with the CDBG program focused largely on the sensitive political issues and key constituencies associated with the program, a greater degree of control over priorities and program initiatives was within his grasp when and if he chose to exercise it. But except for the continuation of model cities and its core of human services, the mayor chose to exercise little authority over the substantive direction of the CDBG program during its early years.

At the same time, a substantial portion of CDBG funds was set loose for what was clearly a more decentralized process of priority-setting focused at the target area level. The institutionalization of formula-based pass-through allocations to each designated CDBG subarea came close to representing the evolution of a system of neighborhood block grants. It provided a clear opportunity to the subarea commissioners for independent priority-setting and program development initiatives within the funds allocated to their respective communities. But the pass-through system functioned as less than a block grant in that it was restricted to neighborhood-specific capital projects and was unable to address service demands in the new target areas. Moreover, the city departments played an important role in approving program proposals submitted by the HRCPC commissioners and in offering their own counterproposals for each target area, and this gave them a degree of initiative in the program. The pass-through process that John Castillo evolved was successful in reducing the anticipated infighting among subareas represented on the HRCPC by letting each of them know in advance the level of CDBG investment to be made in their areas. Although resident commissioners did not end up with unconstrained authority to determine how funds were to be used in their subareas, the Community Development Division became an important institutional nexus for a more decentralized decisionmaking process that promised to facilitate communication between interested residents and the relevant city departments that serviced their communities. This represented a potentially significant institutional change in a city in which that kind of consensus-building dialogue between public officials and lower-income residents had been notably absent.

The program also signaled important changes and some opportunities for the established city departments. The creation of an interdepartmental task force had been an early attempt to increase departmental involvement in CDBG plans and to promote a climate of cooperation between the Community Development Division and the departments during the program execution stage. As already noted, the attempt was a qualified success and encountered serious obstacles. But the increasing availability of federal funds for conventional capital projects was clearly to the advantage of the departments. Although the block grant did not constitute a major incentive for the departments, it marginally expanded their funding base and scope of activities, and it provided them with a higher degree of initiative in CDBG programming than the first-year planners had intended.

The most fundamental substantive change was the rapid expansion of the geographic area targeted for federal enrichment benefits, extending beyond the inner ring of model neighborhoods to outlying low- and moderate-income areas across the map of the city. With only a small increase in HUD funding levels during the initial years, what followed over the short term was a deconcentration of federal funds previously allocated to the model city area and a spreading of those funds to meet the development and service needs of other areas across the poorer half of the city.

Associated with this changing areal pattern was a correlated shift in the distributive effects of federal development funds toward greater benefits in the more numerous moderate-income tracts across the city, and toward lesser benefits than before in the more impoverished and seriously declining areas such as those that had been subsumed by the Model City Program. The expanded geographical scope of the CDBG, however, also included a number of low-income areas of the city in strong need of community development efforts; these areas lay outside the Model City Program's boundaries and had been unserved by both federal grants and local funds. Many of them were the low-density, quasi-rural slums that had long been annexed by the city but still lacked the basic infrastructure necessities and improvements that had been due them upon annexation. As a result, it may be said that greater equities had been achieved under the CDBG in the distribution of federal development funds among all of the city's low- and moderate-income areas and among a wider cross section of racial and ethnic residential enclaves. Nevertheless, the net distributive effect was toward a wider areal dispersion of funds and an evident shift toward development priorities in those moderate-income areas closer to the upper range of income eligibility; that is, a greater spreading, or deconcentration, of benefits across areas and across income groups.

These shifts, as well as the federally prescribed constraints on the CDBG, have also produced important programmatic changes in the city's community development agenda. Unlike the predominantly service-oriented character of the model cities programs, CDBG plans were geared largely to physical improvements in the target areas—primarily conventional capital improvements of streets, parks, and drainage systems, as well as housing code enforcement and rehabilitation, the construction of multiservice center facilities, and expanded public services. Given Houston's traditional unwillingness to apply local revenues to the development and improvement of its more blighted communities, model cities had come to stand for "human resources" in the city. Within that context, it was likely that the dominant image of the CDBG would come closer to "neighborhood renovation."

The Future

Houston was a "winner" city under the federal allocation formula, and its third-year block grant of about $23 million represented two-thirds more than it had received the previous year.[27] But the phasing in of the twenty-one remaining third-stage target areas—some of them the poorer inner areas—expanded the geographic scope of CDBG activities and increased the demands placed on block grant funds. This expansion in geographic scope, coupled with the tremendous backlog of infrastructure development and capital improvements in the target areas, meant that there was little if any slack in the funding that could be applied toward major new initiatives or a reconfiguration of earlier priorities. Procedures for the annual CDBG planning cycle tended to stabilize as a result of accumulated experience on the part of the Community Development Division, HRCPC, and the city departments, and the preparation of the third-year application was a smoother, more predictable, more orderly process than it had been during the first two years. Nevertheless, a number of factors spelled important changes in Houston's CDBG program over the near future.

The Model City Program ceased to exist as a federally recognized program entity with a potential claim on block grant funds. But both its significance as a center of local human service initiatives in an otherwise low-service city and the political influence of its leadership assured the functional continuity of its administrators and core staff in the newly

27. Houston's CDBG rose from its initial hold-harmless level of $13.1 million during the first year to $13.5 million in the second year. Although a "winner" jurisdiction under the federal formula, the city did not experience a major rise in its block grant until its third-year allocation of $22.6 million.

named Human Resources Department. Even the name of the department was a victory of sorts. The department carried the administrative responsibility for contracting all human service programs—apart from manpower programs—for which the city received external funding, including those services funded by the CDBG. Despite small cuts in CDBG funding, the department succeeded in picking up federal funds for the aging and, most important, in breaking city precedent by securing the first allocation from the city's general revenue sharing funds for human services, albeit a small allocation to be used for the operation of completed multiservice centers.

Under John Castillo's direction, the Community Development Division embarked on a new approach to the planning and provision of CDBG-funded human services from the third year on. The service planning rationale stressed three kinds of services—services for the elderly, youth programs, and day-care programs—and used the demographic characteristics of the CDBG target areas to determine the "population at risk" and the resulting mix of services needed in each subarea. The resulting pattern determined the areal distribution of CDBG human service activities and the way in which funds were to be allocated from the 10 percent of the block grant that had been set aside for these efforts. Within that framework, the former model neighborhoods now competed for services with the other subareas targeted by the CDBG for the limited funds available. Those ongoing model city activities that conformed to this pattern of priorities were continued with CDBG funding; those that offered services accorded low priority under the CDBG were either discontinued or found funding elsewhere. The Human Resources Department in turn was responsible for contracting for these services and for ongoing administrative oversight of the programs. Although there remained the question of whether the sparse funds for services were adequate to the needs addressed, the CDBG succeeded in eroding the seemingly arbitrary concentration of human service activities in the model neighborhoods without destroying the core of initiatives they represented in Houston, and it evolved a sensible way of assessing needs throughout the city and distributing limited resources in an equitable fashion.

HUD's increasing presence in the program began to be felt in substantial ways by the third year. The HUD audit had corroborated the position of the area office with respect to the city's questioned activities and had recommended disallowance of funds allocated to the neighborhood service centers. The audit report was also critical of the amount of funds allocated to staff support of citizen participation activities. Leroy's hold on the HRCPC support staff depended on his political currency with the mayor and the council, and by the third year much of that currency had begun to wane. The mayor's own disenchantment with the sluggishness of CDBG implementation was exacerbated by the frequent complaints from HRCPC and Leroy concerning the pace of the program and the mayor's commitment to delivering on promises. More important, Leroy had testified in favor of a charter change to single-member district elections in a suit brought by the National Association for the Advancement of Colored People against the city. His testimony presented a serious political threat to the incumbents on the city council and alienated Leroy from their affections. The HUD audit report on high CDBG administrative expenses fueled the council's hostility toward Leroy and the mayor's concerns about the efficiency and competence of the CDBG component as a whole. As a result, with the mayor's support the council eliminated third-year funds for HRCPC support staff and pressed for further staff reductions in the Community Development Division as a way of weeding out some of the "deadwood." The neighborhood service centers, however, survived the council onslaught. Although the loss of HRCPC's support staff did not do any critical injury to its citizen participation mechanism, Leroy's apparent political decline and the funding cut had been a symbolic blow to the commission that confirmed their mounting sense of impotence in the program and gave CDBG staff an even stronger edge in decisionmaking.

With the changeover in federal administrations after the election of President Carter, HUD began to scrutinize more carefully Houston's CDBG applications beginning in the third year. As a consequence of the "substantive monitoring" memorandum issued by Assistant Secretary Robert C. Embry, Jr., in the spring of 1977, site visits from the area office field representative in Dallas became more frequent, and a third-year allocation for a park improvement project was disapproved by HUD on the grounds that the area directly served by the park was not predominantly low- or moderate-income in character. Subsequent changes in the map of the CDBG target area were made by the city in an effort to tighten up the boundaries so that more affluent areas were not included. Later HUD regulations promoting the concentration of CDBG efforts in specifically designated neighborhoods also caused the city to reverse its tendency to disperse neighborhood improvement activities and to change its target area maps correspondingly, particularly in the preparation of the fourth-year application.

HUD's increased role also extended to questions of program execution. Midway through the third year of CDBG implementation, the city had not yet moved on its rehabilitation loan and grant programs and many conventional capital projects programmed during the first year showed no record of expenditure. Concerned with the city's slow rate of expenditure and the growing local dissatisfaction with the conduct of the program, HUD indicated that it might hold back a substantial portion of the city's fourth-year block grant if there were not signs of substantial progress in execution by the time of the application. The city agreed to supply HUD with monthly progress reports, began to innovate a "fast tracking" system to get work through the departments more rapidly, embarked on its first rehabilitation grants, and managed to comply sufficiently to ward off any further HUD threat of a cutback in the block grant. But Houston's poor record of performance in program implementation made it increasingly vulnerable to HUD pressures and sharpened the city's willingness to comply with changing regulations and the demands of the HUD field office. Houston's original "maverick" image with HUD changed considerably as the city realized the implications of its poor performance.

The decision of Hofheinz not to run again in November 1977 represented another key dimension of potential change in the program. The short history of Houston's CDBG efforts is indicative of the role of local political commitments and alignments in determining some of the key distributive decisions and mechanisms in the program. In that sense the future of the CDBG in Houston is likely to be sensitive to changes in mayoral leadership and to any realignment of coalitions in the city's power structure. The election of James J. McConn and his assumption of the mayor's office in early 1978 did not have a profound effect on the CDBG program for better or for worse, in large part because he assumed Hofheinz's political mantle. Running on a strong platform of "neighborhood revitalization," McConn also managed to obtain broad support from many black voters. Although a new cadre of black leaders entered McConn's inner circle, and those who were close to Hofheinz vacated office, the Community Development Division has been more marked by continuity than by discontinuity, and observers tend to believe that McConn's style—he is a builder, thought to be a man of action in contrast to Hofheinz's image as an intellectual—is more likely to win the necessary cooperation of the city departments in the CDBG enterprise.[28] These assertions, of course, remain to be tested.

28. E. B. Cape, the long-standing and powerful director of the city's Public Works Department under several mayors before Hofheinz, became ill and died as a result of a Heimlich-syndrome type of accident that occurred to him in a Houston restaurant during the summer of 1977. As a result of the accident, and Hofheinz's early announcement of his withdrawal from the 1977 mayoral race, the new mayor taking office in 1978 had an unprecedented opportunity to appoint his own public works director. Informed observers felt that McConn's latitudes in appointing a new department head for public works would give him much greater leverage with the department in future CDBG implementation efforts. That leverage seemed to increase with his subsequent decision to promote the director of the Parks and Recreation Department to the position, thereby opening that position for a consecutive appointment.

CHAPTER FIVE

Chicago, Illinois

LEONARD RUBINOWITZ

THE "CITY THAT WORKS" was born in 1833. From that time until the end of the nineteenth century, Chicago was the fastest growing city in the world. Even the great Chicago fire of 1871 could not stem the tide. The city's location made it the hub of a railroad network, a logical place for the stockyards, and a magnet for people and industry; but its growth was not to continue indefinitely. Around 1950 Chicago's population peaked at about 3.6 million.[1] From then until 1975, the relevant date for this case study, the city's population declined slowly to an estimated 3.1 million, while its suburbs experienced enormous growth.[2]

The People and Their Prospects

The black population of Chicago remained well below 10 percent until the mid-1940s, but has grown steadily since then. By 1950 blacks accounted for about 14 percent of the city's population, and during the 1960s, as the number of whites declined by 500,000, the blacks increased by 290,000.[3] In 1970, 1.1 million blacks lived in Chicago, representing 33 percent of the city's total population of 3.4 million.[4] The city's Latino

1. U.S. Bureau of the Census, *Census of Population, 1950, Number of Inhabitants,* Final Report PC(2)-A13, *Illinois* (Government Printing Office, 1952), table 6.

2. The pace of the decline seems to be quickening—less than 2 percent from 1950 to 1960, over 5 percent from 1960 to 1970, and an estimated 8 percent from 1970 to 1975. U.S. Bureau of the Census, *Census of Population, 1970, Number of Inhabitants,* Final Report PC(1)-A15, *Illinois* (GPO, 1973), table 6; and Bureau of the Census, *Current Population Reports,* series P-25, no. 661, "1973 (Revised) and 1975 Population Estimates and 1972 (Revised) and 1974 Per Capita Income Estimates for Counties and Incorporated Places in Illinois" (GPO, 1977), p. 1.

3. The growth rate of the city's black population may have decreased because of a slowing of in-migration from the South and a reduction in the birthrate. U.S. Bureau of the Census, *Census of Population, 1970, Characteristics of the Population,* Final Report PC(1)-B15, *Illinois* (GPO, 1963), table 23; and ibid. (GPO, 1963), table 21.

4. City of Chicago, Department of Development and Planning, *Chicago's Black Population: Selected Statistics* (City of Chicago, 1975), p. 5.

population has also grown to an estimated 350,000, or slightly over 10 percent of the population.[5]

Chicago has two contrasting faces. The bustling downtown area is dotted with massive new office buildings competing for tenants and public attention, but it also contains older deteriorating, underoccupied office buildings slated for demolition in the city's plans for redeveloping portions of the Loop, as the downtown area is called.

Chicago's diverse neighborhoods manifest a broad range of income, racial, and ethnic groups. Some of the neighborhoods are made up of single-family homes, often the so-called Chicago-style bungalow characteristic of working class neighborhoods, such as Bridgeport, the lifelong home of the late Mayor Richard J. Daley. Others are vertical neighborhoods, such as the Cabrini-Green public housing project on the city's near north side and the block after block of high-rise public housing on the south side. The high-rise areas along the lakefront contain some of the city's most exclusive neighborhoods.

The south side exemplifies Chicago's diversity. The racially integrated, predominantly middle-income Hyde Park area is adjacent to the predominantly black, lower-income area called Woodlawn, which has lost much of its population over the past decade and is dotted with the burned-out and boarded-up hulks of buildings. Farther south is South Shore, a once prosperous white community, which now houses a portion of the city's growing black middle class. And on the southwest side are white, working-class neighborhoods trying to remain intact as south side blacks spread westward, farther from the lake. As a result, tension continues between white ethnic enclaves seeking to retain the social character of their neighborhoods and blacks seeking to expand and better their housing opportunities. The city's white neighborhoods, located primarily southwest and northwest of the Loop, continue to be ethnically identifiable as Polish, Lithuanian, Greek, and so on.

These patterns have made Chicago the most racially segregated of major northern cities.[6] Segregation in turn has produced massive, almost all-black ghettos on the south and west sides of the city. Housing choices for blacks have expanded primarily through rapid racial turnover or re-

5. Estimates of the Latino population are particularly difficult because of the unknown numbers of undocumented aliens in the city. Anthony Downs, "Some Comments on Chicago's Housing Situation," paper presented at a meeting of the Chicago United Deacons, October 18, 1968, p. 3.

6. Pierre de Vise, "Chicago: First in Residential Segregation in 1970," *Integrated Education,* vol. 9 (November-December 1971), pp. 37–42.

segregation of areas adjacent to the ghetto rather than through the movement of black households throughout the city.

Chicago's housing stock is relatively old—over 65 percent of the city's 1.2 million units were constructed before 1940—and its condition resembles that of most older American cities.[7] At the time the community development block grant (CDBG) program began, approximately 278,000 households were considered to be in need of housing assistance because they occupied substandard or overcrowded housing or paid more than 25 percent of their incomes for housing.[8] Like other major cities, Chicago also had a large number of poor people, particularly among its minority populations. Although one out of ten Chicago families were considered low income, the percentage was almost double among black families.[9]

Along with the population decline, Chicago's economic base has slowly eroded in the past twenty-five years. Though Chicago has fared better than other declining cities, in part because of its diversified industrial base, it is still losing jobs. From 1972 to 1975, 3 percent of Chicago's manufacturing establishments moved out of the city.[10] During 1975 fifty-three companies left the city for the suburbs, while only two traveled the reverse

7. U.S. Bureau of the Census, *Census of Housing, 1970, Metropolitan Housing Characteristics,* Final Report HC(2)-44, *Chicago, Illinois SMSA* (GPO, 1972), table E-6.

8. City of Chicago, Community Development and Housing Coordinating Committee, "Housing Assistance Plan for CD Year III," *CD News,* vol. 2 (June 1977), p. 16. Estimates of housing conditions in 1977 indicate that the total stock had undergone a net loss of about 60,000 units between 1970 and 1975 and that about 11 percent of the remaining units were substandard or dilapidated. Ibid.

9. National Urban Coalition, *City Profile: A Statistical Profile of Selected Cities,* vol. 2: *Midwestern Cities* (Washington, D.C.: NUC, 1977), p. 4.

10. Chicago United, "Summary of Chicago Report Card" (report prepared at the 1976 Deacons Retreat), p. 10. In 1976 a group called Chicago United prepared a "Chicago Report Card," which rated the overall social and economic condition of the city on a scale from A to F. (Chicago United is a group of leading black, white, and Latino business executives and professional people who work together to improve the socioeconomic environment of the Chicago metropolitan area. Its membership is limited to ranking executives of twenty major corporations headquartered in Chicago and a like representation of major black and Latino businesses and community organizations. The membership roll reads like a *Who's Who* of the white corporate establishment and black corporate and community leadership.) The report concluded that "for the most part, conditions in Chicago have not improved over the past decade. In most areas they are worsening and positive action is needed to prevent acceleration of deleterious trends." The city was graded in eight topic areas at meetings preparatory to writing the report. These grades were not intended to compare Chicago with other cities but to judge the status of the city. The areas included, among others, housing and community development (C−), employment (C), and business development (C).

route.[11] Of approximately 280 plant location decisions made by Chicago firms from 1973 to 1975, 60 percent chose a suburban location and only five companies made the opposite move. More than three-fourths of the investment dollars involved in these facilities went into the suburbs. Chicago's share of industrial investment (new construction and expansion projects) in the metropolitan area steadily declined, from 33 percent of the total in 1962 to 17 percent in 1974.[12]

The unemployment picture reflects these changes in the economic base. Although here, too, Chicago had fared better than many older cities, unemployment remained a serious, seemingly intractable problem. Between 1970 and 1976 Chicago experienced an average rate of unemployment of 6.31 percent. From a low of 3.9 percent in 1970, the rate rose to a high of 9 percent in 1975 and 1976.[13] Among minorities the unemployment rate is much higher.[14] To counteract these economic trends, the city created an Economic Development Commission to assist and encourage companies to stay in the city and to attract new industry.

Fiscally, Chicago is in a fairly strong position for an older city. The municipal debt, for which Chicago is directly responsible, was very low in 1976 compared with that of other cities—$216 per capita (New York's is $1,529).[15] This is partly because the city government itself handles only a portion of the functions that are administered by municipal governments in other cities. For example, the Chicago Board of Education operates the city's schools, and the Chicago Park District and the City Colleges of Chicago are separate legal entities whose jurisdictions are also coterminous with the city of Chicago. Cook County shares responsibility with the city for providing health services. The major public hospital in Chicago is a Cook County facility, while the city's Department of Health sponsors neighborhood health centers.

Local Government

Chicago's residents are governed by a mayor, who is elected on an at-large basis every four years, and a council consisting of fifty aldermen

11. *Chicago Reporter,* March 1977, p. 3. (The *Reporter* provides information on racial issues.)

12. Judith D. Feins, *Managing Chicago's Urban Dollars* (Chicago: Trust, 1976), p. 38.

13. Unpublished data prepared in 1978 by the Mayor's Office of Manpower in Chicago.

14. National Urban Coalition, *City Profile,* vol. 2, p. 5.

15. First National Bank of Chicago, *The City of Chicago: A Comparative Study* (FNB, 1976), p. 2.

elected from each of the city's wards in a nonpartisan election every four years. Council business is conducted through committees, of which the Finance Committee is the most powerful.

Since the 1920s, Chicago's political scene has been dominated by the Democratic party, known locally as the "regular" Democrats or the "machine." There is little semblance of the two-party system or of nonpartisanship in Chicago. The lone Republican on the city council at the time the CDBG began resigned his seat in 1977 because of his isolation and inability to gain a significant voice in council deliberations. Not all the Democrats, however, are regular Democrats. In the period covered by this study three aldermen from liberal or black wards were Democrats but "independent," as distinguished from the regular Democrats, and they served as the opposition in the council.

The power of the Democratic party leader has made the mayor's office the focus of power in Chicago. From the mid-1950s until his death in 1976, Mayor Daley was that leader.[16] Although the transfer of power after Daley's death seemed to go smoothly, there was also evidence of changing political winds. The Democratic organization quickly rallied around Daley's handpicked successor, Michael Bilandic, urging that he serve as acting mayor until the next election. It was Daley and Bilandic who had dominated city government in the beginning years of the block grant program.

Bilandic, a financially successful lawyer who had been alderman from Daley's Eleventh Ward, committed himself not to run for mayor but later changed his mind in the wake of widespread support for his candidacy. He encountered opposition in the primary from a Democratic alderman (a former congressman) and a black state legislator. His victory in the primary was followed by an easier win over the Republican challenger, but a year after Daley's death it appeared that machine solidarity was waning. Even when Daley was running the machine, some political life had occurred outside the regular Democratic organization. The independents, or minority block, in the city council were one sign of such life. Furthermore, in the past few years Republican Governor James R. Thompson, Republican Cook County State Attorney Bernard Carey, and independent Democratic Congressman Ralph H. Metcalfe have won deci-

16. For an account of Chicago politics during Daley's tenure as mayor and party leader, see Milton Rakove, *Don't Make No Waves—Don't Back No Losers* (Indiana University Press, 1975).

sive victories over the late mayor's handpicked candidates. Bilandic was defeated by Jane Byrne, a dissident member of the machine, in the Democratic primary in 1979; she was subsequently elected mayor.

The Community Development Setting

Chicago's participation in federal categorical programs began when Congress enacted the urban renewal program in 1949. By 1970 the city had received over $150 million in urban renewal funds, which went into residential, commercial, and industrial redevelopment projects. Urban renewal aid was used to carry out major clearance programs as well as for neighborhood conservation. Perhaps the most famous of Chicago's urban renewal projects was in Hyde Park, the south side neighborhood that is the home of the University of Chicago. Urban renewal arrested the decline of that area and replaced deteriorated structures with new townhouses, apartment buildings, and shopping areas, albeit at the cost of the removal of low-income black and white residents of the area.[17]

In the mid-1960s model cities was added to the city's growing involvement in federal urban programs. By the late 1960s and early 1970s model cities grants represented almost two-thirds of the funds the city received from the Department of Housing and Urban Development (HUD), with a funding level of $38 million for each program year. Chicago's model cities program focused on four target areas: three in impoverished, predominantly black neighborhoods and one in a neighborhood with a mix of low-income whites, Latinos, blacks, American Indians, and other minority groups.

Under the model cities program Chicago carried out a variety of social service activities as well as related physical development projects in these communities. Many of the resources went into day-care centers, educational programs, and the training and employment of police-community aides. More frequent garbage collection was provided in target areas, recreational areas and programs were developed, and supportive programs for the elderly and the handicapped were instituted. On the hardware (or redevelopment) side, neighborhood health and multiservice centers were constructed. When the Housing and Community Develop-

17. For an account of the urban renewal process in Chicago in general and of this project in particular, see Harold M. Mayer and Richard C. Wade, *Chicago: Growth of a Metropolis* (University of Chicago Press, 1969), pp. 375–402.

ment Act was enacted in August 1974, Chicago was in the fourth "action year" of its model cities program.[18]

In 1968 Congress enacted the neighborhood development program, which modified the conventional urban renewal program to provide for annual funding of activities instead of long-term project funding. Chicago converted those renewal projects in the early stages of neighborhood development activities and continued the older projects as conventional urban renewal projects. In the first year of the neighborhood development program Chicago received $38 million. Chicago's funding for the program, however, was suspended by HUD in November 1970, along with its model cities grant, because of the city's inadequate performance in providing housing for low- and moderate-income people displaced by public programs such as neighborhood development and code enforcement.

The suspension was related to the Gautreaux case, a federal court decision requiring that low-income public housing in Chicago be provided on a desegregated basis.[19] This case became an important part of subsequent local decisionmaking in the CDBG program. It began in 1966, when low-income black plaintiffs filed lawsuits against the Chicago Housing Authority and HUD. The plaintiffs claimed that the Housing Authority had placed virtually all its public housing projects for families in black neighborhoods and had used quotas to limit the number of blacks in the few family projects located in predominantly white areas. After postponing consideration of HUD's possible responsibility for this pattern of segregation, the district judge in February 1969 decided that the Housing Authority had violated the Constitution and the Civil Rights Act of 1964, which prohibits discrimination in programs receiving federal assistance.[20]

The presiding judge in the case was the late Richard Austin, a feisty little man who had once been a Democratic candidate for governor of Illinois. The case became a cause for bitter dispute between Austin and Mayor Daley—a dispute some say had been brewing for years because Austin felt that the mayor had not made an all-out effort in support of

18. By the end of 1977 HUD and the city had not negotiated a grant assistance completion date for the model cities program. City officials estimated that model cities would not exist as a separate categorical program after September 1978.

19. *Gautreaux* v. *Chicago Housing Authority*, 296 F. Supp. 907 (N.D. Ill., 1969).

20. The case against HUD was revitalized by the plaintiffs and proceedings began in 1970. In 1971 the court of appeals found that HUD's funding and approval of the Housing Authority's discriminatory housing program violated the Constitution and the Civil Rights Act of 1964.

Austin's run for the governor's mansion. In July 1969 Judge Austin ordered the Housing Authority to place public housing primarily in predominantly white areas of the city. The first 700 units of new public housing were to be built in white areas, as well as three out of every four apartments after that,[21] and the Housing Authority was required to increase the supply of public housing as rapidly as possible. But the intransigence of local officials and private citizens impeded progress.[22] In addition bureaucratic delays persisted in the Housing Authority and HUD, and the Nixon administration put a moratorium on subsidized housing programs in 1973.

After the city failed to proceed promptly to provide desegregated public housing and to make sufficient progress on other housing programs for lower-income people, HUD suspended funding for Chicago's model cities and neighborhood development activities in November 1970. In May 1971 HUD and the City of Chicago signed a Letter of Intent that identified steps the city would take to provide the needed housing. One of these activities was the staged approval of sites for public housing to be devel-

21. White areas of the city were designated the "general housing area" in the court order. These were areas outside the "limited housing area," which consisted of census tracts that were 30 percent or more black as of the latest census, as well as census tracts that were within one mile of those census tracts. Thus the judge incorporated the concept of a buffer zone to take into account the probability of future black migration within the city.

22. For example, under Illinois law the Housing Authority must submit proposed sites for public housing to the Chicago City Council for its review and approval. The Housing Authority chairman decided, however, that the agency would not submit proposed sites until after the mayoral election in April 1971. Frustrated by these delays, the district judge required the agency to submit sites to the council according to a specified timetable. This order was affirmed on appeal, but by the time the appeal process was finished, the original deadline had passed. The district judge then set up a new timetable. The Housing Authority waited until the last possible moment and submitted the sites to the council only two weeks before the mayoral election. Mayor Daley opposed the sites because he objected to the federal court dictating where poor people should live; instead, the mayor said, the housing should be provided "where people want it."

The City of Chicago was added as a defendant in the case in 1972, primarily to assure the city's participation in the enforcement of the court's decrees. The district judge ordered that the state law that provided for council approval of public housing sites be ignored because of the council's failure to approve sufficient sites to implement the original court order. More bureaucratic delays followed as the Housing Authority developed specific plans and HUD rejected a number of the proposals as being too expensive. Many of the sites were lost when the land was purchased privately and used for other purposes. Finally, in 1975 ground was broken for housing for approximately sixty-five families in predominantly white neighborhoods.

oped primarily in white neighborhoods. After one month the council had approved sites for only a quarter of the dwelling units it was to have acted on under the Letter of Intent. HUD released model cities funds totaling $26 million but continued the freeze on neighborhood development funds. At that point the plaintiffs in the Gautreaux case went to court to ask the district judge to hold up the model cities funds until the city met its obligations as spelled out in its agreement with HUD. The judge granted an injunction, but the court of appeals lifted it, reasoning that the judge did not have the authority to hold up funding for one program (model cities) because of discrimination in another program (public housing). HUD terminated the neighborhood development program on its own initiative in 1972 because the city had not fulfilled the terms of the Letter of Intent.

In addition to its progress with urban renewal and the model cities program, Chicago had been successful at securing other federal categorical funds that were consolidated into the block grant. In the late 1960s and early 1970s Chicago received an annual average of close to $1 million in water and sewer assistance, almost $1.5 million in funds for housing rehabilitation, and over $1.5 million for the acquisition and development of open space and park projects. Between 1968 and 1972 Chicago received an average of $43.2 million annually under all these programs. However, this hold-harmless level for initial CDBG funding did not accurately reflect the magnitude of the city's prior participation in categorical programs, since it was skewed downward by the suspension of model cities funds and neighborhood development funds during the 1968–72 base period for calculating hold-harmless grants.

The Chicago bureaucracy reflected the city's success in getting federal money; many agencies were established in response to the enactment of public housing, urban renewal, model cities, and other federal programs. Most were city agencies, although the Chicago Housing Authority, which administers the city's public housing program, is a separate legal entity, as is the Board of Education, which has responsibility for the model cities educational programs. City agencies with responsibilities in these program areas include the Department of Urban Renewal, the Department of Development and Planning, the Economic Development Commission, the Mayor's Office of Manpower, and the Department of Human Services.

In the 1960s the Model Cities Administration was created, and the Chicago Committee on Urban Opportunity was established to carry out the city's federally funded antipoverty program. In 1971 the two agencies merged to become Model Cities/CCUO. (In 1977 this agency merged with the Department of Human Resources, continuing a trend toward putting social service programs under a single umbrella.) As the CDBG program began, the community development activities remained divided largely between the Department of Development and Planning and the Department of Urban Renewal, the latter functioning as the local redevelopment agency under the federal categorical programs. (At the end of 1977 these two departments merged to become the Department of Planning, City and Community Development.) The city's activities in the housing area were also divided among a number of agencies, including Development and Planning, Urban Renewal, the Chicago Housing Authority, and the Building Department.

Against this background of active involvement in federally assisted urban programs, Chicago officials were eager for the resumption of federal funding for redevelopment under CDBG. Because of their experience with categorical programs, the bureaucracies did not anticipate problems in securing and spending the funds, and they looked forward to a program with less red tape and more local control than in the past. Furthermore, Chicago was slated to be a "winner" under the CDBG program; its entitlement under the 1974 law was to increase from a level of $43 million in the first year to $61.5 million in the third year of the program. (It became an even greater winner under the 1977 CDBG amendments establishing the dual formula; Chicago's fourth-year grant increased to nearly $118 million.)

Applying for the Block Grant: The First Year

Chicago's first-year CDBG application was prepared in three separate periods. During the first period, which lasted from early November to mid-December 1974, citizens expressed their views about the program and proposed projects and program activities. City officials during that time were doing technical work and making some initial decisions about allocations of funds. During the second period, from mid-December 1974 to early April 1975, the city prepared a draft application. For the most part, citizens were neither involved in nor privy to this process. The third period began in early April with the release of the draft application, which was followed by public comment on the proposed activities and negotiations between citizen groups and city staff on the housing assistance plan. That period concluded with HUD approval of the first-year application in June 1975.

The first period began after Chicago had decided to participate in the community development program. The one necessary ingredient in that decision was the support of Mayor Daley. No important decision could be made in the city without the mayor's blessing, which he gave publicly at a citywide kickoff meeting held in November 1974 in the auditorium of a downtown hotel to introduce the public to the CDBG program and its objectives. Official notices of the meeting had been published in metropolitan dailies as well as neighborhood newspapers. At the meeting the mayor introduced the Community Development and Housing Coordinating Committee that he had just appointed, and gave the committee responsibility for preparing the city's CDBG application. He included on the committee the heads of agencies that had been involved in the folded-in categorical programs because they were thought to have a legitimate claim to participate in the planning and allocation process as well as in the distribution of funds. Other committee members were chosen to represent offices or agencies that cut across departmental lines, such as the Department of Development and Planning, and a final group consisted of representatives of the mayor's office.

The Coordinating Committee included the directors of the Mayor's Office for Senior Citizens and of the Mayor's Budgetary Division, the acting city comptroller, the assistant to the mayor, the acting commissioner of the Department of Streets and Sanitation, the special assistant corporation counsel, the commissioner of the Department of Human Resources (later the Department of Human Services), the mayor's administrative officer, and the acting commissioner of the Department of Public Works.[23] This committee was to facilitate the coordination of the relevant agencies in the city.

The appointed cochairmen were Lewis Hill and Erwin France. Hill represents a Chicago success story, having risen through the ranks from staff planner to serve simultaneously as commissioner of both the Department of Development and Planning and the Department of Urban Renewal. France served as both administrative assistant to the mayor and head of the model cities program. As a result, the cochair arrangement

23. The department heads serving in an acting capacity at the time of their appointment to the Coordinating Committee were shortly thereafter confirmed in their appointments.

could be viewed as a recognition of the central role of the former urban renewal and model cities specialists in the CDBG planning process.

Public Participation

The mayor's presence at the kickoff proceedings communicated his support for the program to the city council, city agencies, and the public. The meeting was complete with a slide show prepared by the National League of Cities that explained the block grant program. The procedures involved in the program were described, the schedule of regional meetings was laid out, and a general invitation to participate in the program was issued to the assembled citizenry. Before the meeting was adjourned, anyone who wanted to express his or her views about the program was given the opportunity to step up to a microphone and do so.

Then followed a series of nine regional meetings held at night in school auditoriums around the city; two were conducted in Spanish. At these meetings the program was explained again, and once more anyone present could state his or her views about the area's needs and the kinds of programs that should be incorporated in the application. These regional meetings were followed by a citywide public hearing before the Coordinating Committee on December 16, 1974.

The city's citizen participation plans also indicated that written comments about and suggestions for the program were welcome. The city proposed to make technical assistance available to civic and community groups that wanted information about eligible activities and other program requirements. During the period before the city began the preparation of the application, the staffs of the Department of Development and Planning and the Model Cities Administration were available to meet with any community group requesting such a meeting. They conducted these meetings either in city offices during the day or in the neighborhoods in the evenings. In the first year, there were about twenty such meetings.

Citizens' groups expressed considerable initial interest in the community development program. The newspapers talked about a new program of $40 million, with amounts increasing over the years, and community groups all over the city considered it a new opportunity to obtain money to deal with their problems. In the first year more than 240 persons chose to speak at the citywide and regional meetings. They spoke of everything from the shortcomings of the citizen participation process to the need for better public services in their neighborhoods, but the most common concern expressed by citizens was the housing problem. The majority of the speakers requested that large amounts of money be allocated for housing rehabilitation. Other housing-related requests were for the demolition of abandoned buildings, the provision of low-rent senior citizen housing, and improved code enforcement programs. Recreational facilities were another high priority on the citizens' lists, and a significant number of residents requested an increase in the model cities program's child care services and other social service programs. Many people also stressed the need for increasing job opportunities and reducing crime in their neighborhoods.

In particular, citizens involved in model cities and antipoverty programs worked to continue to bring federal funds into their neighborhoods. As part of the citizen participation requirements, councils had been set up in four model cities and twelve antipoverty target neighborhoods. In 1971, three years before the CDBG program was enacted, the sixteen councils had been merged. The model cities areas were smaller than the committee's areas and each was entirely contained within a committee area. The merged councils averaged forty members; half were appointed by the mayor and half were elected by area residents. Representatives of some neighborhood groups in these areas claimed that the mayor had the effective appointment power for almost all the council members because the slating process and the electoral process itself operated to exclude nearly everyone who was not acceptable to the regular Democratic party.[24] These citizens' groups saw the new program as both a threat and an opportunity. It would replace previous programs, particularly model cities, thereby endangering the funding of ongoing activities in the area, and at the same time, it would provide new resources that could continue

24. The term of office of the members of the councils are determined by the bylaws of the twelve Chicago Committee on Urban Opportunity areas, except for the model cities areas, which had two-year terms. The city council has extended this two-year term until the model cities programs are phased out. Elections cost around $300,000 to $400,000. Each community council has a substructure of committees: health, housing and environment, education, social services (subcomponents—senior citizens, criminal justice, and so on), and manpower. These subcommittees are open-ended as to membership; one does not have to be a community council member to be on a subcommittee. Each council has an operating budget of between $16,000 and $32,000. In 1976 each council had a base budget of $15,000, and the remaining money was distributed on a proportion of population basis. Ten out of twelve councils have staffs, and a council office is located in each committee area. Staff at the field level provide day-to-day technical assistance.

and possibly expand the programs available in the groups' areas. They could hardly afford to ignore the block grant application process.

The councils shared information concerning the operation of the program with target area residents to help them lobby for a larger share of the funds than might otherwise come their way. For example, the council in the north side target area set up a planning group and invited about forty community groups to participate. Technical assistance was made available to groups that wanted to prepare proposals but were unfamiliar with the intricacies of the program. The council seemed to anticipate that this form of involvement would enable it to serve as an intermediary between north side groups and the Coordinating Committee, making recommendations to the latter body about which proposals should be funded for what part of the city. Many other neighborhood organizations also participated, particularly in the regional meetings; several citywide groups focused primarily on housing assistance and rehabilitation issues.

The financial and business community of Chicago did not participate publicly in the development of the CDBG application. Traditionally, the major Chicago corporations and financial institutions were located in the downtown area, where in the past decade they had spurred a major development of office buildings, banks, and stores, but these corporate interests did not generally assist in the revitalization of city neighborhoods and communities. Real estate developers made profits from the large-scale clearance and redevelopment projects carried out under urban renewal auspices, such as Sandburg Village, a high-rise and town house development on the city's near north side. Some of the major corporations developed a proposal for a massive "new town in town" south of the Loop and secured some CDBG funds to assist in developing the infrastructure. Savings and loan associations had established a service corporation, a joint venture of almost sixty institutions to finance housing rehabilitation in the inner city; they also sought CDBG funds to help support their efforts. But their projects were large-scale ones that replaced old neighborhoods or created new housing, or they were small-scale, isolated efforts that did not address the larger problems of neighborhoods. One vice-president of a major downtown bank conceded that his bank knew more about investing in South Africa than it did about investing in the neighborhoods on the south side of Chicago.

In spite of the numerous opportunities for interested citizens to testify at public meetings, several groups found this to be an inadequate vehicle for involving citizens in the development of the application. They objected that people simply gave testimony and did not engage in dialogue with public officials. At each meeting a succession of speakers approached the microphone and made a statement. Presiding city officials thanked the speakers but did not respond to the concerns expressed. A spokeswoman for the League of Women Voters said: "We believe that there must be an actual opportunity for interchange between the public and the members of the committee and among members of the public on more than a one-time basis. Such interchange cannot take place in this forum."

The Housing Assistance Plan

While the public meetings of the first period were proceeding to secure citizens' views on CDBG priorities, a more private process was initiated concerning the housing assistance plan required to accompany the block grant application. The plan was developed against the background of the Gautreaux case. The parties already knew that Judge Austin was willing to use leverage to see that his original order to provide desegregated public housing was carried out. His attempt to freeze the model cities funds had made his intentions clear. City officials were also aware that an effort by the plaintiffs to tie the receipt of community development funds to the development of an adequate housing assistance plan would probably succeed in court. Earl Neal, a prominent black attorney serving as the city's legal adviser, conceded that because of the connection in the law between CDBG funds and the housing assistance plan, the court might decide that the city should not get its CDBG "entitlement" unless its plan met the applicable requirements.

At the request of the Gautreaux case plaintiffs' counsel, HUD Area Office Director John O. Waner wrote to Mayor Daley in November 1974, stating that HUD would evaluate the city's housing assistance plan in light of its consistency with the Gautreaux decision. Under the 1974 act, if the plan did not meet legal requirements, HUD was not permitted to approve the CDBG application. In December, after city staff had prepared a partial draft of the plan, the cochairmen of the Coordinating Committee, their top staff, and Alexander Polikoff, chief counsel for the plaintiffs in the Gautreaux case held a private discussion. Polikoff, a successful attorney with a major Chicago law firm, had initially represented the plaintiffs as a volunteer lawyer for the American Civil Liberties Union. Later, as the case continued, he became executive director of Business and Professional People for the Public Interest (BPI), a law firm that is particularly active in the areas of housing, the environment, and government corruption.

During the discussion with Polikoff, city officials presented a proposed approach to identifying the general locations where assisted housing was to be provided. This scheme was later incorporated into the draft housing assistance plan. It divided the city into six sectors, each to be allocated a number of new and substantially rehabilitated units built with "section 8" funds.[25] Several of the sectors included both white and black neighborhoods, and the draft did not indicate where the housing was to be located in these sectors—a critical shortcoming since it was impossible to determine how much of the proposed housing would go into white areas or into black areas.[26] Polikoff questioned that approach, but the matter was not pursued seriously by city officials until after the release of the draft application in April 1975.

Drafting the Application

After the last public hearing on December 16 the second period of the preparation of the first-year application began. The process became invisible to the general public until early April 1975. In the interim the aldermanic elections and mayoral primary were held at the end of February, and the mayoral general election took place in the beginning of April. At the end of the initial public process in mid-December some community groups predicted that the draft application would not ap-

25. Section 8 is explained in note 35, chapter 3.

26. The basis for drawing the boundaries of the sectors is not clear. They followed generally the boundaries of some of the seventy-six "community areas" in the city, but they did not appear to have any particular meaning beyond that. Community areas were defined by a University of Chicago study of the demography of the city about fifty years ago in an attempt to delineate discrete neighborhoods. (Charles S. Newcomb and Richard O. Lang, eds., *Census Data of the City of Chicago, 1934* [University of Chicago Press, 1934], pp. 703–29.) Although these definitions are less valid now than when they were established, they remain the most widely used set of definitions of Chicago neighborhoods, but city officials had no concrete explanation for the groupings of community areas used to define "sectors" in the draft housing assistance plan.

pear until after the mayoral election, to ensure that no controversial issues about the program would surface during election season, as had occurred with the release of proposed sites for public housing shortly before the previous mayoral election.

Community groups objected strenuously that they had insufficient opportunity to be involved in drafting and reviewing drafts of the application and contended that the city had not complied with the Housing and Community Development Act. Meetings of the Coordinating Committee had not been open to the public, nor were minutes or reports of these meetings made available to citizens. In Evanston, Chicago's immediate neighbor to the north, the Community Development Committee's meetings not only were open to the public but also provided an opportunity for citizens to make their views known. Their voices of protest helped bring about a total revamping of the first-year application that had been drafted by the city planning department. In contrast, Chicago groups could not get access to the city's working drafts. When community groups asked to see working drafts of the application during this period, they were told by city officials that the application was not in a form that could be released to the public. When those organizations requested the Coordinating Committee to open its meetings to the public so that community groups could observe and participate in the planning process, they were told that these were private meetings.

Some community groups continued to meet with city staff through early 1975. Organizations that were part of the Metropolitan Area Housing Alliance coalition met several times with David Larson, deputy commissioner of the Department of Development and Planning and the department's senior executive for the program. These groups pressed for allocation of a major share of first-year funds for housing rehabilitation, particularly in older neighborhoods that needed major infusions of funds. But most of the CDBG planning effort between mid-December and early April centered on the decision process of the Coordinating Committee, supported by staff work of city agencies. Largely on the basis of staff recommendations, the Coordinating Committee made the fundamental decisions during this period concerning the kinds of activities to be funded and in some cases where the projects were to be carried out. The process constituted an internal competition among city agencies for pieces of the $43 million pie in which Cochairmen Hill and France played the lead roles. One alderman described the process as one in which the cochairmen negotiated with each other for the bulk of the funds, while the leftovers were relegated to agencies or community groups with the clout to secure funds for their programs.

In short, the two lead agencies and their top staff were highly influential in shaping the major decisions concerning the activities to be funded by CDBG and their locations. Although the Coordinating Committee decided to conduct some activities on a citywide basis, it designated more than twenty areas of the city where CDBG activities were to be targeted. Most of these areas were inherited from prior programs. Some were model cities target areas. Others had been designated by the city as slum and blighted areas or conservation areas under the state's urban renewal law; almost all the conservation areas were made into CDBG target areas. In still other instances neighborhoods where the city's urban homesteading program was in operation were defined as CDBG areas in order to facilitate the flow of additional resources for neighborhood upgrading.

The Coordinating Committee also determined to carry out some activities on a narrower geographical basis than the CDBG area as a whole. The model cities activities were, of course, focused on the four specific target areas, and other activities were targeted beyond the model cities areas to specific locations. For example, a $500,000 mortgage guarantee pool was established with CDBG funds to be used in seven designated neighborhoods. These areas were agreed upon mutually by city officials and the agency administering the program, the Community Service and Research Corporation. Four were model cities target areas; the other three were selected for diverse reasons, such as the presence of a strong community organization, the quality of the housing stock, or concern about the level of mortgage money available in the area.

The locational decisions by the Coordinating Committee were not made independently of the decisions about activities to fund. Proposals had come in from the public. In addition, priorities and appropriate funding levels were proposed by city staff, particularly those of the lead agencies. Members of the city council wrote letters to the committee expressing support for various activities in their wards and got in touch with agency staff developing the application in an attempt to influence decisions on behalf of their constituents. Some aldermen gave their support to specific proposals by community groups in their wards. For example, Voice of the People, an organization active in the Uptown area on Chicago's north side, submitted a proposal to the Coordinating Committee for $1 million for housing rehabilitation and supportive services. The proposal was accompanied by the endorsement of the two aldermen from the area. Although the organization received a portion of the requested funding, it was difficult to determine whether aldermanic influence was decisive.

Members of the Coordinating Committee and agency staff reviewed the proposals and recommendations from various agencies and the public. The committee's response to these competing demands was to provide some funds for each area of the city and to each of the agencies previously involved in categorical programs. There was to be something for everyone. It was hoped that this would generate a broad base of political support for the program.

Perhaps the most basic decisions involved the allocations to France's and Hill's programs and agencies. France was able to secure a relatively high proportion of first-year entitlement funds, 42 percent of the $43 million grant, to continue model cities programs because there was a full-blown program already under way that could expend funds promptly. In addition, model cities officials subsequently secured an additional $7 million through a program amendment.

Hill, the other prime competitor for funds, was well aware of the time-consuming difficulties in mobilizing new urban renewal and housing rehabilitation efforts. As a result, he did not press for large sums for the first year. The year would provide sufficient lead time for his staff to do the necessary planning for subsequent years. In the meantime he was willing to settle for some funding for a limited number of physical improvement projects and several new, untried housing rehabilitation programs to be administered under his aegis.

Once the funding split between these two agencies had been decided, each exercised discretion over the kinds of activities to be carried out. It was essentially left to France, Leroy Whiting, and other model cities staff to determine which activities would be funded in each of the model cities target areas, as it was left to Hill, Larson, and their staff to divide up their money, programmatically and geographically. This deference to agency discretion was also evidenced in other agencies that got smaller shares of the pie. For example, in the process of ensuring that each relevant agency received what was judged to be an equitable share, a significant amount was set aside for the Park District for parks and open space development, in effect continuing the flow of federal funds that had been coming under the open space categorical program. But further programmatic decisions were left to the Park District. As Commissioner Hill stated, "Where the Park District spent its funds that are allocated under Community Development is the decision of the Park District."[27] The Park District decided to spend its funds on a citywide basis rather than to concentrate them in the designated CDBG areas. Park District officials worked closely with council members, who provided priority lists for park improvements to be undertaken in their wards. As a result, the Park District's activities included funds for a park in Sauganash, one of the city's most affluent neighborhoods.

In sum, the Coordinating Committee's decisionmaking process was orchestrated by its cochairmen, who staked a claim on the lion's share of the funds. At the same time, they and the rest of the committee saw to it that some portion of the block grant funds were available to any city agency that seemed to have a legitimate claim to be operating in the community development sphere. This meant that the funds were to be spread over numerous agencies, activities, and areas, with the heaviest funding concentrations in the control of France and Hill and targeted in the areas where their agencies had been active previously.

The Coordinating Committee was able to make decisions about the many projects that were proposed because the staff screened these projects and identified priority proposals for the committee's consideration. The major staff work and day-to-day decisionmaking was done by the agencies that had operated the previous categorical programs, model cities, the Department of Urban Renewal, and the Department of Development and Planning. Thus the agencies that had been the central decisionmakers under the categorical framework continued to play that role. Other city agencies played a more significant role than under previous programs, but the working relationships did not change dramatically under the community development program. Urban Renewal and Development and Planning, both headed by Hill, had worked closely together under the city's neighborhood development program and did so under the community development program. In both instances staff were loaned from one agency to the other when the need arose.

By late March the committee had wound up its initial work, and the staff had prepared a draft application, the Preliminary Report, which was ready to be printed and circulated to the public for comment. The mayoral election was held on Tuesday, April 1, 1975. Those on the city's mailing list received copies of the draft application within four days after the

27. Television interview with Commissioner Lewis Hill, "Chicago Feedback," WTTW, Channel 11, Chicago, February 27, 1978.

election. According to a local newspaper story, city officials took pains to guarantee that a draft did not see the light of day before they were ready to release it publicly.[28] The newspaper reported that the city sent a draft application to the Northeastern Illinois Planning Commission for its preliminary "A-95 review" a couple of weeks before the public release of the Preliminary Report.[29] A newspaper reporter discovered the existence of the document and requested to see it. The Planning Commission staff person involved called Commissioner Hill's office to see whether the reporter should be given access to the document. Hill's response was to send a messenger to the commission to retrieve it. Some citizens' groups speculated that the draft was withheld from public view until after the mayoral election for political reasons. City officials countered that the draft sent to the Northeastern Illinois Planning Commission was incomplete and was subject to final editorial and program changes and that the Preliminary Report was mailed out to citizens on the day it was returned from the printer.

Moving toward HUD Approval

The third period in the preparation of the CDBG application began in early April with the release of the Preliminary Report. Shortly thereafter the Coordinating Committee held a hearing to receive comments from the public on the document. Some community groups protested that because insufficient advance notice had been given, they had too little time to review the draft and thus could not comment intelligently on it. Nevertheless, the hearing proceeded, with much of the testimony focusing on the ways in which the city's housing problems were addressed in the report. This testimony reiterated themes that had emerged in the first round of public meetings in November-December 1974. As in the earlier stages, two distinct positions were put forward. Some people emphasized the Gautreaux thrust of providing lower-income housing throughout the city on a scattered-site basis, while others concentrated on the need to build or rehabilitate housing in older neighborhoods. One of the most active community organizations was the Metropolitan Area Housing Alliance, a citywide organization that had worked aggressively for several years on issues related to neighborhood preservation, such as red-lining and disinvestment. Its moving force was Gail Cincotta, who had achieved a na-

28. Dennis Byrne, *Chicago Daily News,* March 27, 1975.
29. See note 22, chapter 4, which explains the A-95 review.

tional reputation for her efforts to combat disinvestment and other problems of urban neighborhoods and who had been instrumental in getting Congress to enact the Home Mortgage Disclosure Act in 1975.[30] The Housing Alliance operated as a coalition of groups from older neighborhoods, including community organizations that were white, black, and integrated. They ranged from the Kenwood-Oakland Community Organization in a black model cities target area on the city's south side to the Northwest Community Organization in an increasingly Latino area on the near northwest side. Robert Lucas, chairman of the Kenwood-Oakland Community Organization, was the main spokesman for the Metropolitan Area Housing Alliance in the public hearings and the meetings with city officials. From the outset the alliance pushed hard for using CDBG funds for housing rehabilitation in these older areas.

The other highly visible organization pressing for an emphasis on housing in the inner city was The Woodlawn Organization, one of the city's oldest community organizations, located in a black neighborhood adjacent to the University of Chicago on the south side of the city. It grew out of the early community organizing efforts of Saul Alinsky and had since grown and become "establishment" to the point that its economic development arm had a two-thirds ownership interest in a supermarket and owned and managed a movie theater in Woodlawn. The organization's director, Leon Finney, was its spokesman in the CDBG process; he stressed the need for new housing in neighborhoods such as Woodlawn as well as rehabilitation of the existing housing stock.

At the same time, a number of citywide and regional organizations actively supported a scattered-site, Gautreaux-type housing assistance plan (although not to the exclusion of rehabilitation in the older areas). Many of these organizations were participants in the Regional Housing Study and Action Group, a forum of representatives of private agencies working toward fair housing goals and the expansion of housing oppor-

30. This law requires lending institutions to disclose where they are making mortgage loans so that the public can know whether these institutions are meeting their communities' credit needs. A newspaper article described Cincotta as a "street fighter who has built her reputation on carefully planning the kind of dramatic, messy confrontation that embarrasses public officials. As leader of MAHA [the Housing Alliance] and chairwoman of the National People's Action on Housing, she has led shouting demonstrations against City Hall, tramped across the lawns of federal officials' suburban homes and confronted real estate agents and bankers in late night, noisy, angry community meetings." Patricia O'Brien, *Chicago Sun-Times,* January 20, 1976.

tunities for lower-income people. Participants in this "group of groups" included the League of Women Voters of both Chicago and Cook County, the Chicago and the Cook County Legal Assistance Foundation, the Chicago Lawyers' Committee for Civil Rights under Law, the Metropolitan Housing and Planning Council (a thirty-year-old civic organization with a board composed primarily of progressive corporate executives in the city), the Home Investments Fund (a ten-year-old fair-housing organization), the Leadership Council for Metropolitan Open Communities (an organization formed in the mid-1960s as an outgrowth of a series of open-housing demonstrations conducted by Martin Luther King for the purpose of opening up the housing market throughout the metropolitan area to minorities), BPI, and the Chicago Urban League, among others.

During the April public hearing Commissioner Hill asked witnesses from each of several of these organizations to meet with him to discuss their organization's concerns. Although the groups assumed they were being invited to a series of separate meetings, city officials had arranged a single meeting with all the groups interested in the housing question. From the commissioner's point of view, it was useful to have all groups interested in the same set of issues meet together, to have all points of view aired, and to move toward a resolution of the differences among these groups and with city officials. Some representatives of the groups, however, felt that the purpose of the joint meeting was to pit the groups against each other and relieve pressure on the city to respond to their specific concerns.

The first meeting of city officials and community groups was very lengthy. The Metropolitan Area Housing Alliance, The Woodlawn Organization, and others argued for the program to emphasize building and rehabilitation in older and inner-city neighborhoods. BPI and other groups stressed the need for expanding housing choices. Some of the representatives of community and civic organizations present at that meeting were convinced that the city officials were attempting to encourage conflict and dissension among these groups. The only agreement reached was on the need to reconvene to resolve differences. Before the second meeting the citizens' groups had worked out a compromise. The basic Gautreaux order required that 75 percent of the public housing be located in white neighborhoods and 25 percent in black neighborhoods. The citizens' groups agreed on a modified ratio under the housing assistance plan of 60 and 40 percent respectively. Polikoff had negotiated the compromise primarily with Finney of The Woodlawn Organization who wanted to have the thrust of the Gautreaux case modified to provide additional housing subsidies in black neighborhoods. After the first meeting the Housing Alliance decided to watch from the sidelines the discussion about the legal impact of the Gautreaux case on the housing assistance plan. The groups' primary agenda was to argue for the use of large amounts of CDBG funds for housing rehabilitation and related activities in their neighborhoods.

At the next meeting Hill reversed his previous position. He had originally proposed that the housing assistance plan funnel housing subsidies into areas where there were concentrations of abandoned buildings and housing code violations—primarily in black neighborhoods. Hill's assumption was that the various Gautreaux judgment orders did not apply to HUD's section 8 housing assistance payments program, which was to be emphasized in the housing assistance plan. By the time of the second meeting, however, it was clear that the Gautreaux plaintiffs would challenge a plan that provided all or most of the subsidized housing in black neighborhoods. It also appeared that HUD would not approve such a housing plan. Thus Hill argued that the housing assistance plan should be literally consistent with the 75–25 pattern of the court orders. Ironically, the negotiating positions then switched around, since the community groups had reached a 60–40 compromise. Hill would not agree to *any* deviation from the 75–25 formula unless it received explicit judicial sanction, because a modification could result in HUD disapproving the housing assistance plan or in the judge holding up the city's community development grant. Consequently the plaintiffs' counsel requested and obtained a modified court order. The city amended the plan accordingly, thus finishing its work on the first-year application.

Once the Coordinating Committee had completed the application, it submitted it to the city council for review and approval. The review of the first-year application by the council's Finance Committee was somewhat perfunctory. The application escaped the notice of Chairman Michael Bilandic. When asked about the availability of a transcript of the hearing on the city's application, Bilandic could not recall such a hearing having been held. The issue of the location of subsidized housing in white neighborhoods might ordinarily have provoked considerable discussion and debate within the council, but it did not. Although individual council members may have had their own private objections to the housing assistance plan, the matter had been "resolved" before it reached the council. Key council members had been briefed by top staff, and the plan was not discussed beyond the presentation to the Finance Committee by Commissioner Hill. After the council approved the application and the compromise plan, a newspaper reported that Commissioner Hill said he had gone along with the changes in the plan to assure that the city would not lose the federal funds: "Let's get the $43.2 million. Although we're not satisfied with (Austin's) order, we can take care of that later."[31]

Local approval of the application was followed promptly by a favorable A-95 review by the Northeastern Illinois Planning Commission at the regional level. The review was completed in one day, and the commission found the application to be consistent with regional plans and programs. The statewide A-95 clearinghouse located in the Bureau of the Budget of the Executive Office of the Governor, prepared a brief review, stating that the proposal was not in conflict with state plans or policies. Its review was dated April 11, 1975, before the submission of the final application to the council's Finance Committee. The dates of the reviews by the commission and the state clearinghouse are indicative of the pro forma nature of the A-95 review process. For the regional and state agencies, it was a responsibility to be fulfilled. For city officials, it was of no utility, just a minor nuisance.

It remained only for HUD to approve the CDBG application. That too was a routine process. The housing assistance plan had provided the only controversy in the program that involved HUD. HUD had stated its official position on the matter early and had stayed out of the picture as the negotiations proceeded locally, except for a second letter reiterating its interpretation of the housing plan requirement. When the application reached the HUD area office, the plan reflected a compromise among city officials, representatives of the Gautreaux plaintiffs, and other community groups. The area office found Chicago's first-year application to be letter perfect. The city's Preliminary Report had contained a proposed expenditure for a library for the blind, declared ineligible by HUD. The city removed the item and the application was approved "as is" when submitted in final form. Approval took only thirty days. (HUD subsequently reconsidered and determined that the library for the blind was an eligible activity, but model cities officials who had sponsored the project decided not to go ahead with it, having already reallocated those funds.)

Program Amendment

Late in the first program year Chicago requested HUD approval of a program amendment of approximately $10.5 million, or almost one-fourth of the first-year grant. Since the proposed revision was in excess

31. Michael Flannery, *Chicago Sun-Times,* May 8, 1975.

of 10 percent of the CDBG annual budget, HUD approval was required. The request for a program change followed HUD approval of a prior city request for a three-month extension of the first program year, which as changed, ran from June 15, 1975, to September 16, 1976. City officials indicated that the extension was requested because revisions in HUD regulations early in 1976 made it impossible to complete the citizen participation process for the second year of the program and to prepare the application for A-95 review by February 1976. In addition federal regulations permitted extensions to allow the CDBG program year to conform with local budgeting requirements. Chicago's budget functions on a calendar year basis, and the extension brought the CDBG program year more closely into conformity with the city's budget process, theoretically permitting better coordination of city and federal resources for community development.

Once the three-month extension was granted, the Coordinating Committee concluded that it was necessary to shift funds into model cities activities to enable them to continue uninterrupted through the longer first program year. Model cities had received approximately $7.5 million from the first-year entitlement grant as a transition fund to support that program from January 1975 through approval of the first-year application in June 1975. The extension of the first program year to September 1976 meant that model cities activities would be funded for twenty-one months. The program amendment provided the funds for these activities for the additional period.

City officials also justified their reprogramming request by acknowledging that "delays in implementing first year program activities caused by the environmental review process made it possible to shift program funds without seriously affecting the operation of other program activities."[32] In fact, the city had fallen seriously behind schedule with a number of activities, particularly development projects, and the program amendment permitted the shift of some of these funds to social services and other activities that were already under way. In short, an important impetus for the proposal was to facilitate getting the first-year money spent, an unlikely prospect without such a shift. Most of the cutbacks were in hardware programs; in particular, allocations for housing rehabilitation activities were reduced by substantial sums because of their slow progress.

Several neighborhood and communitywide groups objected vigorously to the submission of the request for a program change to HUD without

32. "HUD Approves 3-Month-Extension of First Year Program: City Plans Budget Revision," *CD News*, vol. 1, no. 1 (n.d.), p. 6.

adequate opportunity for citizen involvement in its preparation. They cited the city's citizen participation plan, which stressed the continuing nature of citizen participation and provided that program amendments that had a citywide impact would be subject to a public hearing before approval. City officials responded by inviting comments on the program amendment at the hearings for the second-year application, but this did not satisfy the organizations. Citywide and neighborhood organizations, ranging from the Urban League and the League of Women Voters to the Kenwood-Oakland Community Organization, charged that approval of the amendment would permit the city to shift funds without the participation of citizens that was required under federal regulations. These groups found support only among the minority bloc in the city council, and only these council members voted against the program amendment. Their primary concern was that the city was transferring money to model cities activities in order to maintain a "patronage army" in that program, and they were not persuaded that it was worth taking money out of hardware programs to use for model cities purposes. They also objected to the abbreviated process that one independent alderman referred to as the city's "midnight method."

While the request for the budget revision was being processed at HUD, the city went ahead on its own with an interim budget revision of almost $3.3 million, which was part of the larger total. HUD approved the full revision in August 1976. The $10.5 million was reallocated to twenty-two model cities activities. Since about $3.5 million was simply moved from some model cities projects to others, the net increase in model cities funding was slightly under $7 million. As a result of this revision, model cities funding became the most important feature of the first-year community development program. Many of the non–model cities projects had not progressed to the stage where all the money allocated would be committed by the end of the first program year. At the same time, some ongoing model cities projects were in need of additional funds. City officials emphasized, however, that this was not a shift in priorities but of timing.

Year Two

In planning for the second year the Coordinating Committee continued to shoulder the responsibility for preparing the CDBG application, but France by then had left his position as head of the model cities agency to wage a battle for a south side congressional seat.

After an interim appointee replaced France as model cities director and Coordinating Committee cochairman, Cecil Partee was selected to head the newly consolidated Department of Human Services, which now incorporated the model cities activities. Partee had been the President of the Illinois Senate and had run unsuccessfully for state attorney general before his appointment as head of the department. The position also carried with it the cochairmanship of the Coordinating Committee.

The public process was again initiated in the second year with a citywide meeting to introduce the community to the CDBG program and its purposes. After the program was explained and the schedule for regional meetings was set out, those attending were invited to step to a floor microphone and comment on the program. These opening ceremonies were again followed by public meetings throughout the city. During the second year the Coordinating Committee began to publish a community development newsletter—*CD News*—to disseminate information to the public; the newsletter described program activities and reported on their progress.

In the second round citizens demonstrated a better understanding of the program and its limitations. There was less testimony advocating ineligible programs and less participation by residents of better-off neighborhoods that were unlikely to receive significant allocations under the program. As in the first year, housing was of great concern to people testifying at the public hearings, accounting for about one-fourth of the comments; another 20 percent of the statements focused on the need for increased social services, such as child care and multiservice centers. Other frequently expressed concerns included environmental problems, the need for increased park facilities, and programs to improve health and education and the lot of senior citizens. Finally, other citizens focused on the need for economic development initiatives and programs to reduce crime.

The development of the second-year housing assistance plan was somewhat less contentious. In May 1976 Commissioner Hill and his top staff met with leaders of civic and community groups and suggested that a proposal be made to the court to modify its order in the Gautreaux case to permit a larger share of the housing to go to the elderly than had been allowed in the first year. The experience of the first year indicated little interest among developers in building or rehabilitating housing for families and far greater interest in developing housing for the elderly. Hill and his staff thought that the second-year housing assistance plan should realistically reflect feasible uses of available section 8 funds. The groups rejected the premise of the suggestion and urged that efforts be increased to find developers willing to make use of the program for families and that, if necessary, the city or the Chicago Housing Authority act as a developer. Hill dropped the matter and the second-year plan contained the same locational and family-elderly allocations as the first-year plan. But what had been a "bang" in the first year had become a "whimper" by the second; city officials did not subscribe to the scattered-site principle in the housing assistance plan, but they were reluctant to risk the cutoff of the CDBG funds.

As was the case in the first year, after the last of the predraft public meetings the process was removed from public view and participation. An interagency negotiation process again produced the kinds and locations of activities; an in-house staff again produced the technical work, the housing assistance plan, and the other components of the draft application. Then the draft application was again made available, and the public was invited to comment on it, both at a hearing of the Coordinating Committee and at a city council Finance Committee public hearing. Neither of these forums produced any dissension, and the application went quickly through the city council, the regional and state A-95 review agencies, and on to HUD.

In light of criticism it had received around the country after the first-year review of CDBG applications, HUD had instituted more rigorous review procedures, including a mandatory legal review of applications. The stricter scrutiny involved a legal review of Chicago's application that raised thirty questions regarding the eligibility of proposed activities. None of these issues, however, was especially significant; HUD lawyers simply raised every technical question possible. Over a third of the questions had to do with whether model cities continuation activities were permissible under CDBG regulations. Six questions attempted to determine whether proposed public service activities were clearly linked to physical development activities.

Chicago's characteristic response to HUD's questions consisted of providing clarifications and supplemental material, but only two changes were made in the program. With regard to a questioned allocation of $500,000 for a new Economic Development Commission, it was too early for city officials to identify the locations of the activities to be undertaken or their precise nature; the project was dropped and the money moved to the local option category. The city also eliminated the model cities relocation program ($40,000) because it was not needed and reallocated that money to another model cities activity. These changes and justifications were sufficient to secure HUD approval of the application.

Plans, Allocations, and Benefits

Chicago's first two years of the community development program passed without the emergence of a comprehensive community development and housing strategy. City officials had not had time to seriously consider such a strategy; they were too busy getting CDBG in operation—conceiving projects, preparing and carrying out citizen participation plans, preparing the applications, and getting programs under way. Nor did the HUD area office attempt to influence city officials to plan and program more comprehensively or strategically. It sufficed that the proposed activities were eligible under HUD's specifications. As a result, Chicago developed bits and pieces of strategy rather than a comprehensive approach to its community development problems.

Strategy and Patterns

A central theme for the first two years was the continuation of model cities activities. This meant a commitment to programs and projects that would tend to benefit low- and moderate-income people. At the same time, however, substantial sums were also to be spent in basically sound, relatively affluent areas to enhance the quality of life there as well. The city's purposes were substantive—to prevent or eliminate slums and blight—and also political—to satisfy residents and politicians throughout the city. This was particularly true of the expenditures for park development, where the Park District was responsive to the wishes of city council members from those areas.

Preservation of older neighborhoods was also a theme of the first two years, although the first-year allocations did not reflect the priority that community groups attached to this goal, particularly after the program amendment removed substantial sums from program activities that would help achieve this purpose. In the second year the funding for housing rehabilitation and urban renewal projects in older residential areas was increased. At the same time, some citizens' groups had influenced the city to adopt a scattered-site, desegregation strategy in locating subsidized housing in the housing assistance plan. The compromise agreed upon (the 60–40 ratio) reflected a balancing of the objectives of providing subsidies for new construction and rehabilitation in the inner city and expanding housing opportunities geographically.

Given this wide range of development needs, city officials recognized that the CDBG grant did not come close to meeting the total cost, and efforts were made to use CDBG funds to leverage private money, particularly for neighborhood preservation projects. In a less systematic way the city also used some of the block grant money to leverage other federal funds.

Efforts were undertaken to get financial institutions to make money available for the purchase and rehabilitation of housing in older neighborhoods. It is difficult to know whether the city would have embarked on this effort without the CDBG program. But community efforts to combat red-lining and other forms of disinvestment had been very extensive in Chicago over the past seven years. Community groups such as the Metropolitan Area Housing Alliance and the Citizens' Action Program, along with numerous neighborhood groups, had put these issues at the top of their agendas. They organized demonstrations at the largest savings and loan association in the city and carried out "green-lining" campaigns threatening to withdraw deposits from uncooperative lending institutions in favor of more cooperative ones, negotiated with federal regulatory officials to get them to require savings and loan associations to disclose where deposits came from and where mortgage loans were made, and successfully demanded that the governor of Illinois establish a Commission on Mortgage Practices. Against this background, it is likely that even without the CDBG program, the city would have allocated some local funds to reinvestment or at least would have provided for the mortgage guarantee pool contemplated in the CDBG program. It is perhaps less likely that direct aid through the Financial Assistance and Rehabilitation Program (discussed below) would have been initiated without CDBG funds. In general, however, the city at least articulated an affirmative position on the need for conventional mortgages and rehabilitation funds in older neighborhoods, and perhaps would have sought capital in those areas even if it had not had CDBG funds to use for leveraging purposes.

Program Effects

In the first year, Chicago allocated a high percentage of its grant to model cities continuation activities, with lesser amounts for housing-related activities and urban renewal projects. This pattern began to shift in the second year; the amount budgeted to continue model cities programs declined, and the emphasis on housing and renewal activities increased. The city's small allocation of CDBG funds for completion of prior renewal projects was a consequence of the fact that Chicago had few such projects in motion. In 1968, when the neighborhood development program was enacted, only the conventional urban renewal projects that were at a relatively advanced stage of execution were not incorporated into the new neighborhood development approach; in 1972 HUD terminated Chicago's neighborhood development funding. Thus as it developed its CDBG plans Chicago was not faced with a substantial backlog of ongoing renewal projects.

In the first year a relatively small portion of the budget was committed to housing and neighborhood conservation activities, in contrast with both citizen concerns and the demonstrable need. If there was any proposition that could have come close to achieving consensus among community groups involved in the program, it was that a major portion of the funds should be targeted for housing rehabilitation and related activities. Of the $18 million originally allocated for model cities activities, none was for housing activities such as rehabilitation or construction. Approximately $5.2 million was allocated separately for housing programs.

The city created a $500,000 mortgage guarantee pool with community development funds, with the goal of stimulating $7 million in private mortgage funds for seven designated neighborhoods. These included the four model cities target areas, a black neighborhood on the south side of Chicago, a black neighborhood on the west side, and a predominantly white neighborhood on the far north side of the city. Chicago also set aside $3 million to establish the Chicago Financial Assistance to Property Owners program. This amount was reduced to $2 million and then to $1.25 million in the program amendment. The city allocated an additional $3 million for the program in the second year. Chicago Financial Assistance to Property Owners was to aid property owners (one to four units) so that they could rehabilitate their structures up to housing code standards. Originally the assistance was in the form of a grant, which was to be matched with a loan to reduce the interest rate on the loan portion to 5 percent. The package was the same regardless of the family's income. When it became apparent that the majority of the applicants could not qualify for loan funds, the program was revised. A central feature of the revised approach was that the size of the grant relative to the cost of the work was based on the income of the property owner. The city hoped to leverage $12 million in private funds through this program.

In the first year the city also allocated $100,000 for Neighborhood Housing Services, a federally assisted program operating in a number of cities to bring together neighborhood organizations, financial institutions, and city governments to preserve viable older neighborhoods by injecting private credit for housing reinvestment and public resources for improved services and facilities. The federal government acts as a catalyst by providing the seed money needed to bring together the diverse parties at the local level. The city's allocation to the organization was designed to provide the local government's contribution to this coordinated effort in Chicago's several Neighborhood Housing Service neighborhoods.

The first-year program amendment reduced the $5.3 million housing allocation because the city was unable to start up activities quickly enough to spend the funds. There were cutbacks in programs that assisted in the rehabilitation of single-family housing, as well as rehabilitation employment training, code enforcement, and relocation. The money available for housing and neighborhood conservation activities dropped to $2.7 million. That the first-year reduction resulted from implementation problems rather than a shift in priorities was evidenced by the somewhat increased allocations in the second year for housing-related activities. The second-year application increased the allocations for most of the activities begun in the first year and added $5.3 million for residential urban renewal projects, which were to be small-scale neighborhood conservation efforts. The total second-year allocation for housing-related activities was $13 million, more than double the original first-year level.

Economic development activities also received a higher funding priority in the second year than they had in the first. The first-year total of approximately $2.5 million provided for improvements in commercial areas, site improvements to attract industrial development, and a small program of low-interest loans for minority business persons and contractors. In the second year Chicago doubled the allocation to about $5 million, of which approximately $2.8 million was for renewal related to industrial development, for site acquisition, and site preparation in three predominantly minority, lower-income areas. Most of the remainder was again to be spent on business area improvements, such as street adjustments, expanded on-street parking, aesthetic sidewalk paving, landscaping, pedestrian lighting, new alleys, and parking facilities.

While housing-related and economic development activities expanded from the first program year to the second, the allocation for social service activities and facilities decreased. The initially heavy emphasis on social service activities and the construction of social service facilities—about $18 million, or 42 percent, of the grant—was directed toward the continuation of model cities programs. Even this high percentage of the CDBG funds appeared to be a substantial cutback in funding for model cities; the city had been receiving $38 million annually in model cities funds. The program year for model cities, however, had often extended well beyond a twelve-month period, so the reduction was smaller than the annual figures suggest, although still a significant cutback. Forty percent of the model cities total allocated was for software (social service) programs and 60 percent for hardware, service-related facilities. As a result, Chicago allocated approximately 20 percent of its total entitlement for software activities, the upper limit suggested by HUD. The amendment for the extended first-year program allocated substantial additional funds to these social service activities. Much of the shift was from hardware, non–model cities activities into model cities activities. As a result of this change, model cities activities received over 50 percent of the first year's funds.

The second year saw the beginning of a trend away from activities related to social services and facilities. About $13.5 million, or 31 percent, of the second-year budget was for these programs.[33] Non–model cities activities gained a greater share of the second-year funds, and many of these were physical development rather than social programs. Part of this apparent shift in emphasis could be accounted for by the fact that the first-year model cities funds were spent over a period of almost twenty-one months, including a six-month "transition" period before the CDBG application was approved and a three-month extension at the end of the first program year. As a result, the reduced model cities allocation

33. This percentage is based on a $47 million second-year budget, which included over $4 million in reprogrammed funds from the first year.

for the second year provided roughly similar resources, on an annual basis, to those allocated in the program's first year.

A major difference between the first and second year occurred in the area of commercial development. In the first year $100,000 was budgeted for public improvements in a far western section of the city where the majority of the residents were middle income. During the second year, the city budgeted almost $2 million on four different types of projects. Two of these projects were designed to improve the neighborhoods by street adjustments, expanded on-street parking, landscaping, pedestrian lighting, and new alley development in order to support private rehabilitation and improvement efforts. Seven of the eight neighborhoods in which improvements were to be made were in the far northern and northwest part of the city where the majority of the residents were middle income; in only one area on the west side of the city were the majority of the residents lower income. The third project created a partial shopping mall on the north side of the city where the majority of the families were above the lower-income level. The fourth project widened a street so that adjacent industries in a lower-income area would be better served.

Repackaging the previous activities in terms of new, expanded, or continued programs, Chicago spent most of its CDBG funds in the first two years on continuing programs previously funded by federal categorical grants and on undertaking new development initiatives; only small amounts were used to expand ongoing city programs. Under the first-year allocations, roughly equal amounts went into program continuation and new activities, but in the second year a discernible shift occurred away from the ongoing categorical efforts toward new, locally initiated activities.

These trends can be seen in the changing distribution of fund allocations. In the first year 45 percent of the block grant was allocated to new expenditures, decreasing to 33 percent as a result of program amendments that reflected the changed program year calendar and the slow pace of the new efforts. In the second year new activities were allocated 65 percent of the grant. Only 7 percent of the first-year grant was allocated to the expansion of ongoing city programs, most notably code enforcement, demolition of abandoned buildings, park activities, and technical assistance to homeowners. The remainder went for the continuation of the categorical activities, largely the model cities program. Overall, these changes also meant a shift in emphasis to capital spending and away from operating expenditures.

Social Targeting

At the start the CDBG program was designed to provide some benefits to most income groups in the city. Although the city emphasized providing benefits to low- and moderate-income people, it also allocated substantial amounts to activities that could benefit relatively affluent groups. In the second year more of the benefits were targeted to lower-income areas and residents. In part this shift reflected the one away from citywide activities (about 40 percent of the funds) to activities directed to more clearly delineated areas.

In the first year, activities designated by the city as citywide included some likely to be targeted to the more than twenty designated CDBG areas. For example, some of the citywide housing rehabilitation programs could not be used literally throughout the city, although they were to be available to many of the city's neighborhoods that needed such resources. Some activities, though, could be implemented anywhere in the city, such as assistance for child care centers, parks, and open space and landmark preservation projects. Still another kind of citywide activity involved programs, such as code enforcement and demolition programs, whose locations were unspecified but in practice would probably be concentrated.

The second-year application showed more clearly the areas that would be targeted for various activities; only three activities (totaling $3.7 million) had a citywide focus, and about three-fourths of the funds appeared headed for areas that would benefit low- and moderate-income people. Other projects, however, such as park facilities and the improvements in commercial areas discussed earlier, were likely to benefit relatively affluent groups. More than 40 percent of the second-year entitlement was designated for the CDBG target areas, while another one-fourth of the funds was allocated for the four model cities neighborhoods. Another quarter of the budget was slated to go into neighborhood activities outside the CDBG and model cities areas. These latter projects tended to disperse some benefits in the second year.

The second-year shift away from citywide activities indicated in part that priorities had been established more precisely at the time of the preparation of the second-year application than at the beginning of the program, when a number of activities were characterized as citywide even though they were to be focused on localized areas. HUD also requested more specific project descriptions in the second year, and this encouraged the city to define the locus of the activities in more detail.

In Chicago the "politics of distribution" were at work, resulting in some spreading of intended benefits, but spreading was limited by the realities of the need to get money spent, the clout of the model cities and urban renewal bureaucracies, and the fact that the pie being divided was smaller than in the pre-1972 period, when large model cities and neighborhood development grants were arriving annually. The resulting configuration showed close to one-half of the funds in the first two years going into the four model cities target areas, one in Uptown on the north side of the city, one on the west side, and two on the south side. The next largest set of beneficiaries was the designated CDBG target areas that were predominantly low- and moderate-income areas, primarily on the west and south sides of the city, where earlier programs had been operated or where previous determinations had been made by the city that the areas were slum and blighted or appropriate conservation areas. Two of the CDBG areas, however, were middle- to upper-middle income.

Since the single largest package of CDBG funds in the first two years went into model cities programs, residents of the model cities target areas, made up primarily of lower-income families, became the single largest class of beneficiaries of these activities.[34] In the first year these areas benefited from the program amendment that shifted more funds into model cities activities. In some of the programs, such as increased garbage collection and other "environmental services," everyone in the target area received the services regardless of their income. The rich as well as the poor were entitled to have their garbage collected twice a week rather than the customary once a week. Other services, such as day-care centers, require individuals and families to take the initiative to make use of them, and the city was able to concentrate benefits on low- and moderate-income people, through eligibility criteria, fee schedules with sliding scales, and other means. Overall, the benefits of the model cities activities accrued to low- and moderate-income people at least in proportion to their numbers. Although precise indicators are not available, it is likely that these groups received a greater share of the benefits than their numbers would suggest because of the concentration of some of the programs in meeting their needs.

Initiatives that were not under the model cities umbrella, however, were spread more widely throughout the city, and middle- and upper-

34. Each of the model cities target areas is occupied predominantly by low- and moderate-income people. About 40 percent of the residents are low income and 25 percent moderate income.

income groups were more directly and consciously assisted. This spreading-of-benefits phenomenon was particularly evident in the expenditures for parks and commercial improvements. If park usage by various economic and racial groups is proportionate to their numbers in the area, the first two years of the parks program was primarily for middle-income white people. Thirty-three park projects involved neighborhood parks rather than major city parks such as Grant or Lincoln Park. The benefits of these investments flowed to the neighborhood residents, most of whom were relatively affluent. Only six of the thirty-three parks were in predominantly low- and moderate-income areas. Even those areas, however, included middle-income residents as well, and it is safe to assume that they received benefits from these expenditures. These six projects accounted for 30 percent ($573,000) of the funds spent on parks in the first two years of the program.[35]

White residents were the major gainers from the park projects. Twenty-one parks were in predominantly (over 90 percent) white areas. These projects represented approximately 60 percent of the park funds spent. Only four of the projects were located in predominantly minority areas; that is, more than 90 percent black or Latino. The parks in minority areas received about one-fourth of the park development dollars.

The flow of money for commercial improvements followed a similar route. Most of these improvements were made in white middle-income areas for improved streets, sidewalks, and other physical amenities in neighborhood shopping areas and on commercial strips. The city spent CDBG funds on twelve commercial improvement and redevelopment projects in the first two years; but only one was carried out in an area where most of the residents were low- and moderate-income people. Ten of the projects were undertaken in areas with minority populations of less than 1 percent.

Overall, the impact of the first two years' expenditures was mixed. Lower-income groups probably received the lion's share of the benefits from the model cities expenditures, but middle-income people were the

35. The census tract was used as the unit for estimating which income groups benefited from the park improvements. The composition of the tracts was based on 1970 census data. In an attempt to derive a more up-to-date picture, Chicago based its estimates of the income characteristics of census tracts on the percentage of recipients of assistance to families with dependent children living in the tract in 1975. These estimates showed that four additional park projects were located in primarily low- and moderate-income census tracts; approximately 46 percent of the park expenditures were used for the benefit of these tracts.

major beneficiaries of park and commercial improvements. This varied picture was a result of conscious choice by local officials. They felt strongly that the program's purposes were not limited to benefiting low- and moderate-income people but that the statutory purpose of preventing and eliminating slums and blight was to be taken seriously as well. Consequently the city decided to target funds for basically sound neighborhoods to improve park facilities, assist commercial areas, and other activities that would help assure the continued viability of those areas and prevent their becoming blighted. This process of spreading physical improvements to areas throughout the city was one of the more pronounced effects of the program in the first two years.

What Difference Has the CDBG Made?

In a city with a $1.2 billion annual budget the injection of $43 million of federal funds was unlikely to bring about major changes in well-established institutional structures. This was particularly the case because the city had a long history of involvement in federally assisted programs and had long since adapted to the institutional demands of those programs. In addition the resources involved in the CDBG were at best on a scale comparable to what the city was receiving from HUD in the late 1960s and early 1970s under model cities, the neighborhood development program, neighborhood facilities, urban beautification, and other categorical grant programs. Thus the community development funds did not provide the leverage or the resources necessary to make a quantum jump in the city's planning and management capacity.

The city did not develop a comprehensive community development strategy or a comprehensive housing strategy, much less an integrated housing and community development strategy. As one city official stated: "Chicago has been dealing with this since 1949, and CDBG is the latest kind of way to get money—you name it, we'll write it."[36] This grantsmanship approach that Chicago had developed for the categorical programs carried over to the CDBG program. The new program was seen by local officials as the latest in a series of urban federal grants to apply for, using whatever staff could most efficiently develop the application and implement the program under federal requirements.

With the community development program, Chicago was able to con-

36. Interview with a Chicago official.

tinue programs that might have been terminated without it and to begin new ones that would not have been undertaken without federal funds. The model cities activities that were so central to the CDBG effort probably would have been severely reduced or phased out entirely if the model cities program had been discontinued without a new injection of federal dollars. Since the urban renewal and neighborhood development taps had already been shut off, the hardware projects of the first two years would probably have remained a gleam in a city planner's eye if the block grant had not come along. The city had never taken all the steps to provide housing for low- and moderate-income people that it had agreed to take in the Letter of Intent of 1971; that lack of progress had cost the city its neighborhood development program. At that point HUD officials lost track of the city's progress, or lack thereof, on housing programs because there were no HUD redevelopment dollars at stake. The CDBG program served to wipe the slate clean.

The Chicago area office of HUD did not reopen the inquiry into the city's progress under the Letter of Intent. The matter was closed. It was history. The city was entitled to a new start under the block grant program. It was not required to remedy the deficiencies that had caused the termination of the neighborhood development program three years earlier in order to qualify for CDBG funds. But while the CDBG may have taken Chicago off an old housing "hook," it immediately put the city on a new one.

Through the vehicle of the housing assistance plan that accompanied the grant application, the Gautreaux case plaintiffs were able to influence the city's housing planning process to focus on providing low-income housing for families on a desegregated basis throughout the city. As a result of negotiations between the plaintiffs' counsel and inner-city community leaders, the housing assistance plan also targeted housing resources for inner-city neighborhoods. The result was a plan with the same kind of desegregation thrust that HUD had required of the city for a brief period at the beginning of the 1970s. As in that earlier time, however, the city made little progress toward achieving those housing objectives in the first two years of the CDBG program. In those first two years the HUD area office talked softly and carried a very small stick. It was not until the review of the city's progress during the third-year application process that the area office began to raise serious questions about how the city was doing in its efforts to make the housing available that was provided for in the housing assistance plan.

Having satisfied HUD and the Gautreaux plaintiffs with its plan, the city in the first two years carried out a multitude of activities identified in its CDBG application. Gearing up was a slow and arduous task, particularly in the first year and particularly for the hardware projects that had not been a visible part of Chicago's immediate past. The model cities activities proceeded more promptly, since to a great extent they represented a continuation of programs already well under way. Providing those services also meant that the jobs of the "service providers" remained intact. If model cities had ended without being replaced, many (if not most) of those jobs would have been lost and the ranks of the unemployed would have swelled proportionately.

In the hardware, or redevelopment, area most activity had ceased with the termination of the city's neighborhood development program. The coming of the community development program signaled a new beginning for neighborhood preservation, rehabilitation, and redevelopment efforts in the city. But a new beginning takes time. Progress was slow. Plans had to be made before they could be carried out. And obstacles to implementation had to be faced and overcome. In the first two years little visible change occurred in the neighborhoods as a result of having the federal faucet turned on again. More than anything perhaps, CDBG funding had created a new opportunity for the city to become actively involved in neighborhood revitalization activities. The city budget lacked the funds needed for this purpose, and the HUD funds permitted the planning, the gearing up, and the beginning of a variety of rehabilitation and other programs that were just starting to get off the ground in the second year of the program. The city now had at least a portion of the resources needed to pay attention to these critical problems of neighborhood viability. It also had the challenge of using this money efficiently to address these problems.

In response to this need to increase its capacity to operate the program, the city made some limited but useful institutional changes. The Community Development and Housing Coordinating Committee helped to regularize the communication and coordination among the city agencies involved in community development activities. The CDBG funds assisted in increasing once again the planning and administrative staffs of the key community development agencies.

Aside from these changes, however, the basic decisionmaking processes remained intact from the days of the categorical programs. Although the mayor continued to have the ultimate formal responsibility for the program, the bureaucracies retained the central day-to-day task of dividing up the money and carrying out the programs. As under the categorical programs, formal citizen participation was extensive. Public meetings were held, council hearings were held, and city staff were available to consult with citizens. And as in the earlier period, citizens were able to have some influence on the general shape of the program, but they continued to express frustration about their inability to participate in the actual drafting process.

The city council retained its familiar role of holding committee hearings and approving the submission of the application to the federal government. For the most part, only the few independent council members continued to raise questions about how the funds would be spent and who would be the beneficiaries. Once the council gave its seal of approval, the mayor forwarded the application to HUD, where it received a narrow technical review of the kind the area office had been doing of the model cities program for the previous several years.

Thus the first two years of community development in Chicago saw the preservation of existing ways of doing things, with a sprinkling of innovative processes and programs. New ground remained to be broken. *Plus ça change, plus c'est la même chose.*

The Third Year and Beyond

Chicago submitted its third-year application to the HUD area office for review on July 15, 1977. The application process had proceeded much as in the previous two years, with the new mayor, Michael Bilandic, supporting the city's participation but playing no active role. The Coordinating Committee continued to have responsibility for preparing the application; the bulk of the staff work took place in the Department of Development and Planning, the Department of Urban Renewal, and the Department of Human Services. The city again held a series of regional meetings around the city, as well as citywide public hearings before the Coordinating Committee and the council's Finance Committee. The citizens' advisory council proposed by community groups was still nonexistent. Once again the council routinely approved the application. This formal process seems relatively fixed for the future, unless changes in HUD requirements make modification necessary.

In July 1977, however, the Coordinating Committee announced that it had recommended to the mayor "that a broad cross section of responsible, civic-minded individuals representative of the city's diverse communities and interests be brought more directly into the process of reviewing program priorities, evaluating program effectiveness, and advising in regard to program content in coming years."[37] Since Congress initially had authorized the CDBG program for only a three-year period, city officials had decided to rely on existing citizen participation structures rather than to take the time to create a new one. When it appeared that Congress would extend the life of the program for another three years, the Coordinating Committee concluded that this was an appropriate time to develop a citizen participation structure specifically for the community development program. At the end of 1977, however, the citizens' advisory committee remained to be established. City officials indicated that they were waiting for the publication of HUD's revised CDBG regulations to ensure that any mechanism they established would be in compliance with any new citizen participation requirements.

Although the formal processes of the third year followed the pattern of the first two years, certain events raised questions about the future directions of the city's program. These events revolved around several citizen complaints about the city's performance in implementing housing programs as well as a challenge by a community group to the city's plan for its neighborhood.

The third-year application for almost $61.5 million bore a considerable resemblance to documents of the earlier years. It continued the trend of a slow reduction of model cities funds and increased the emphasis on small-scale urban renewal-type activities, presumably because projects on the drawing boards had reached the point where they were ready to proceed. These projects were to be carried out in residential areas, with the activities including property acquisition, demolition, sale of land for residential development, rehabilitation of properties, and relocation of displaced residents.The third-year program proposed to reduce the funding for some of the housing rehabilitation activities, apparently because they had been slow in getting started and officials had reassessed the city's ability to spend money for them. This reduction was a point of contention with citizens' groups that criticized the program.

There were also some big gainers in the third-year program, since some activities received major increases over their funding for the first two years. Spending for public facilities was increased by almost 25 percent to provide resources for projects such as a senior citizens' clinic,

37. "Status of Housing Assistance Provided," *CD News*, vol. 2 (July 1977), p. 6.

the relocation of a social hygiene clinic, and a multipurpose center for the elderly and the handicapped. The biggest third-year gainer was economic development, for which allocations more than doubled to almost $12 million. Forty percent of Chicago's increase in funding in the third year was devoted to economic development activities; much of the increase was to go into urban renewal-type projects. The funds were to be used for planning how to use land for business and industrial purposes and to eliminate or prevent blight in commercial and industrial areas.

Chicago's third-year program targets resources more heavily on activities that will benefit low- and moderate-income people. In the first two years money for parks and commercial redevelopment was spread among relatively affluent areas. The third-year application, however, seemed to retreat from this position, perhaps partly in response to a HUD memorandum to area offices and recipient communities in April 1977, instructing area offices to pay close attention to whether proposed activities would fulfill one of the following statutory objectives: benefiting low- and moderate-income people, preventing or eliminating slums and blight, or meeting other urgent community needs.

The third-year application process saw renewed hostility between citizens and the city over the housing assistance plan. This time citizens were complaining about the implementation, or lack thereof, of the plans for the first two years. The HUD area office took seriously two administrative complaints relative to the third-year application and the city's performance in the first two years of the program. One of the complaints was filed by BPI and focused primarily on the city's alleged failure to implement its housing assistance plan in accordance with HUD regulations. In addition to following its customary procedure of forwarding the complaint to the city for its response within fifteen days, the area office invited BPI to recommend actions that should be taken to improve the city's performance.

The second complaint was filed by the local legal services office, the Legal Assistance Foundation, on behalf of three neighborhood organizations. The complaint emphasized the city's alleged failure to implement its housing rehabilitation programs adequately and to ensure that these programs would serve low- and moderate-income people rather than displace them from their housing. The HUD area office also forwarded this complaint to the city for its response.

The city's response to the BPI complaint disputed the shortfall in performance and indicated that whatever disparity existed between the city's goals and the housing assistance plan performance was the fault of HUD in its administration of the section 8 program. In reply to the city BPI indicated that even using the city's new figures, it found a very substantial failure to achieve the housing assistance plan goals. Although BPI conceded that part of the problem lay at HUD's doorstep, its letter suggested that the city had not taken all the actions within its control to implement the housing assistance plan and that it should be required to do so as a condition of receiving third-year CDBG funds.

The city's plans for redevelopment of the so-called Chicago-Oakley area also encountered vigorous and persistent citizen opposition. After an examination of the residential and commercial structures in the area, the city officially designated it as "slum and blighted." Residents opposed this classification, fearing that it would result in the demolition of their homes and a recently constructed medical center. Neighborhood residents went to their ward committeeman, their alderman, Commissioner Hill, HUD officials in Washington, and council committee meetings in an attempt to block the use of CDBG funds for demolition in their neighborhood. In August 1977 they filed an administrative complaint with HUD, protesting the use of CDBG funds for that purpose since the project would injure rather than benefit low- and moderate-income people, and it would not prevent or eliminate blight, because their neighborhood was viable and stable. A local television channel joined the controversy, editorializing that the project should be stopped and the neighborhood saved.

Before the area office acted on Chicago's third-year application, it experienced a change of leadership. John Waner, who had headed the office since 1971, resigned his post and Secretary Patricia R. Harris replaced him with Elmer Binford, a veteran HUD professional.[38] Ironi-

38. Waner was a former Republican candidate for mayor, one of a long line of opponents that was swamped by Richard J. Daley on election day. He had also served as the director of the Federal Housing Administration Insuring Office in Chicago in the 1960s. In the early 1970s he had returned to the federal government as assistant regional administrator in charge of FHA housing programs for HUD's Midwest region. When the Chicago area office was established, Waner was appointed its first director. His successor, Elmer Binford, was a well-traveled and highly regarded career bureaucrat. He had served HUD and its predecessor agency for fifteen years and had directed the HUD offices in Milwaukee, Columbus, and Detroit before being named to the position in Chicago. In 1974 he had been sent to Detroit to clean up an office plagued by corruption and incompetence. Having earned a reputation as a troubleshooter, he was then assigned by Secretary Harris to straighten out the Chicago area office.

cally, Binford had been head of the Workable Program Division of the Chicago regional office during much of the period when the HUD-city team was doing its housing analysis that led to the suspension of HUD funds in 1970. After being in various HUD offices in the Midwest, he returned to Chicago in 1977 to a position in which he was again involved in Chicago's housing issue.

On September 28, 1977, the HUD area office approved the city's third-year program, but the approval contained several conditions related to the implementation of the housing assistance plan. The three major conditions were that the city must develop (1) an affirmative program to implement the plan, (2) a program to solicit landlords and counsel clients to ensure occupancy under the section 8 existing housing program, and (3) a program to ensure construction of subsidized housing in specified areas of the city. These programs were to be developed and submitted to HUD for its approval within ninety days, and the city was to report on progress in implementing the program every three months.

Director Binford also included a special condition respecting the Chicago-Oakley project. The city would not be permitted to spend CDBG funds for that project unless it could demonstrate within sixty days that the designation of the area as blighted conformed with HUD's revised requirements for defining slums and blight. On the sixtieth day Commissioner Hill responded to Binford, reiterating that the area was eligible but withdrawing the Chicago-Oakley project from its third-year program because of the delays involved, including possible litigation.

The imposition by the HUD area office of conditions on Chicago's third-year grant was a marked departure from HUD's response to the applications for the first two years. The Binford letter was seen as a victory by the neighborhood group in Chicago-Oakley, as well as by housing groups throughout the city. Neither those with a rehabilitation focus nor those who concentrated on desegregation were satisfied with the city's housing performance in the first two years. Although city officials protested that the implementation of those programs was largely beyond their control, the citizens thought otherwise. And for the first time, the HUD area office seemed to be on their side. Whether the city would be subject to continuing pressure to improve its performance in the housing area remained to be seen. With an entitlement of over $117 million for the fourth year, the stakes involved, as well as the resources available to do the job, were mounting.

CHAPTER SIX

Allegheny County, Pennsylvania

LEON L. HALEY

THE COUNTY of Allegheny was formed in 1787, one hundred and six years after the chartering of Pennsylvania, in an area the Indians called Allegheny because of its "endless mountains and rivers."[1] Between 1790 and 1865 the development of Allegheny County paralleled the economic growth of the state, which had a rich resource base and was emerging as a major national center of industrial production. Pittsburgh, the hub and county seat, by virtue of its position in what was then the busiest interior valley of North America became known as the "Gateway of the West." From here, settlers moved into the vast unsettled areas of the Mississippi Valley, supplied by goods produced in Pittsburgh.

The County's Vital Statistics

In the post–Civil War period western Pennsylvania and Allegheny County experienced phenomenal growth and prosperity as the nation began to shift from an agricultural to an industrial economy. Buoyed by their proximity to coal and iron deposits, Pittsburgh and Allegheny County became, after Philadelphia, the state's second largest industrial and commercial center. The availability of unskilled factory jobs made the county particularly attractive to many European immigrant groups. The greatest economic and population booms in Allegheny County's history occurred, however, in the years following World War I and World War II, when steel production grew rapidly to meet the rising demands of the auto and other steel-consuming industries. By 1950 the county's population had grown to over 1.5 million, of which about half lived in Pittsburgh.

1. Allegheny County, Bureau of Public Information, *Guide to the Government of Allegheny County* (Pittsburgh, Pa.: BPI, 1976), p. 1.

In the past two decades, Allegheny County has undergone significant demographic changes. From 1960, when the county population reached 1.6 million, to 1970, it experienced a small population decline of 1.4 percent. Most of this was the result of a decline of 13.9 percent in the population of Pittsburgh. The county area outside Pittsburgh, however, continued to grow at the rate of approximately 6,000 people a year. Between 1970 and 1975 the county experienced an accelerated population decline of about 5 percent, again reflecting a decrease in Pittsburgh's population. By 1975 the central city portion was estimated at 31 percent of the total county population of 1.5 million, a fact that spelled important changes in city-county relationships.[2]

Allegheny County is a highly urban area. Occupying an area slightly over 730 square miles, the county has an overall population density of about 2,200 persons per square mile; although it drops to 1,600 outside Pittsburgh.[3] Allegheny County is a fully incorporated jurisdiction consisting of 130 separate and independent municipalities, ranging in population from 520,117 in the city of Pittsburgh to 95 in the borough of Trafford.[4]

In recent years Allegheny County has begun to show signs of fiscal strain brought on by inflation, increased costs of personnel services, and the expansion of urban services, especially transportation, education, and social services. Despite recent increases in the tax base, the county's resources have failed to keep pace with rising expenditures.[5] The county's budget increased over 200 percent from 1968 to 1977, while the real estate tax rate remained stable at 15.5 mills and revenue from state and federal funds increased by only 14 percent. To meet the higher spending demands in the 1978 budget, an increase in county real estate taxes of 5.87 mills was adopted by the county commissioners.[6]

The county is governed by the three-member Board of County Commissioners and eight other officials elected at large every four years. As

2. Population data in this paragraph are from the *Pittsburgh Post Gazette,* May 31, 1977.

3. "Allegheny County Overall Economic Development Plan," prepared by the Allegheny County Department of Planning and Development in Pittsburgh in October 1977.

4. U.S. Bureau of the Census, *Census of the Population, 1970, Characteristics of the Population, Pennsylvania,* sec. 1, vol. 1, pt. 40 (Government Printing Office, 1973), pp. 40-6, 40-26.

5. Between 1970 and 1975 the assessed value of taxable real estate increased 11.8 percent. *Pittsburgh Post Gazette,* April 16, 1977.

6. Ibid.

the principal legislative-executive body of the county, the board administers elections; assesses property; prepares and administers the budget; administers health, recreation, welfare, and educational programs; and exercises final policymaking authority in the areas of urban development, planning, zoning, land use, and transportation. In their respective spheres the eight other independently elected county officials share, on a limited basis, administrative and policymaking authority.[7]

The Democratic party holds an almost two-to-one edge in voter registration among county residents and has controlled the County Commission without interruption since the early 1930s. Nevertheless, a provision in the state constitution that requires minority party representation on the Board of County Commissioners, coupled with the numerical strength of the Republican party outside of Pittsburgh, has enabled the Republicans to remain a moderately strong force in Allegheny County politics; the party has controlled one or two elected offices outside the commission for brief periods of time.

Allegheny County is socioeconomically mixed. It is a cluster of old industrial towns located along the banks of three rivers that converge in downtown Pittsburgh, but it also contains newer middle- and upper-income suburbs. Median family incomes in 1970 ranged from $4,500 in Braddock to $29,500 in Ben Avon Heights. In 1970 the Census Bureau estimated that 5.2 percent of the families living in Allegheny County outside of Pittsburgh were below the poverty level, while in Pittsburgh about 15 percent were below the poverty level.[8]

While socioeconomic disparities can be found throughout the county, the single largest concentration of low-income families and housing deprivation outside of Pittsburgh is clustered in a group of communities known as Turtle Creek Valley, located in the eastern part of the county. This area contains the largest clustering of nonwhites in the county and the largest concentration of older housing outside the central city. Housing conditions in the county, however, are better than in Pittsburgh. Slightly more than 13 percent of the dwelling units in the county (excluding Pittsburgh) were considered to be substandard in 1975, compared

7. The eight independently elected officials are the sheriff, treasurer, clerk of the courts, registrar of wills, district attorney, coroner, recorder of deeds, and prothonotary.

8. U.S. Bureau of the Census, *1970 Census of Population and Housing, Census Tracts,* PHC(1)-162, *Pittsburgh, Pa. Standard Metropolitan Statistical Area* (GPO, 1972), p. 4.

with a conservative estimate of 20 percent in Pittsburgh. In some jurisdictions in the county, however, the percentage of substandard housing rises to levels comparable to those in the city, especially in the older industrial towns and in the more rural areas of the county.[9]

A rise in the proportion of people over 65 years of age has been of significance to Allegheny County. This group constituted 11 percent of the population in 1970 and was projected to be 14 percent of the population by 1980.[10] The largest pockets of elderly people are in the older boroughs and cities of the county; this reflects both the residential stability of older people and the out-migration of younger households to the newer, nonindustrial suburbs in the county.

Long Experience in Development Activities

Allegheny County had a long and extensive involvement in urban renewal, public housing, model cities, and other federal programs before receiving the community development block grant (CDBG). These activities were carried out by a multiplicity of county agencies and special authorities, including the Allegheny County Redevelopment Authority, the Housing Authority, the Port Authority (public transportation), and the Industrial Development Authority.

The special authorities generally acted on the basis of requests from individual municipalities for specific projects. When a municipality made such a request, the appropriate agency drew up proposals for federal, state, or other funding and would then usually implement the program. The rationale for county special authorities was that municipalities lacked sufficient resources and expertise to conduct these activities autonomously. For example, the Redevelopment Authority would prepare the application for an urban renewal project, acquire the land, handle bidding and contracting, and do the accounting. In some cases the authority might choose a private firm to perform some of the tasks, such as project engineering.

9. Housing data are from "Community Development Block Grant Program, 1976," prepared by the Allegheny County Department of Planning and Development, n.d., p. 20. The figures are based on 1970 housing estimates from the Southwestern Pennsylvania Regional Planning Commission in Pittsburgh.

10. "Allegheny County Third Year Community Development Plan," prepared by the Allegheny County Department of Planning and Development, March 17, 1977, p. 10. This projection is based on 1980 population for Allegheny County, using fertility and survival rates from 1960–70.

The Redevelopment Authority, a major development agency in the county, was established under state charter in 1950. It is governed by a five-member board appointed by the county commissioners for five-year terms; the terms are staggered with one appointment each year. The five-year appointment means that members are less subject than regular department heads to direct control by the county commissioners. (The city of Pittsburgh has its own redevelopment authority.) Moreover, the five board members are frequently wealthy and politically or economically active in the county and thus are less susceptible to control by the county commissioners. The Redevelopment Authority implemented major urban renewal projects in fifteen different jurisdictions, including both commercial redevelopment and large-scale housing projects. Since most of the renewal projects had been completed or were near completion in 1975, however, urban renewal activity in Allegheny County had reached a low level by the time the CDBG program began; the authority's major remaining activities were two flood disaster projects that provided the bulk of the agency's operating money.

A countywide public housing program is administered by the Housing Authority. While the public housing activities are not directly related to the programs consolidated into the block grant, they are mentioned here to show the extensive experience of the county in a wide range of federally funded projects. The Housing Authority was created in 1938 under state charter to build and manage dwellings for low-income families and elderly citizens; it serves at the request of any municipality in the county except Pittsburgh and the city of McKeesport, which have their own housing authorities. Like the Redevelopment Authority, the housing agency is governed by a five-member board appointed by the county commissioners for five-year, staggered terms. As of 1977 over 4,000 housing units were under the management of the Housing Authority, most of them built before 1968. While these units are geographically scattered, large concentrations (especially the large-family units) are located in the southeastern section of the county and in the industrial communities of the Allegheny River Valley. This pattern of public housing distribution resulted from both the greater concentration of low-income and elderly people in these areas and the willingness of these communities to have public housing built.

The county's model cities program was administered by an agency of the general county government. Model cities operated in eleven adjoining communities in the Turtle Creek Valley area, sponsoring projects in housing, health, recreation, and services to the elderly until the program was terminated in 1975. Model cities, which received $6.4 million a year, was highly important to Allegheny County since it was the basis for the county's hold-harmless allocation at the beginning of the CDBG program. But because the county's hold-harmless amount was based entirely on model cities participation, its hold-harmless grant was scheduled to decline substantially during the early years of the new program.

The general rule for hold-harmless funds was that a community was guaranteed as much CDBG funding during the first three years of the new program as the average of what it had received under the previous grants during the period 1968–72. Model cities was treated in a special way, however, because it had originally been established as a five-year demonstration program. Therefore the CDBG law provided the full hold-harmless guarantee on model cities for a period of five years—referred to as "action years"—during which the program was in full operation. At the end of these five action years a community's hold-harmless credit for the model cities program would be phased down in three yearly steps to 80, 60, and 40 percent, after which it would be treated the same as other hold-harmless funds and be phased down to zero by the sixth year of the CDBG program. By contrast, a community that received its hold-harmless guarantee solely on the basis of urban renewal would not have any phase-down until the fourth year of CDBG. In the case of Allegheny County, four action years of the model cities program had been completed at the time the CDBG started, leaving only one year of the full hold-harmless guarantee. In the second year of the CDBG the county's hold-harmless amount declined by 20 percent to about $5.1 million since it was based entirely on model cities. The law, however, also provided that the allocation of an entitlement jurisdiction would be the larger of either the hold-harmless or formula amount. Therefore, for Allegheny County the early phasedown provisions of model cities provided an extra incentive to quickly become a formula entitlement community with as large a grant as possible (discussed further below).

County departments were also active in funding development and service activities such as public works, parks, and recreation. In the social services area programs in aging, mental health and retardation, and other human services were also the responsibility of county agencies. Allegheny County's extensive involvement in federal programs (both those included in the CDBG consolidation as well as some others) was the result of several factors. The most important was the presence of energetic leaders among the county commissioners who were willing to seek intergovernmental assistance as a means of improving the economic and social welfare conditions of county residents. The effects of this leadership were visible in the number of new community agencies created in the past decade and in the expansion of programs under the Department of Health, Parks and Recreation, and Economic Opportunity. Another factor was the presence of Democratic party machinery, which pursued categorical programs to maintain its strong support from the residents and elected municipal officials of the aging industrial communities in the county. The cumulative effect of this growing county role was to make the county government a more visible participant in a variety of development and service activities around the county.

County-Municipality Cooperation in Getting Grants

The urban county, as a category of recipients within the CDBG entitlement system, was a different kind of jurisdiction from the entitlement cities, and the difference had important effects on decisionmaking and the kinds of CDBG activities carried out in Allegheny County.

The CDBG legislation defines an urban county as one that has a population of at least 200,000, excluding any formula entitlement jurisdictions (its central city and suburban cities with populations of 50,000 or more), and any other municipalities that choose not to participate in the CDBG program. Thus an urban county does not necessarily include the entire geographic area of the county or all of its population; it is a "residual" entitlement area made up typically of suburban and rural areas, and in some cases, unincorporated rural areas. Even where a county has sufficient population to qualify in unincorporated areas alone, there is an advantage to the county in gaining the participation of incorporated municipalities since the county's grant increases as its entitlement population increases. Participation can also be advantageous to the municipality, since individually it could receive CDBG assistance only from HUD's much smaller discretionary block grant funds.

The second eligibility requirement of the CDBG law specifies that the urban county must have powers to perform essential community development and housing activities. This condition is met if the county is authorized by state law to carry out community development activities (specifically urban renewal and publicly assisted housing) in its unincorporated areas and incorporated municipalities.

If a county is deficient in population, community development authority, or both, it can still become an entitlement jurisdiction by entering into cooperative agreements with incorporated, nonentitlement municipalities in the county. These agreements permit the population of the participating municipalities to be counted toward the 200,000 and allow the municipality's own development authority to be shared with the county.

Under these requirements, seventy-three urban counties were qualified as entitlement areas in the first year of the program. Allegheny County was one of four CDBG urban counties in the Pittsburgh metropolitan area. Besides Allegheny, the others were Beaver, Washington, and Westmoreland Counties, which were substantially less populous than Allegheny County. Beaver County had not participated in the previous categorical programs, and Washington and Westmoreland Counties had only very limited involvement. In the case of Allegheny County, because the required development powers were exercised by special authorities, the Department of Housing and Urban Development (HUD) at one point during the first-year application process questioned whether the county itself had such authority. To avoid any risk of having its grant application rejected, the county relied initially on the cooperative agreement approach. As a result of the county officials' decision to play it safe and take the more complex route to qualifying and of the short period that remained to submit the application after the HUD challenge, the county met the minimum 200,000 population requirement only at the outset of the program. The low population level, however, did not adversely affect the amount of the first-year grant, which was based on a hold-harmless amount of $6.4 million. As discussed below, the state subsequently certified that the county had its own community development authority and was therefore not dependent on the participation of the municipalities. In the second year the county's entitlement population was nearly 850,000.

Where an urban county was dependent on the participation of the municipalities to get the necessary population or community development powers, there was sometimes an arrangement in the distribution of the county's CDBG funds that gave the municipalities more program control than the county government. For example, in Hennepin County, Minnesota (Minneapolis), negotiations between the county and the municipalities resulted in 90 percent of the county's grant being passed through to the municipalities that decided on the specific use of the funds. Allegheny County, however, retained all funds, largely because of the early certification by the state that the county was not dependent on the participation of the municipalities to qualify for a grant. County officials, although influenced by municipal officials, decided who got the money and the kinds of projects that would be funded.

In addition to the county's own grant, eleven municipalities in the county had hold-harmless grants ranging from $46,000 to $642,000 as a result of participation in the urban renewal program; these grants totaled $2.9 million. (A total of fifteen communities had participated in urban renewal, but only eleven had active projects between the years 1968 and 1972, the base period for calculating hold-harmless grants.) These eleven communities, which directly received the hold-harmless grants, also participated in the county program in order to gain access to a share of the county's grant and to a large bond issue to be floated by the county for various capital projects. They were also apparently looking toward the future when their hold-harmless funds would be phased out; they wanted to be built into the county's broader development program at the outset. The county's view on why municipalities should participate was expressed pointedly by the chairman of the Board of County Commissioners, Leonard Staisey: "My feeling is this. Perhaps it is wiser to go through the County because if you go it alone to the federal government and if you flunk out there, you are out. At least if you go with the County, it's possible that some of the $6.4 million [the County's first-year grant] can be used to help in your particular project."[11]

First-Year Planning

By the time the block grant legislation was signed into law, Allegheny County had already made progress in preparing for the new program. One of the earliest decisions that shaped the CDBG program in Allegheny County concerned the organizational responsibilities for the planning and implementation of community development efforts. The apparent choice for running the new program was between the Redevelopment Authority and the county's Department of Planning and Development. The department was an operating agency under the County Planning Commission, a nine-member policy advisory group appointed by and responsible to the county commissioners.

In 1972, two years before the CDBG program, the newly created Department of Planning attempted a merger with the Redevelopment

11. Quotation is from the author's field report.

Authority. The effort was not endorsed by the Board of County Commissioners and left the county with two agencies having important and related development functions. The issue of overlapping functions resurfaced in 1973 when the Department of Planning added a development component to provide the county government with a comprehensive priority-setting capability located within an agency directly under the control of elected officials, the county commissioners. The department, with the strong endorsement of the Board of County Commissioners, secured a $50,000 HUD 701 planning grant to restructure the overall planning and development activities of the county.[12] This resulted in several changes in the department, including the creation of the Community Development Division. In anticipation of congressional passage of the CDBG legislation, the department began staffing the new division with personnel from the county's model cities program. The expanded department was renamed the Department of Planning and Development. Jack Milberger, who had directed model cities since its inception, was appointed acting department head when the director became county solicitor. Milberger kept informed about the impending block grant legislation through the National Association of Counties and helped the county get an early start on CDBG planning.

Although the Board of County Commissioners did not formally designate the Department of Planning and Development as the responsible CDBG agency until November 1974, the department's early lead in CDBG planning had the strong endorsement of the commissioners, especially of Commissioner Staisey, the dominant influence on the board and the member most active in CDBG decisionmaking. The decision to put the CDBG into the expanded department was dictated by several considerations. The commissioners preferred not to create a new agency, and they were satisfied with the demonstrated capabilities of the former model cities staff that was now integrated into the department. Officials of the Redevelopment Authority were interested in administering the CDBG program, but that agency was never seriously considered. The major reason was that the commissioners preferred to put the CDBG program under one of the county's own agencies rather than the semi-autonomous Redevelopment Authority. But several other factors worked against the authority. It had become unpopular around the county be-

12. Section 701 of the Housing Act of 1954 provides grants to states and areawide planning bodies to assist in comprehensive planning for urban and rural development.

cause of its slowness in getting projects under way and completed. In addition, while Staisey was chairman of the Board of County Commissioners, he had also served as chairman of the model cities citizens' committee and thus had close ties with that program. With the shift of much of the model cities staff over to the Department of Planning and Development, the close ties between model cities personnel and Staisey could be continued by putting the block grant program into the county department. Exclusion of the Redevelopment Authority meant increased centralization of development decisions in the county government; thus the immediate effect of the block grant on the local process in Allegheny County was that it strengthened the authority of the local executive in development decisions.

In September 1974, following the enactment of the CDBG, the department's role as the dominant development agency for the county was further advanced when a working group of housing experts, organized earlier by the department to assist in 701 planning, was designated the Housing Task Force to assist in formulating the housing assistance plan for the county's CDBG application. The twelve-member task force included representatives of several county departments and authorities, the local home builders association, the mortgage bankers association, the area Council of Governments, and several nonprofit housing sponsors.

Another important part of the centralization of the CDBG decision process in the department concerned the county's relations with the municipalities. In October the department invited the Allegheny League of Municipalities—a federation of elected public officials from cities, boroughs, and townships in the county—to present its views regarding the overall direction of community development efforts in the county. League members were asked to channel their formal requests for assistance to the department for consideration in the final drafting of the CDBG plan.

As preparation of the application speeded up during the fall and early winter, county departments—including Health, Public Works, and Adult Services—were asked to prepare specific projects for consideration.[13] The Redevelopment Authority was not asked to participate; as noted above, it had already been excluded from the planning process. Although

13. For example, the Adult Services Department request was for funding of senior citizen centers in the program application. The Department of Public Works requested inclusion of housing demolition, waste disposal facilities, and road repair activities.

the slight could be viewed as insignificant since the authority was not a formal operating department of county government, the exclusion from the pool of potential recipients of funds meant that the Redevelopment Authority was being isolated from the implementation as well as the planning process.

The Citizen Participation Process

Another early procedural decision of importance concerned citizen participation. The citizen advisory structure for the county's block grant program had been a point of contention between Milberger and the County Planning Commission. Milberger wanted to create a new, representative citizen advisory body to participate in the development and review of CDBG plans and programs. He preferred a decentralized citizen participation process with a citizen committee in each of ten community development districts. The Planning Commission, however, preferred a centralized system and to reserve the citizen advisory function for itself, taking the view that it possessed the statutory responsibility to act in this capacity for all planning activities. Moreover, the Planning Commission was dubious about the potential effectiveness of a large network of community-based citizen organizations in getting agreement on program priorities.

Milberger questioned the representativeness of the commission, which was dominated by a group of influential public and civic agency representatives, including the executive director of the County Housing Authority, the head of a large industrial development concern, and a former head of Pittsburgh's Urban Redevelopment Authority. The lone minority member of the commission was the executive director of a large multiservice community agency in Pittsburgh. The issue was decided when the Planning Commission submitted a resolution to the Board of County Commissioners recommending itself as the citizen participation mechanism, and the board approved. Milberger, not wanting to prolong the issue, acquiesced. Thus the Planning Commission had a dual role in the CDBG process. As a policy body, it reviewed the work and recommendations prepared by the Department of Planning and Development before sending them on to the Board of County Commissioners. In this capacity the Planning Commission could accept or reject the department's recommendations, although in practice the two agencies maintained continuous liaison that reduced the likelihood of serious disagree-

ment. In its second role, it was acting as a citizen advisory committee and became a part of the citizen participation process.

The citizen participation process had two parts. The first related only to entitlement funds allocated directly to the county as a separate jurisdiction; it included public hearings in which the County Planning Commission functioned as the formal mechanism for citizen input. The second part related to the participation requirements governing the eleven hold-harmless municipalities in the county that had indicated their intent to participate in the countywide CDBG program; these municipalities were required to hold their own formal public hearings as part of the process to decide the use of their hold-harmless funds.

The county's process for registering citizen concerns began in late November with a series of five public hearings held in various locations. These hearings were preceded by mailings to civic groups, special interest groups, municipal public officials, and others, describing the block grant program. A tentative list of program areas and proposed CDBG activities was also made available to the participants. Despite the large population of the county and the fairly extensive publicity, attendance at the five hearings totaled only 373, of whom 112 people actually made statements. About sixty people presented specific program proposals for inclusion in the application; others addressed more general questions about the program's administration and its overall objectives. Specific recommendations were made by such groups as the League of Women Voters, Open Doors for the Handicapped, the Urban League of Pittsburgh, the Lutheran Service Society, the American Association of Retired People, the National Council of Senior Citizens, and the National Association for the Advancement of Colored People (NAACP). In addition municipal officials—councilmen, mayors, managers—were represented; their requests primarily concerned code enforcement and housing rehabilitation loan programs, senior citizen centers and services, and municipal capital improvements. Thus as the geographic area of activity spread beyond the model cities area, an expanded set of demands began to be requested.

The one area in which citizen participation was translated into influence was programs for the elderly. Focus on Renewal, a highly vocal group from the McKees Rocks area, argued for an increase in the number of senior citizen centers in the development plan. Well-organized senior citizen groups also pressed for increased services. The prominence

of senior citizen centers in the final CDBG application reflected the pressures from these groups. The relatively low turnout at the public hearings and the dominance of representatives of areawide groups with special constituent interests indicated that the county's public hearing process would have little effect in mobilizing broad community or neighborhood-based interest and involvement in the CDBG program. The size of the county and the multiplicity of political units tended to constrain the mobilization of resident and community-based interests. It may well be, however, that the crucial factor was neither size nor political fragmentation, but rather public indifference.

In addition to its role as convener of the public hearings, the Planning Commission was involved in working with the staff of the Department of Planning and Development in analyzing overall county needs, sorting out priorities mentioned at the public hearings, determining strategies and objectives, and choosing the first-year CDBG program to be recommended to the Board of County Commissioners. The Planning Commission met between early December and early January to draw up its priorities for the first-year application.

Preparation and Review of the Application

A major constraint on participants in the process was an early decision by the Board of County Commissioners to allocate one-third of the CDBG to continue some model cities activities through the first year of the grant. Nevertheless, funding for model cities was substantially reduced compared with the categorical period. The reduction was possible because about 60 percent of the county's model cities program had been for physical development projects, and many of these had been completed or were nearing completion. Moreover, the model cities staff, anticipating the end of their separate program, had succeeded in spinning off a number of social services to other county agencies. Staisey's ties to model cities and the presence of Milberger, who had directed the model cities program, in a key CDBG decision role were important factors in continued funding of model cities activities. But the decision to continue model cities was clearly understood to apply *only* through the first year of the CDBG program, thus fulfilling the commitment to five action years of model cities. This understanding foreclosed any further consideration of model cities continuation into the second year.

The largest new development activity was the neighborhood preservation program, a strategy for rehabilitating housing stock in combination with related public improvements such as streets, lighting, sidewalks, and sewers. The preservation program was initiated by former model cities personnel who had shifted to the Department of Planning and Development. Staisey, who preferred to assist municipalities with public works money, was not enthusiastic about housing rehabilitation aid, which he thought was a local responsibility; nevertheless, he did not object to the inclusion of the preservation program. The county refrained from selecting or identifying communities to participate in the program in the original application until a careful evaluation of alternative sites could be made. County officials seemed to be sensitive to potential charges of political favoritism if communities were identified before such a screening. And even though the state certified that the county possessed development powers, county officials held the view that they must "negotiate" with the municipalities before proceeding with development. This illustrated an important difference between an urban county and entitlement cities, where there are no legally independent subunits.

A factor affecting the CDBG program in the first year was the imminent primary election in the county in the spring of 1975 and the general election in November. A viable and very visible community development program—especially in the areas of bedrock Democratic party support such as the model cities area—was seen by Staisey, titular head of the Democratic party in the county, as a factor both in his bid for reelection and in control of the powerful Board of County Commissioners. The effects of the election on the program are discussed below.

As the grant application was in the final stages of preparation, the issue of the county's development authority was raised. In January HUD questioned whether Allegheny County possessed the power to initiate and carry out activities without cooperation agreements with municipalities. Although the county asserted its constitutional authority to carry out community development activities, it agreed to obtain written cooperation agreements to avoid any risk of having its application rejected by HUD. As stated earlier, the short time available for obtaining the cooperation agreements forced the county to settle for the minimum population required to qualify. By mid-February the county had obtained the necessary agreements to ensure its qualifying as an urban county. The question was settled two months later when State Attorney General Robert P. Kane affirmed the authority of all Pennsylvania counties to carry out urban renewal and publicly assisted housing activities without first securing cooperation agreements from incorporated areas.

For all practical purposes the preparation of the county's first-year application ended quietly and without controversy on January 27, 1975, when the Planning Commission held its final public hearing. Citizens and community groups were invited to react to the county's draft application, but the reaction raised no substantive issues. Among the seventy-five persons who came, several spoke strongly in favor of the plan, particularly the proposed senior citizen centers and neighborhood preservation project. One week later the Board of County Commissioners approved the CDBG application and submitted it to the area's regional and statewide clearinghouses for A-95 review.[14]

Because the newly formed Pennsylvania State Clearinghouse, the formally designated state review agency, was not yet in operation, the review was performed by the Department of Community Affairs. The department reported merely that it could not assess the application's proposed recreation projects because the county's open space study had not yet been completed, and that the county's application had erred in the amount of state funds it assumed would be available for land acquisition and development related to recreation.[15] The absence of comment on the major programs reflected the state agency's general lack of involvement in community development. Before the CDBG, its role was confined primarily to modest state funding of the urban renewal activities of individual municipalities, at the request of the County Redevelopment Authority.

The regional review agency was the Southwestern Pennsylvania Regional Planning Commission (SPRPC), composed of representatives of six counties and the city of Pittsburgh. As with the state review, the regional group did not closely scrutinize the application and concluded that the county's CDBG plans were consistent with the data contained in the application and with the SPRPC's own plans and programs. By mid-March the state and regional A-95 reviews were completed, and the county's application was submitted to the HUD area office in Pittsburgh. HUD gave preliminary approval to the application on June 1, 1975, with final approval subject to identification of the specific project sites.

14. The A-95 review is explained in note 22, chapter 4.

15. The application had given the figure of $250,000 instead of the $187,000 the state had actually committed.

Site Selection and Application Approval

While awaiting HUD approval, county planning officials began to identify first-year project sites with the assistance of Action-Housing, Inc., a nonprofit housing sponsor. The process of screening sites began in May, just before HUD's approval of the application, when the Department of Planning and Development sent letters to the 129 municipalities in the county to determine their interest in participating in the neighborhood preservation program. The conditions for participation were spelled out in the letter: (1) proposed target neighborhoods would consist primarily of homeowners, with household incomes averaging no less than $7,500 annually,[16] (2) the municipality would permit the County Health Department to expand its housing inspections to determine conformance with both county and municipal codes, and (3) the municipality agreed to contribute to needed capital improvements in the proposed neighborhood preservation area. Forty municipalities initially expressed an interest, but by the mid-June deadline only seventeen had submitted formal applications.

The responsibility for determining the final sites was delegated to a task force composed of representatives of the Health Department, the Department of Planning and Development, and Action-Housing. The team developed criteria to rank the seventeen applications, including factors related to environmental considerations, structural conditions of housing, attitudes of residents and local officials (did they understand and support the program?), favorable loan market conditions, needed public improvements, and socioeconomic characteristics of neighborhoods.[17] The task force and county planners believed that resident property owners should have a sufficiently high income to generate loan activity in the target areas. Neighborhoods that had median income levels of less than $7,500 (using 1970 data) were judged so in need as to require more than the limited resources could provide.

In mid-August, following a series of three meetings, the task force selected the sites. Neighborhoods in the five municipalities of Munhall, Duquesne, Homestead, Wilkinsburg, and Bethel Park were recom-

16. The income criterion was subsequently changed to a median income of not less than $10,090.

17. Jonathan Zimmer and Dennis K. E. Pittman, "Status Report and Recommendations: Allegheny County Neighborhood Preservation Program," August 11, 1975, p. 4.

mended. There was a suggestion of politics in the final choice; Duquesne was Chairman Staisey's hometown. Before the final agreements were negotiated, Bethel Park, a large and moderately affluent community, withdrew its application as a result of growing uncertainties about the municipality's commitment to participate.[18]

On August 19, after receiving the report of the neighborhood preservation task force, the County Planning Commission approved the report's recommendation of the four municipalities. In keeping with the procedures prescribed by the task force, each municipality subsequently held a public hearing to determine the extent of resident support for the program. Controversy arose only in Duquesne, where the NAACP chapter complained to HUD that the designated neighborhood preservation neighborhood—predominantly white—was chosen over a more deteriorated area for racial reasons. The NAACP also noted that two of the municipality's councilmen lived in the target area. HUD stated in its reply that the target area met the low- and moderate-income requirements of the program but said it would be alert to the needs of black areas in future program allocations. The response apparently satisfied the NAACP and the issue faded.

On the day the Board of County Commissioners took formal action on the neighborhood preservation program, it also reduced from $5 million to $1.75 million a bond issue that was intended to supplement the county's CDBG grant. The reduction was made because of a tight bond market. The effect was to cut the first-year development program from $11.4 million to $8.2 million. The commissioners' reduction of the bond issue freed some CDBG funds that had been earmarked to pay interest on the bonds. Because the program change exceeded 10 percent of the total, HUD regulations required additional public hearings.

These hearings were held in September and early October 1975 and unexpectedly elicited considerable citizen interest. At all three meetings citizen witnesses argued strongly for an expanded program of senior citizen centers throughout the county. On October 2 the Planning and Development Department and the County Planning Commission formally recommended that the number of senior centers to be funded be expanded from ten to fifteen, with a corresponding increase in funding of $125,000.

18. Bethel Park's decision was reversed by the time the second-year planning began. This resulted in its inclusion as one of the second-year municipalities selected for neighborhood preservation.

In the amending process the county commissioners had to contend with some unexpected problems. Although only mildly intruding into the decision process, HUD surprised the Department of Planning and Development in early September by informing it that two comprehensive human service centers proposed in the first-year application were not eligible. The decision was based on a belief that the program would not sufficiently benefit low- and moderate-income residents but also reflected HUD's preference for physical development rather than human services activities. While the HUD decision was a disruptive reversal of earlier approval, the county did not protest, and the centers were dropped.

In November 1975, almost six months after the original CDBG application had received tentative approval, HUD finally approved the amended application, thus beginning the county's first-year CDBG program. The election soon had a major impact on the county program, however.

Elections and Reprogramming

In the November 1975 election two incumbent commissioners, Staisey and William Hunt, a Republican, both ran with party endorsements and lost to a maverick Democrat, James Flaherty, and a Republican, Robert Pierce. The new Board of County Commissioners was dominated by a Flaherty-Pierce coalition that relegated the Democratic incumbent, Thomas Foerster, to a minority policy role. Two months after taking office, the new commissioners were clearly in control of the CDBG program and proceeded immediately to make several changes in it. They canceled the proposed bond issue altogether; canceled a $200,000 housing demolition program on the grounds that this was a municipal rather than a county function, although staff planners attached much importance to it; approved a $453,000 reduction (28 percent) in the neighborhood preservation budget, based on reports from the Department of Planning and Development that the program could not absorb the full allocation for the initial funding period; and cut $150,000 in technical assistance for housing development.

Once again the senior citizen groups won. The commissioners approved an additional $209,000 for senior citizen centers, raising the first-year funding for them to over a half-million dollars. The funds cut from the neighborhood preservation program were reallocated to the nonprofit Turtle Creek Housing Development Corporation to help finance the construction of eighty low- and moderate-income units in a part of the county badly in need of housing. Thus Turtle Creek Valley, which faced the loss of its model cities funds, was slated to get another slice of CDBG money. The other major piece of reallocated funds went for a county flood control project.

Surprisingly, these reprogramming decisions did not arouse significant controversy. Apparently the losses were sufficiently spread to cause no reaction, and there were some clearly identifiable winners among lower-income groups.

Second-Year Planning

At the time the newly elected Board of County Commissioners took office in early 1976, preparation of the second-year application was just beginning. This provided the new commissioners with the opportunity to influence both the general direction of the program early in the planning process and the specific allocation of a sizable amount of uncommitted money. The $7.6 million grant for the second year provided an additional $1.2 million over the first-year grant. The county had been active during the first year in enlisting the participation of municipalities in the county program and succeeded in getting an entitlement population of 850,000. The county was aided by a HUD ruling that unless municipalities specifically chose not to participate, they were to be automatically included as part of the urban county. The county was also motivated to develop goodwill with the municipalities to prevent individual communities from seeking discretionary grants through the Redevelopment Authority. In the first year Wilmerding received a $600,000 discretionary grant, which was administered by the Redevelopment Authority. Thus the active county wooing of the municipalities during the first years was in part to head off free-lancing for clients by the Redevelopment Authority. Beside the added formula amount, another chunk of uncommitted money came from the decision made earlier to discontinue the model cities activities, which had received $2.4 million in the first year. In effect the commissioners had about $3.6 million in new money.

In a pattern similar to the first year, the Planning and Development Department sent special information mailings to municipalities and interested groups describing preliminary allocations and inviting participation in the public hearings scheduled for January. This time, however, the county's operating departments were not asked to submit project requests for consideration in the block grant application. The decision reflected the judgment of the staff of the Planning and Development Department about the capability of the county's line departments to carry out community development activities. It also had the effect of reducing the demand side and leaving more room for the commissioners to determine priorities. The County Redevelopment Authority continued to be excluded.

As in the first year, the Department of Planning and Development, now headed by a new director, William Dodge, proposed programs to the Planning Commission for review. (Milberger, who had been serving as acting director, was replaced before the election. Dodge, who came from Ohio, was hired by the Planning Commission after a recruitment search for a new director.) The general public was involved primarily through five regional hearings held in January. Once more, however, citizen participation in CDBG decisionmaking fell short of expectations; attendance at the public hearings was lower than that of the first year. And once more, the only significant instance of citizen influence occurred when organized activity developed in favor of senior citizen centers and the number of centers in the plan was further increased.

One of the more heated issues during the preparation of the second-year application was whether the neighborhood preservation program should continue to be the centerpiece of the county's CDBG program. The new board majority held views similar to Staisey's, and suggested that housing was a municipal, not a county, responsibility. Flaherty and Pierce preferred to use CDBG funds to ease the pressure on the county's budget and to finance countywide activities such as the development of parks and reconstruction of bridges and roads. But Dodge and his community development director, Al Pelinsky, wanted to maintain the county's involvement in housing. Armed with their interpretation of HUD regulations, the national goals under CDBG, and the Department of Planning and Development's analysis of local housing needs, they urged the new Board of Commissioners not to abandon the neighborhood preservation program. They succeeded in obtaining the commissioners' reluctant agreement to continue the program; $1 million was budgeted for rehabilitation assistance and $150,000 for code enforcement. In the second year three additional communities were included in the neighborhood preservation program.

Just before submitting the application to HUD the new Board of

County Commissioners made a key decision. Responding to continuing pressures from municipal officials for more direct and visible assistance under the CDBG, the board added two new municipally oriented programs to the application. CDBG funds for recreation facilities were provided to municipalities with a demonstrated need for them, particularly for low- and moderate-income residents. Funds were also provided for municipalities to undertake public improvements such as sewers, water lines, and streets. Although new to the CDBG program, such county-funded activities had a precedent. County funds had earlier been loaned or granted to municipalities for locally initiated public improvements in a program run by a county agency known as AIM (Authority for the Improvement of Municipalities). To accommodate the recreation and municipal improvement programs, the commissioners eliminated from the application a home winterization program and the homeowners and tenant counseling service, two projects that had been proposed by the Planning and Development Department and the Planning Commission. Although both Dodge and the commission were opposed to the new municipal programs, they were unable to change the decision.

Thus as the program progressed, the municipalities became increasingly successful in getting a share of the block grant. This increased influence appeared to be aided in part by the absence of competition from other significant constituent groups either among organized interest groups or neighborhood-based organizations; the one exception was the senior citizen groups. It appears, however, that even the municipalities were not the dominant influence, since the centralization of CDBG administration tended to reinforce the power of countywide authorities. Moreover, the increasing municipal orientation of the program appeared to result as much from the interest of the Board of Commissioners in securing its power base as from responsiveness to municipal demands.

The final application was approved by the Board of County Commissioners in March 1976. The subsequent A-95 reviews raised no issues; state review officials deferred to the regional agency and authorized the county to proceed if that agency had no comments warranting delay. As in the first year, the regional review was a pro forma recommendation that the county's application be approved by HUD.

In its review of the second-year application, HUD questioned the failure to identify specific sites for certain activities—a recurrent issue in Allegheny County—such as the senior centers, and the emphasis on capital public works projects. HUD's objection to the capital improvements was stimulated in large part by congressional criticism of the use of CDBG funds for purposes that did not directly benefit low- and moderate-income residents. Taking a somewhat harder line than in the first year, the HUD area office asked the county to withdraw its second-year application and to resubmit it when these concerns had been adequately addressed. The questions about site specificity were relatively easy to respond to, but the county did not alter its emphasis on public works, and HUD was apparently unwilling to pursue its challenge. It approved the application, leaving the county's original public works plan intact.

The strategy of the first-year program had been to expand assistance beyond the model cities communities in Turtle Creek Valley and to shift program emphasis from social services to the physical development needs of the county's older mill towns through neighborhood revitalization. The shift to capital projects was virtually completed in the second year, when the county no longer funded the continuation of model cities services. The only remaining social service activity of significance was the network of senior citizen centers that was started in the first year and expanded in the second, and these funds were used primarily for building renovation and equipment purchases. The second year also saw a change in the revitalization objective. While continuing to fund the neighborhood preservation program, which emphasized housing rehabilitation and which was the centerpiece of the first-year strategy, the new centerpiece was general development activities, such as park and recreation facilities, and public improvements, such as storm sewers, streets, and bridge reconstruction. Overall, the strategy that evolved over the first two years was a shift away from assisting individual citizens through services and housing rehabilitation to assisting governments, both municipal and county, through conventional public works projects. Such a shift within two years would not have been possible under the categorical approach where federal policymakers determined the kind and quantity of assisted goods and services.

Balancing Program Needs

As stated, one of the earliest major decisions was to continue a variety of model cities projects but to end this assistance after the first year. Continued support for one year fulfilled the county's commitment to the model cities program, which had started as a five-year demonstration project. When the CDBG began, the county had just one year to go in the five-year demonstration. Furthermore, the CDBG was intended to be a capital-intensive program, thus making it easier to discontinue the service-oriented activities of model cities such as preschool centers, primary health centers, housing counseling, youth recreation, and drug rehabilitation. While services represented less than half of model cities spending, it was unlikely that HUD would have allowed both indefinitely continuing those services and funding the large network of senior citizen centers that became the service emphasis of the county's program. HUD's rejection of the two pilot human service centers in the first-year application indicated the agency's opposition to an overemphasis on service-oriented activities.

The decision by county officials to deemphasize social services and end the concentration of spending in Turtle Creek Valley freed CDBG funds for needed physical revitalization of the older mill towns scattered throughout the county. This new priority was reflected in the neighborhood preservation program, which was to be targeted to a small number of municipalities. The four communities selected for program participation in the first year were all outside the model cities area and three of the four were older mill towns. In the second year three communities were added, also outside the model cities area.

The neighborhood preservation program consisted of housing rehabilitation and related neighborhood improvements such as street and sidewalk repair; the related improvements were to be funded primarily through locally raised funds. Housing rehabilitation was to be financed through bank loans, with the interest rate reduced to 3 percent through subsidies from CDBG funds. Direct CDBG loans from the county were also available. In the selected communities the rehabilitation funds were to be directed toward salvageable neighborhoods by limiting assistance to moderate- rather than low-income areas. Another component of the revitalization effort was a $335,000 allocation to Action-Housing to provide planning and technical assistance to developers who would build federally subsidized housing for low- and moderate-income residents in the neighborhood preservation communities. Thus the CDBG funds were designed to induce additional expenditures for revitalization from municipal funds and housing investments by private lending institutions and developers.

In both program years substantial CDBG funds were directed toward the neighborhood preservation project, although in the second year it received a smaller share of block grant funds, and officials in the Department of Planning and Development had to resist efforts by the new commissioners to drop the program entirely. In the first year 44 percent of the county's grant went for neighborhood revitalization; in the second year 35 percent went for this purpose. Despite the nine percentage point decline, the amount of money going for neighborhood preservation activities declined only slightly, from $2.8 million to $2.7 million; the percentage drop resulted from the increase in the county's grant in the second year.

Besides the revitalization objective, another significant activity in the first-year application was economic development in the underdeveloped areas of the county. County officials planned to use county bonds to finance construction of water and sewer systems and roads to open up new industrial parks. CDBG funds were to pay $209,000 in interest costs on the bonds. Like the neighborhood preservation projects, the economic development activities were to be placed outside the model cities area. County officials viewed these activities as an extension of the county's traditional concern for encouraging planned economic growth. When the bond issue was canceled the economic development activities were dropped, and the CDBG funds earmarked for interest payments were reprogrammed over to the senior citizen centers. No economic development activities were included in the second-year program, which had a much different emphasis.

The new commissioners elected in November 1975 appeared to have a dual strategy: (1) to ease the county's fiscal pressure by using CDBG funds for county functions; and (2) to give more direct aid to municipalities to keep them interested in participation and to strengthen the political support of the commissioners among municipal officials. To support this two-part strategy, the commissioners earmarked over half (55 percent) of the second-year funds for general development projects; the amount allocated for general development increased from about $325,000 in the first year to about $4.2 million in the second.

The much larger funds for general development came from the additional $1.2 million in the county grant, the cutoff of the model cities services, and a drop in funds for planning and administration, most of which had been related to the continuation of the model cities program. The lion's share of the general development money, $3.4 million, was allocated for direct county use for projects such as county park and recreation facilities and public improvements such as storm sewers, roads, and bridge reconstruction; $800,000 was set aside for similar public works projects through grants to municipalities. The general purpose of the municipal assistance program was to fund activities that would increase the attractiveness of the communities and help prevent population loss. Preference for municipal public works was to be given to those that addressed an urgent need, were not revenue producing, and represented a reasonably complete solution to the existing problem. For the municipal recreation projects (such as tennis courts, lighted ball fields, basketball courts, and tot-lots), the selection criteria included low family income in the area to be served, lack of recreation facilities, and the absence of other funding sources.

The general rule governing the municipal projects appeared to be that they were to be relatively small, one-shot capital projects that would enable the county to continually circulate CDBG funds among municipalities throughout the county. Thus a community that could not participate in the neighborhood preservation program might get some money from the municipal fund. This would avert any political problems that might stem from making commitments to a few large, long-term projects that favored certain communities or sections of the county (the eastern part of the county did very well the first year).

Overall, Allegheny County's first two years of the CDBG reflected the programmatic need to deal with deteriorating housing and infrastructure in the older mill towns that dotted the county. At the same time, the programs showed a clear response to the special composition of constituents in an urban county, the participating municipalities. And the major change in strategy that accompanied the election of two new commissioners showed the extent to which development decisions had become closely linked to local political factors and disconnected from federal policy controls.

Social Targeting

The block grant program had a notable impact on the distribution of projects and benefits. The geographical scope of the county's development activities expanded and so did the income and racial groups served.

The communities receiving projects were scattered throughout the county, doubling from about twenty-five communities in the first year to nearly fifty in the second. There was no particular geographic pattern to the spreading, although the second year seemed to bring more activities to the northern and western parts of the county. It was clear, however, that the general flow of CDBG dollars during the first two years was out of the Turtle Creek Valley area, which had been the site of model cities, and toward more communities that can be characterized as low- to moderate-income areas; the shift also tended to move funds from a heavily minority area to a more racially diverse constituency.

About 60 percent of the first-year allocations were intended to benefit low- and moderate-income persons. The principal project benefiting this group was the continuation of model cities. The neighborhood preservation program was directed at homeowners in moderate-income census tracts, leaving out the worst-off areas. In 1970 incomes, the lowest median income level for the neighborhood preservation tracts was $8,000 and the highest was $8,940.[19] The criteria of willingness to participate and the need to secure loans screened out potential lower-income beneficiaries; moderate-income families were more likely to qualify. This was borne out in a report assessing early neighborhood preservation performance prepared by Action-Housing.[20] But the report also indicated that sixty-four households whose low income prevented their borrowing from other sources received direct loans through the preservation program for housing repairs. Overall, while the neighborhood preservation program served a varied-income population, the principal beneficiaries were in moderate-income neighborhoods.

In the second year low- and moderate-income group benefits declined when the model cities program ended and the county shifted emphasis to conventional public works projects. Both the countywide and municipal projects diluted the neighborhood focus and provided a greater share of direct benefits to the general population. In the case of recreation facilities, however, the Planning and Development Department did place emphasis on sites close to lower-income areas that previously had no recreational outlets, and lower-income residents were intended to benefit from the senior citizen center programs. When completely operational, each facility was expected to serve an estimated 7,000–12,000 senior

19. Zimmer and Pittman, "Status Report," pp. 13–26. The 1970 Pittsburgh standard metropolitan statistical area median income was $9,737; the low-moderate level was below $7,498 (80 percent of the median). See U.S. Department of Housing and Urban Development, Community Planning and Development, Office of Evaluation, *Community Development Block Grant Program, Urban Counties: The First Year Experience,* Evaluation Series (GPO, 1977), table 2.2, p. 9.

20. Action-Housing, Inc., "First Year Neighborhood Preservation Program: A Preliminary Assessment" (Pittsburgh, Pa.: December 22, 1977).

residents in the surrounding area. Most of these were likely to fall in the lower-income groups.

It is important to note that the decline in lower-income benefits in the second year was not the result of any explicit decision to spread the benefits among a broader range of income groups. The drop primarily resulted from the shift in the kinds of projects to be funded, away from person-oriented activities that could be more directly targeted to activities that yielded locational benefits and were less easily targeted to a specific income group.

Overall Effects of the Block Grant

The institutional impact of the block grant was felt before it was formally legislated in the county's pre-CDBG decision to centralize community development functions in the Department of Planning in anticipation of the block grant program. The centralization of CDBG functions in the expanded Department of Planning and Development lessened bureaucratic fragmentation and tied planning more directly to allocation decisions. This increased the department's clout not only with other county agencies but also with the municipalities seeking CDBG funds. The centralization was achieved partly at the expense of the Redevelopment Authority. With the end of the urban renewal program and by being left outside the CDBG process, the authority lost its position as a major player in county development. County planning capabilities were augmented through the recruitment of new staff and the realignment of existing staff to perform planning tasks and environmental reviews, to oversee citizen participation, and to coordinate project execution.

Programmatically, CDBG provided a boost to housing rehabilitation and neighborhood preservation activities and, with the phaseout of model cities, adversely affected social service programs. The installation of the new commissioners in the second year again changed the block grant into an infrastructure program to aid the county in maintaining bridges and roads and carrying out public improvements in the municipalities. In the transitional years, however, the impact of the program was more potential than real since actual implementation was slow.

The county was able to prevail in establishing local spending priorities against sometimes reluctant but generally permissive HUD officials. Because Allegheny County had considerable experience with the categorical programs, extensive interaction with HUD on procedural issues and paperwork was not considered unusual. But in the second year, when HUD objected to the emphasis on capital projects and the limited benefits of such projects for low- and moderate-income groups, it appeared to county officials that the department was setting the groundwork for bringing the jurisdiction into compliance with a set of national priorities. HUD, however, did not attempt to force a change in the local program.

The Future

The county's third-year grant was $8.4 million. Of this, $4.3 million was allocated for general development activities such as bridge and road reconstruction.[21] Local insistence on high expenditures for general development again elicited objections from HUD because of the lack of targeting to low- and moderate-income areas. Eventually HUD accepted many of the expenditures under the "urgent needs" section of the law (see chapter 2). In the fourth year, however, general development expenditures declined significantly and emphasis on housing rehabilitation and economic development increased. In the fourth year the county received $13.2 million, the large increase coming from the impact of the new dual formula that benefited the county (see chapter 9). The shift to housing projects came from the growing awareness of county officials that housing conservation strategies were essential in a county that was not growing and that had complied with HUD pressure for more social targeting. The neighborhood preservation activities were to be better targeted than in the past toward predominantly minority and low-income areas.

The county also came under pressure from citizen groups for more social targeting. In 1977 a coalition of dissatisfied community groups filed a suit against the county in federal court charging mismanagement and misallocation of CDBG funds. Among the specific allegations, the suit charged that money intended for improving the housing and living environment of the poor was being misallocated for bridge repair, flood relief, and sewers. The suit was withdrawn by the plaintiffs after a similar one filed against the city of Pittsburgh was dismissed by the court, but the targeting of CDBG program benefits remained an issue facing this jurisdiction in the implementation of its block grant program.

21. "Allegheny County Third Year Community Development Program," pp. 27–28.

CHAPTER SEVEN

Carbondale, Illinois

JOHN S. JACKSON III

CARBONDALE is a small city of some 27,000 people centrally located in deep southern Illinois, 320 miles south of Chicago and 220 miles north of Memphis, Tennessee. Newcomers who move to Carbondale from the East or West coasts are often surprised to find that their new home is closer to Mississippi than it is to Chicago. The nearest metropolitan area is St. Louis, which is 100 miles northwest of Carbondale. Thus the rural and small town people of southern Illinois regard Carbondale as their "city."

Carbondale was founded in 1852 by a local entrepreneur who wanted to take advantage of the opportunities offered by the coming of the Illinois Central Railroad. When the railroad was built, Carbondale became a switching center and transportation hub, and the railroad and coal industries have always been an important part of the economic base of the area.[1] The city was built along the railroad, and multiple strands of Illinois Central tracks still run right down through the center of Carbondale, physically dividing it. Slow freights often create frustrating traffic jams that sometimes threaten to make raving antirailroad Populists out of even the most staid and patient of the city's drivers.[2]

A Small but Cosmopolitan City

In this setting one might expect to find a very homogeneous, parochial, and conservative small city of the type that seems to abound in the Mid-

THE AUTHOR wishes to thank John Baker, associate professor of Political Science at Southern Illinois University (Carbondale), and William L. Shade, assistant to the governor of Florida for planning, for their helpful comments on this chapter.

1. John W. D. Wright, *A History of Early Carbondale, Illinois 1852–1905* (Southern Illinois University Press, 1977), chap. 1.

2. In 1980, with the help of a federal transportation grant, the city undertook a major project to put the tracks underground throughout most of the city.

west. After all, who has not heard the phrase made famous in the Nixon era: "But will it play in Peoria?"—a cliché that was supposed to epitomize the Midwest and indeed all of Middle America. Peoria is Carbondale's neighbor to the north, and the two cities share a state and other outward characteristics, but Carbondale is more complex than one might expect a small midwestern city to be.

Carbondale is a diverse, heterogeneous, and even cosmopolitan place for its size and location. The city is 13 percent black, with a significant black ghetto on the northeast side of town.[3] It is a city where representatives of virtually every race, culture, and nationality make their homes—at least temporarily. It is a city whose labor force ranges from the marginal and seasonal migrants in the neighboring fields and orchards to sophisticated research scientists manning laboratories and computers. It is a city formerly dominated by a socioeconomic elite of longtime families who now find themselves having to compete daily with an endless stream of newcomers. It is a city where as many residents were born in Cook County and Chicago as were born locally. It is a city where dilapidated and substandard housing stands virtually back-to-back with comfortable upper-middle-class suburban homes. It is a city where the pressure on housing is so great that the official vacancy rate hovers between 1 and 3 percent. It is a city where a decaying central business district has left several burned-out and vacant store buildings on the main street, while further decline is hastened by a gleaming new shopping mall on the outskirts of town.

The major source of the diversity in this small city is a large state university, Southern Illinois University, which sits half in and half out of the city's official limits. SIU and Carbondale have a totally symbiotic but frequently suspicious and hostile relationship. The city often does not know what to make of the university and vice versa. SIU has about 22,000 students, 1,800 faculty members, and 2,000 staff.[4] The university

3. U.S. Bureau of the Census, *1970 Census of Housing, Block Statistics,* HC(3)-74, *Selected Areas in Illinois* (Government Printing Office, 1971), table 2, p. 8. Carbondale is one of the few cities in southern Illinois with so large a black population, which originated with the employment opportunities originally offered by the Illinois Central Railroad. These jobs have long since declined.

4. Because of the location of the university and the housing patterns of the students, there is no official estimate of what percentage of Carbondale's total population consists of college students, but surveys indicate that this figure may be as high as 50 percent. The students obviously could exercise a great deal of political clout if mobilized; they have never been successfully mobilized in city politics, however.

is clearly the mainstay of the city's economy and is by far the area's largest single employer. By comparison, the second largest employer in the city is a small industry with approximately 425 employees, and there are very few others of similar size. SIU students, faculty, and staff make up a large proportion of the city's population, although many of them also live outside the city limits and in other surrounding towns. SIU has both a law school and a medical school, numerous graduate programs, and a comprehensive undergraduate curriculum. Consequently it attracts a diverse student body and faculty from all over the nation and the world. Much of the complexity and heterogeneity of the city results from the presence of the university.

Carbondale, in short, contains virtually all the problems of urban America today. To be sure, the problems are smaller scale. The smaller scale, however, also means that the resources are proportionately smaller. This is the backdrop for the case study.

Local Government

Carbondale has a council-manager government in which the city council is composed of five members elected at large on a nonpartisan basis. The elections are largely nonpartisan in reality as well as in name.[5] Although the local parties are fairly strong, they do not consistently get involved in city campaigns, and one often finds progressive or liberal Democrats and Republicans facing conservative Democrats and Republicans in the city council races. The mayor is popularly elected, holds a seat on the council, and is "first among equals" on the council in the sense of presiding at council meetings and representing the city at most ceremonial functions. The chief executive officer is the city manager, and it is he who runs the executive branch of government.

There is a lot of rhetoric, particularly at election time, about how the council-manager plan is supposed to work and how it is working in Carbondale. The supposed dichotomy between policy and administration is frequently defended and even extolled. Many people seem to believe it exists, and that if it does not, it should. Few doubt that the city manager runs the administration, but there is considerable room for skepticism about whether the council is the source of all policy. The city manager

5. Charles R. Adrian, "A Typology for Nonpartisan Elections," *Western Political Quarterly*, vol. 12 (June 1959), pp. 449–58.

often makes important policy-related decisions, but only some of these have to be ratified by the council.

Carroll J. Fry has been city manager of Carbondale since 1971, and thus his tenure spanned the entire period of this case study. Fry is a strong, activist leader who enjoys solid council support. He is a forceful personality who runs the city's staff with an iron hand (some say "fist"). He expects a lot from his staff and usually gets it. The manager's detractors see him as undiplomatic at best and abrasive and authoritarian at worst. His admirers see him as the only person who has ever really successfully made the city manager system work in Carbondale and the only administrator to ever weld a formerly factious group of city employees into a coherent staff. No one accuses him of being either timid or weak.

The city manager and his method of operation is a major part of this story. Fry's role and the staff he has assembled are key ingredients in explaining how and why Carbondale's community development block grant (CDBG) program operates as it does. In subsequent pages references are made to the city staff's position or actions. While the staff often takes initiatives, its efforts have to be approved by the city manager, so these references are to policies and actions that are ultimately his responsibility. In summary, Carbondale's governmental structure features the typical reform package characteristics with a perhaps unusually strong city manager.

Carbondale's political history is complex. For decades the city had a commission form of government dominated politically by a coalition of old-line Carbondale families and interests. Generally this ancien régime seemed to look after the economic interests of the downtown businessmen and an array of real estate and financial institutions. SIU experienced very rapid growth in the 1950s and 1960s, generating large amounts of business, particularly in real estate. The city generally provided not much more than whatever services were necessary to support the continued growth of the university, which in turn was solicitous of those who wanted to make a profit. SIU, for example, built far fewer dormitories than were necessary to house its resident student population, preferring instead to encourage the building of private dormitories around the edge of the campus and mobile home parks in the countryside. All in all, it was a mutually beneficial and, some critics say, a much too cozy arrangement.

In 1967 the old order passed away in a significant political upheaval. The precipitating issue was a drive to change the city charter from the commission to the council-manager form of government. The precipitating political force was a group called the Blue Ribbon Commission, a coalition of predominantly upper-middle-class reformers, many of whom had university ties. After a long and bitter fight the new city charter was adopted, and the Blue Ribbon Commission won three seats on the city council, including the office of mayor.

Since 1968 Carbondale's government and politics have been dominated by the Blue Ribbon group and its successors. Most of these upper-middle-class activists and most elected officials live in the southwestern quadrant of the city, which clearly holds the most effective political power in town. Many of the activists are imbued with the spirit of volunteerism, "public-regardingness," and good government.[6] They are very prominent in the plethora of volunteer boards and commissions that are an important component of the city's government. Most of them vote in city elections and will respond to candidates who make the reform and good government appeals one would expect in such a context.

The old-line families have grown increasingly apathetic. They know there once was a lot of money that could be made in a small city such as Carbondale, money that often depended on benign or supportive government officials and favorable policies and programs. But the private sector cannot make a lot of money from welfare, educational, and community development programs that are the focus of Carbondale government today; consequently they are ignored by the old-line residents.

This is not to say that the representatives of the formerly dominant economic interests have entirely left the scene. They are still an important feature of the political landscape when their interests are involved. They can still mobilize significant political muscle when the occasion demands and when they are exercised about some issue or candidate. The difference, however, is that they are ordinarily aroused only about the issues that have rather clear and direct business and economic implications. If a zoning exception is needed, if a new shopping center requires that a city street be built, or if a new industry can potentially be

6. See James Q. Wilson and Edward C. Banfield, "Public Regardingness as a Value Premise in Voting Behavior," *American Political Science Review,* vol. 58 (December 1964), pp. 876–87; and John O. Field, "Political Ethos and the Structure of City Government," ibid., vol. 60 (June 1966), 306–26.

attracted, then the economic elites will become involved. Otherwise they generally stay out of the nitty-gritty of operating the government on a daily basis.

In this partial vacuum the upper-middle-class good government political activists, following the path of the Blue Ribbon Commission, are able to dominate almost by default. They are sometimes supported and sometimes opposed by the lower- and lower-middle-class members of the community who are often the clients of the governmental programs. When the good government activists make common cause with the clients of these programs, the coalition is formidable. They usually prevail unless the issue happens to arouse the economic elites, which CDBG activities rarely do. The old-line economic elites often choose not to enter the competition, because their immediate interests are not involved. This leaves the field to the activist elite, whose motivations are ideological and issue oriented, and to the clients of the social programs.

Four Distinct Neighborhoods

Understanding Carbondale's geography and its extensive involvement in categorical grants is important to understanding why the city's CDBG program took the particular shape it did. The categorical experience was framed by Carbondale's geography, which divided the city into four sections that are distinct physically, socially, and politically. The Illinois Central Railroad runs north and south through the heart of the city and bisects more than just the traffic pattern. Illinois Highway 13 (Main Street) runs east and west and provides the other axis dividing the city into four parts.

The northeast section of the city, predominantly black and containing a high percentage of low- and moderate-income residents, had suffered for many years from discrimination and racism at worst and "benign neglect" at best. The streets were narrow, filled with potholes, and often covered with brick or worn asphalt. Curbs, storm sewers, and sidewalks put in only occasional appearances. Approximately 30 percent of the housing stock was well below the city's code standards. The city's own wastewater treatment plant often polluted the neighborhood's atmosphere with a pervasive, offensive odor.

Some attention to the Northeast was long overdue when the city began to move on its problems in the early 1970s. It was the site of two urban renewal projects, and parts of these projects remained incomplete when the block grant program began. In addition the Northeast was the designated "model neighborhood" under the model cities program. Finally, Carbondale had a $594,000 grant under the neighborhood facilities program with which a large, modern structure—the Eurma C. Hayes Neighborhood Center—was built in the heart of this section. It opened in 1973, just before the CDBG began. Many of the social welfare programs operated with model cities, and other state and federal funds were housed in the Hayes Center.

The bulk of the categorical grants money, from the former Office of Economic Opportunity, model cities, and urban renewal, had been devoted to the Northeast, and some notable changes in the physical appearance of the neighborhood had been achieved by the time the renewal and model cities programs ended in 1974. In addition the social and political characteristics of the neighborhood changed. For several years the most significant social and political organization in that section, and one of the most important in all of Carbondale, was the Northeast Congress. The Northeast Congress, organized in the mid-1960s, was the officially designated citizen participation unit for the neighborhood during the War on Poverty days. It was also the official model cities neighborhood organization during the life of that program.

As it became clearer at the national level that the model cities and urban renewal programs were likely to be replaced by the CDBG, progress slowed and these two programs were left in something of a holding pattern at the local level. In the summer of 1974, when CDBG planning began in Carbondale, the model cities program was entering the fourth of five planned "action" years. Urban renewal was entering what was to become its last full year of operation. The concrete was not yet poured for a lot of projects that had been promised to the Northeast. Sidewalks and streets literally remained half finished. The Hayes facility had just opened and needed maintenance and staffing. In short, a variety of capital improvements that needed to be finished were under way, and social programs on which staff and clients depended were in place. After all, Carbondale officials reasoned, we got into these programs willingly but also with the very positive stimulus and encouragement of the federal government. How can we just abandon ship now?

Facing many of the same problems of physical deterioration evident in the Northeast, the Northwest was a neighborhood in transition toward blight and decay. It was more heterogeneous, with a large population of students, renters, and the elderly as well as scattered enclaves of upper-middle-class affluence. The Northwest was also predominantly white, while the Northeast was predominantly black. When the Northwest residents saw the bulk of federal and city attention being focused on the Northeast, they looked at their own area and judged its needs to be just as pressing. In an effort to get their own programs a number of residents organized the Northwest Homeowners Association, a group comparable to the Northeast Congress. Before the CDBG the city staff and the council decided that the Springmore section of the Northwest would be the city's next urban renewal neighborhood; soon after the decision the federal government announced plans to end that program.

In terms of the CDBG program the other important section of town was the Southwest, a relatively well-off area. The streets are generally wide and well maintained, and city services are generally adequate, although there are pockets in the Southwest where some city money could be well spent. The Southwest is a newer section of town and has not suffered the years of neglect, both public and private, that undermined the vitality of the Northeast and the Northwest. The Southwest's political clout is underscored by the fact that four of the five city council members, including the mayor and the city manager, all lived in the Southwest during the early phase of the CDBG program.

The fourth section of town, the Southeast, contains part of SIU and large concentrations of students, multifamily homes, and mobile home parks. The residents are the most heterogeneous and least cohesive population in the city. They are generally transient, and virtually the only common identity they share is that many are SIU students. In the recent past the students ran candidates for city council and mayor, but in each case they lost badly.[7] The common factor of being students is just not sufficient to create a mutually perceived set of interests that are strong enough to mobilize the students politically.

If councilmanic seats were based on districts rather than at-large elections, students would control one or more seats. The Student Government Organization at SIU had petitioned for this change but failed. In defending against the petition drive, the current members of the city council argued that at-large elections better serve a general interest or public interest than would representation by districts.

7. It is also notable that neither the city nor the county have tried to prevent students from registering to vote and have even encouraged it.

Beginning the Program

Carbondale officials were aware very early of the CDBG legislation as it worked its way through Congress. The city's biggest concern was that the program might overlook smaller cities such as Carbondale, which had received substantial categorical funding, by eliminating them altogether or greatly reducing their allocation. Through several trips, letters, and telephone calls, the mayor and the city manager directly lobbied Illinois senators and congressmen. Both officials also attended the Congressional-Cities Conference (sponsored by the National League of Cities) held in Washington in March 1974. They came back from that meeting armed with considerable information concerning the potential shape of the anticipated new program.

The final legislation gave the city three years of hold-harmless funding, which as a result of Carbondale's successful history with categorical grants, resulted in a fairly generous level of funding. In the first year the city received $2.9 million; the second-year grant was $2.7 million.[8] One can better appreciate the magnitude of these funds when it is realized that they constituted almost 20 percent of the city's total budget for each of the first two CDBG years, about the same percentage as under the categoricals. But a painful fact of life for Carbondale was that it was not a formula entitlement city under the CDBG and thus would suffer major reductions of funds. The grant amount was scheduled to drop from $2.5 million in the third year to $1.5 million the fourth year and $600,000 in the fifth year. With no guarantee of discretionary funding, Carbondale faced the possibility of receiving no CDBG funds in the sixth program year.

The Players: Local Officials

The city manager, the council, and the city staff all played crucial roles in shaping the CDBG program in Carbondale. Once the legislation passed and the Department of Housing and Urban Development (HUD) issued the final regulations, the city manager immediately assembled a

8. For the size of the city this is very high, and it works out to an average of $100 per capita per year. The national per capita grant to assisted communities was $17.63. For comparisons see Richard P. Nathan and others, *Block Grants for Community Development* (U.S. Department of Housing and Urban Development, January 1977), chap. 4.

task force of three city staff members to begin preparing the application. The task force, headed by Donald Monte, a young SIU graduate and formerly staff director of a planning effort called Goals for Carbondale, included one member each from the model cities and urban renewal agencies. Because of their experience with federal programs, they were able to prepare the CDBG grant application rapidly. Speed was essential because applications were due April 15, 1975, barely five months after the final HUD regulations were issued.

The staff, under the supervision of City Manager Fry, made the basic plans for the program.[9] Although policies ultimately had to be approved by the council, Fry's recommendations carried great weight. The council and the mayor, however, were more than a rubber stamp and played an important role in setting a number of basic program directions and making some of the crucial political decisions.

Another early step taken by the city manager was the creation of the Department of Community Development from a number of existing agencies; the department became the critical staff unit in the CDBG program. Fry made himself the department director, signifying his strong desire to maintain control over the staff. Monte was made assistant director and ran the day-to-day operations of the department. He combined bureaucratic efficiency and attention to detail with a commitment to citizen participation and a concern for the disadvantaged. Monte enjoyed a good reputation with the city council and had the manager's confidence.

The department was composed of five divisions: Human Resources, Renewal and Housing, Codes Enforcement, Planning, and Industrial Development. (The director of the Department of Public Works was an ex-officio member of the Community Development Department.) The first two divisions were the most active and important for the CDBG program.

The Division of Human Resources was essentially the former model cities agency. Robert A. Stalls, who had directed the model cities program, became the division director, and many of the staff were also carried over. Carbondale officials had regarded the model cities program as an opportunity to try a variety of new approaches to community prob-

9. This structure is explained in Carroll J. Fry and Robert A. Stalls, "Gearing Up for Community Development," *Public Management*, vol. 56 (December 1974), pp. 15–17 (the authors are the city manager and director of human resources, respectively).

lems and some of the activities, such as the Comprehensive Health Program, the Comprehensive Child Care Program, and the Career Opportunities Programs, continued with CDBG funds. As a result there was substantial continuity in both the programs and the staff of model cities.

Similarly, the Division of Renewal and Housing was staffed from the Urban Renewal Agency. It was headed by Eldon Gosnell, the former director of urban renewal. The division's emphasis under the CDBG changed from demolition in blighted areas to housing rehabilitation. The division also prepared the housing assistance plan, which ordinarily was approved without controversy by the other actors in the CDBG process.

The availability of experienced specialists allowed Carbondale to gear up quickly to take maximum advantage of the CDBG program. The fact that the city had substantial experience with categorical programs, including interaction with HUD staffs in Chicago and Washington, was important in achieving a smooth transition to the new program.

The importance of the CDBG to other city bureaucracies varied. For the Codes Enforcement Division, the Planning Division, and the Department of Public Works the CDBG program constituted only a fraction of their overall responsibilities. For the Industrial Development Division the CDBG was slightly more important. If the CDBG money were to end, Carbondale would continue to have about the same planning, codes, and public works operations, but it was likely that the Renewal and Housing Division would be significantly reduced and that the Human Resources Division might not survive at all.

The Players: Local Citizens

Citizen participation was one of the most controversial early problems in the CDBG program. The city manager recommended that a new citizen participation unit be created. He knew that several members of the council placed great importance on active citizen participation, whereas his own attitude ranged from hostility to lukewarm support, depending on the circumstances.

Stimulated and sustained by federal requirements, formal citizen participation had become an important component of politics in Carbondale. The first citizen participation unit, the Citizens Advisory Committee, had been established in 1963 to comply with HUD's requirements for the development of a "Workable Program" under urban renewal. The committee was instrumental in helping to monitor both the War on

Poverty and the model cities programs that came later. This overarching, communitywide citizen participation organization for Carbondale was composed of 25–30 persons appointed by the mayor and city council. These members gave a great deal of volunteer time to developing the recertification requirements every two years for the city's Workable Program and to conducting a wide variety of studies. Many of the committee members went on to the city council, city boards, or commissions.

There was a lot of overlap between Citizens Advisory Committee members and the political activists who successfully fought for a council-manager form of government. In fact, the committee originated the study with which the charter reform movement began. Thus city council members who had served on the committee before being elected to the council harbored a strong commitment to citizen participation. In recognition of the city's high level of citizen activism, Carbondale was chosen as an "All-American City" in 1971 by the National League of Cities, a designation ever since emblazoned on all city property from letterheads to garbage trucks.

Another important element in Carbondale's citizen participation experience was the Northeast Congress, a quasi-official vehicle for neighborhood participation in the urban renewal and model cities programs. As citizen participation groups, the Citizens Advisory Committee and the Northeast Congress often made common cause; the committee, however, represented the city as a whole, whereas the congress was devoted primarily to improving the Northeast. The congress, at one point, had a modest staff paid with model cities funds ($42,000 in the final year), and its president had considerable prestige in the community. The visible success of the Northeast Congress was an important stimulus for other sections of town to form their own groups. For example, in addition to the Northwest Homeowners Association, the Tatum Heights Improvement Association (Southeast) and the Southwest Homeowners Protective Association were organized, although none have ever reached the prominence of the Northeast Congress.

It was in this context of intense and growing activism that planning for citizen participation in the CDBG program began. The law required only that there be adequate public notice of planning for the grant's expenditure and that at least two public meetings be held for each application. There was never any question that Carbondale would do considerably more than the bare minimum. Local officials wanted to impress HUD with the good job they were doing. They felt that Carbondale and other small cities were on trial during the first three years, because if Congress did not change the law, the program would dry up in the sixth year. Local officials wanted to show HUD and Congress that Carbondale had problems just as serious as those of larger neighbors and that it could do just as good a job as the entitlement cities in fighting its problems with federal money. They believed that citizen participation was one of the criteria by which their performance would be judged.

Many people thought the Citizens Advisory Committee should be designated the vehicle for citizen participation. Some residents of the Northeast, however, urged that the Northeast Congress be chosen. The city manager maintained that a new group was necessary because the committee was too broad and the congress too narrow. Fry also maintained that the committee had come to be dominated by upper-middle-class activists from the Southwest, whereas the congress was exclusively based in the Northeast. The manager's critics charged that he preferred a new group because he had already battled the committee and the congress and could not dominate them.

The city manager recommended, and Mayor Neal Eckert and the council agreed, that a new group should be devised to allow for citizen participation under CDBG. This new group was called the Community Development Citizens Steering Committee. To set up the Steering Committee Mayor Eckert asked several groups, including the Northeast Congress, the Citizens Advisory Committee, the Chamber of Commerce, and the SIU Student Government, for nominations; he got more than a hundred candidates. He and Monte put all one hundred names on the map and coded them according to where they lived and other demographic characteristics. The mayor then selected twenty of these people, seven of whom were black and ten of whom were female. Occupationally, the group consisted of two businessmen, one union business agent, two ministers, two blue-collar workers; two clerical workers, two SIU professors, one doctor, two retired persons, one unemployed person, and two housewives.

Seven SIU students were added to the original group shortly after it was formed in response to a demand by SIU Student Government Organization officials that they be given 50 percent of the seats on the committee. While the mayor never seriously entertained this possibility, he decided to provide the students with some seats and requested nominees from the Student Government. The twenty-seven names finally selected were submitted to the council, which ratified them.

The Steering Committee represented all sections of the city, but the Northeast, with 25 percent of the representatives, and the Northwest, with 40 percent, dominated. The final group tended to be middle class in economic composition and probably in outlook.[10] As a new group, the Steering Committee had the advantage of fresh blood and ideas but the disadvantage of being totally unprepared for dealing with the complexity of the programs or the city staff. It took the Steering Committee a while to learn its way around. By then, some strategic decisions had already been made.

Interaction of Players

From the outset the city staff drew up the plans, established the priorities, developed the major programs and projects to be funded, shepherded the paperwork, saw that the right forms were used, paid attention to the meticulous detail of the HUD guidelines, and worried about meeting all the deadlines. In short, as noted earlier, the city manager through the staff was very much in control of the executive branch operation of the program, but in some major policy decisions the council also played an important role. It had final authority over all CDBG plans and acted as the court of last resort when the staff and citizen groups disagreed.

Some of the members of the Steering Committee were accustomed to the strong, active citizen participation that had developed in Carbondale before the CDBG. They thought the committee should have an equal, and perhaps predominant, role in the formulation of policies and programs. Some members, accustomed to the heady days of the antipoverty program or the model cities experience, did not want to defer to the city staff. In one important early meeting of the Steering Committee the issue of their role vis-à-vis that of the city staff came to a climax. The following exchange is taken from the Steering Committee minutes of December 5, 1974:

> Mr. [Richard] Hayes [black member of the Steering Committee and affirmative action officer at SIU] said he did not feel comfortable with the plan respecting the function of the committee. He stated that he didn't want to be part of a committee which simply rubber stamps programs after submitting needs. He felt that the committee should participate in the development of programs.
>
> Mr. Fry [city manager] responded that this would not be a feasible proce-

10. Craig S. Conolly, "Citizen Participation: The First Year of Carbondale's Community Development Program" (Master of Public Affairs internship paper, Southern Illinois University at Carbondale, 1975).

dure and that it would be simpler for the committee to react to programs than to go through the nuts and bolts of programs.

Mr. Hayes stated that the committee should go back to the community before establishing the priority of the needs so that the people could have an input in the establishing of priorities. He questioned the criteria used by the committee in establishing priorities if it is not based on input from the citizens. Mr. Hayes indicated that the Northeast Congress had rated a list of needs by the five categories of "critical" through "not significant" and this list could be considered by the committee.

Mrs. [Sammye] Aikman [citizen member from Northwest] noted that time pressures have been a significant factor in the process taken by the committee.

Mr. Fry noted that every need identified in the public hearings held by the committee was included in the list and that it was amazing how many items were included on both lists. He stated he would guess that the needs were probably ranked very closely as well. He felt that the citizen committee was highly representative and could prioritize the needs without getting bogged down with needless meetings.

Mr. Hayes repeated his concern that the committee would be limited to review and could not have a role in developing programs.

Mr. Fry stated that it would be an impossible administrative situation to have committee members developing programs.

Mr. [George] Crim [citizen member from Northeast] stated that he felt putting programs together would take more time than he or other members could give to the committee and that the staff was paid to do this job. . . .

The Chairman [Reverend Charles Watkins] asked whether the committee wished to continue the meeting in accordance with the agenda. A motion was made, seconded and passed to continue the meeting as scheduled. . . .

A week later Hayes resigned from the committee. As the transcript shows, he was at odds not only with the city manager but also with some of his fellow Steering Committee members.

The result of the struggle to define the role of citizen participation was a division of labor. The staff took the initiative in developing plans and programs, with Monte ordinarily spelling out the options and presenting a proposed program to the Steering Committee. The Steering Committee reacted, asked questions, gathered information about the public's reactions, and indicated what its priorities and preferences were, thus serving as a sounding board for program proposals. It also participated in the original decision to establish the 65:35 spending ratio between capital and services activities (discussed below). The Steering Committee was somewhat more protective of social programs than the staff was and was also agreeable to some shifting of emphasis to the Northwest.

The Steering Committee remained an important route of access to the decisionmaking process. Members listened carefully to various persons and groups that wanted funding, and they also heard complaints about how the programs were being operated. The committee set up its own program evaluation subcommittees, visited the sites of the major projects, and brought back reports on how they operated.

There were inherent limitations, however, on the committee's ability to play a major role in program formulation. It was the staff, especially Monte, who had the ability to read the federal regulations and determine what they meant; the Steering Committee ordinarily deferred to his expertise. In the end the most important function served by the Steering Committee was to "legitimize" planning with grass roots approval.

It must be emphasized, however, that in most areas most of the time there were no major disagreements between the staff and the Steering Committee. There was more consensus than conflict in Carbondale. The consensus was the result of several factors. First, there was an identifiable set of problems and needs that most participants agreed should be high on the public agenda in Carbondale—jobs, housing, new streets, and other facilities. The fact that Carbondale's problems conformed well to the direction of federal policy also aided local consensus-building. While the CDBG program was not a categorical grant, many people learned early and somewhat to their surprise that it also was not general revenue sharing. The various participants in Carbondale read the CDBG law and regulations as explicitly requiring the funding of programs for low- and moderate-income people.

After Hayes left the Steering Committee the level of conflict in the group was ordinarily very low. Most votes were unanimous, and discussions that uncovered disagreements were usually conducted without much acrimony. But one or two others, like Hayes, became disenchanted and stopped coming to meetings or resigned.

It is surprising that there were not more major disagreements between the staff and the Steering Committee. Most disagreements were muted, but occasionally disputes had to be referred to the city council, which functioned as a safety valve. For example, of the fifty-five projects funded in the first year's program, the staff and Steering Committee reached a common position on forty-seven. Eight were taken to the council for final decision. Of the eight, the staff prevailed on three, the Steering Committee on three, and the council split the difference on two decisions.[11]

11. John Trimble, "Council Agrees to Fund 55 Community Projects," *Southern Illinoisan* (Carbondale), February 11, 1975. Information was also gained from personal interviews with all principal parties in January 1976.

Where there was disagreement, it was generally because the Steering Committee was more aggressive than the staff in wanting to fund innovative social programs. For example, the Steering Committee consistently supported the Women's Center, whereas the staff opposed it. The committee consistently asked for higher levels of funding for the senior citizen programs than the staff desired. In general the council sided with the committee rather than with the staff on these matters. The council, however, sided with the staff against funding for a new solid waste recycling proposal submitted by a private nonprofit agency and supported by the Steering Committee.

To be sure, there were dissidents who criticized both the CDBG process and the project it produced. Some critics came from the more activist days of the 1960s, when citizen participation had more teeth; they saw the arrangements between the staff and the Steering Committee as being all too cozy and an elaborate cop-out by the Steering Committee. A number of Northeast residents were unhappy that the Northeast Congress had lost the premier citizen participation role it had once enjoyed, and some resented the spread of the CDBG efforts into the Northwest. Others, again particularly in the Northeast, resented the staff taking over more and more of the operation of the CDBG social programs, and they often criticized the city manager for what they considered his hard-nosed and abrasive style. Others were disgruntled because their programs were not funded, and some of those who did receive funds were dissatisfied because the funds were too little. But many of the critics themselves were engaged in operating CDBG programs or otherwise benefiting from them, and this somewhat muted the intensity of their criticisms. The three major participants—the Steering Committee, the staff, and the city council—put up a fairly solid front against the disgruntled, and basic directions, once determined, were not changed.

Outside of Carbondale the major potential sources for influencing the direction of the city's program generally took a hands-off stance. The A-95 process at the regional and state levels provided only pro forma reviews of the Carbondale program and routine approval of the plans.[12]

HUD's role was larger, but the agency provided only general guidance and broad limits within which the program was designed and executed. HUD sent out its regulations and program directives, processed the paperwork submitted to it, and the HUD staff answered questions and

12. See note 22, chapter 4, for an explanation of the A-95 process.

made occasional site visits. Generally they left Carbondale on a very loose leash. They declared only two minor programs ineligible during the first two years of the program, and their site visits resulted in only minor suggestions and no serious criticisms of the way the Carbondale program was executed. Carbondale's program apparently enjoyed a good reputation with HUD area and regional offices in Chicago.

Allocating CDBG Funds

Two early strategic decisions had major implications for the kind of program that Carbondale would have. The first of these, made even before the CDBG program began, was the decision to commit new city money to the Northwest section of town. Between 1972 and 1974, near the end of the urban renewal program, city officials, including both the city council and the staff, became increasingly aware of the decay that was beginning to beset the Northwest. Many of the streets were narrow and brick-paved, and sidewalks and sanitary sewers were poor. The housing stock ranged from upper-middle-class suburban enclaves at the edges of the area through stately old turn-of-the-century mansions closer to downtown to dilapidated one-family and multifamily houses in other areas. In the late 1960s and early 1970s more and more SIU students discovered the northwest section as a way to live close to the campus yet remain free from the university's influence in on-campus housing. The social tenor of the times and the university's steady relaxation of rules requiring on-campus living combined to produce an immigrant wave of students.

As students moved in, homeowners moved out or battled the decay of their section of town. The Northwest Homeowners Association was organized to protect property values and restore a sense of community, and it lobbied the city council for money to deal with the deterioration of the Northwest. After finding that the blighted central core of the Northwest was eligible for urban renewal, the city staff recommended it as the city's next major renewal site. The council agreed, but shortly thereafter it became evident that the Nixon administration was planning to phase out urban renewal and consolidate it with other programs in what was to become the CDBG. Thus funds for an additional urban renewal project would not be available. Plans for the Northwest were put in abeyance while the federal program changes were clarified. The council was expected to allot some of the CDBG money to the Northwest while continuing to give high priority to the Northeast. This expectation was based on the city council's decision to concentrate on one neighborhood until it showed significant signs of improvement, then shift the focus to another neighborhood with a reduced emphasis on the first neighborhood. This dual approach was the most basic policy decision for the program.

Another important strategic decision made in the fall of 1974 was to allot 65 percent of the funds for capital projects and 35 percent for social services. The share of funds for social services was well above the national norm of 20 percent suggested by the legislative history of the CDBG. The ratio grew out of Steering Committee and city staff recommendations about what programs and projects should be funded the first year. The overall breakdown of the first tentative budget was approximately 65:35, and this figure became a standard agreed to by both groups, including the city manager and the council.

The 35 percent for social services was not out of line with Carbondale's past program mix. If one takes into account all the consolidated grants, Carbondale's capital expenditures accounted for 65 percent and social expenditures, 35 percent. While Carbondale officials were somewhat nervous about the unorthodox capital-social expenditure mix, HUD officials in the area and regional offices in Chicago never complained to the city about exceeding the 20 percent limit. During the first year they accepted Carbondale's plans without significant modification. In the second year, however, they insisted that the social programs be tied to physical improvements in the target neighborhood. When city CDBG officials were able to document this tie, HUD went along although somewhat reluctantly. Carbondale officials constantly sensed that they were pushing the limits of HUD's tolerance in the area of social spending, but it was a risk they felt local conditions compelled them to take.

CDBG Program Directions

The initial decision to adopt the 65:35 ratio of capital expenditures to social services was adhered to tenaciously throughout the early years of the program. It meant that a number of social programs begun under earlier federal grants could be continued. Programs carried over from federally aided programs in the first two years of the CDBG are shown

Table 7-1. *Model Cities Activities Continued in Carbondale, Illinois, under the Block Grant*
Thousands of dollars

Project	Program year	
	First	*Second*
Comprehensive Health Program	213	261
Comprehensive Child Care Program	200	240
Career Opportunities Program	35	55
Unified service support for Hayes Center	32	45
Minority Business Program	44	50
Comprehensive Job Training	50	50
Senior citizens	13	28
Total	587	739

Source: Carbondale CDBG applications. Figures are rounded.

in table 7-1. These programs represented a very broad range of health, educational, training, and other services primarily for low- and moderate-income clients and were located primarily in the northeast section of town. Carbondale was determined to protect programs that had already demonstrated success or the probability of success. The CDBG funds allowed Carbondale three more years of breathing room, and in most respects the transition from model cities to CDBG funding was smooth for these programs.

Although there was strong support for these programs in Carbondale, it would have been very difficult to find city funds to keep them afloat. When Mayor Eckert was asked what would have happened without the CDBG money to cushion the transition from model cities and urban renewal, he replied that Carbondale would have had "riots in the streets" if those programs had been terminated abruptly, and that there would have been "hell to pay" politically if the city had tried to raise taxes or curtail other essential services to support them.[13]

While model cities activities provided the foundation of the CDBG-funded social program, some new software, or service, programs were also funded (see table 7-2). The new programs to some extent were responsive to new constituencies and demands. The Women's Center program, for example, was sought by a newly active group of women in the city. The Women's Center provided social services, counseling, and tem-

13. Interview with Mayor Eckert, January 1976.

Table 7-2. *New Social Services in Carbondale, Illinois, under the Block Grant*

Thousands of dollars

New projects	*Program year*	
	First	*Second*
Coordinated youth program	29	40
Women's Center program	13	13
Community information and referral	6	8
Equal opportunity officer	13	1
Money and housing management program	25	0
Arts and crafts program	18	30
Needs of the handicapped study	3	0
Comprehensive human services plan study	5	3
Community education program	0	0
Economic development officer[a]	15	0
Animal control	7	0
Total	134	95

Source: Carbondale CDBG applications. Figures are rounded.
a. Although there may be some debate about listing this (and other programs) under the "social" category, this is the way Carbondale, at HUD's direction, counts them.

porary shelter and was administered by a nonprofit agency that predated the CDBG. The use of CDBG money for such purposes was controversial (in the third year the cost was shifted to other sources in the city's budget). In other cases the demands had been long-standing and new programs were devised to meet them. The Coordinated Youth Program and the Equal Opportunity Office were both new attempts to deal with problems perennially faced by low- and moderate-income minorities. Some of the new programs were vulnerable, however, and when pressure increased to reduce the budget, these programs were often the first to go.

As with social services, the 65 percent of Carbondale's money designated for capital improvements included both continuation and new spending. Table 7-3 shows that the bulk of this money (70 percent) during the first year was designated for the continuation and completion of the urban renewal program in the Northeast. There was never any doubt that a significant commitment of funds would be made to finish the project. A substantial portion of funds was also devoted to various housing programs. These programs provided the local administrative costs of HUD-sponsored section 312 rehabilitation loan programs and a local version of the section 115 rehabilitation grants to low-income persons

Table 7-3. *Capital Projects in Carbondale, Illinois, Continued from Categorical Programs*
Thousands of dollars

Project	Program year	
	First	*Second*
Northeast neighborhood streets and infrastructure	658	108
Completion of neighborhood development program (interest and reimbursement)[a]	239	0
Housing rehabilitation grants[b]	300	281
Housing loans[c]	0	50
Code enforcement	74	70
Total	1,271	509

Source: Carbondale CDBG applications. Figures are rounded.
a. The neighborhood development program expenditure was one time only and thus did not appear in the second-year budget.
b. Listed as a "continuation" program because it is a local version of the former section 115 grants program.
c. The loan program is the local share of administering the section 312 grants program.

that had been folded into the block grant.[14] In Carbondale a low- or moderate-income homeowner in the target area who qualified could get a grant of up to $5,000,[15] compared with the $3,500 limit in the former federal grant. (To be eligible, a homeowner could have no more than 80 percent of the Jackson County median income.) In addition the city developed a small grant program for housing weatherization and insulation. These grants were available to low- and moderate-income residents of both the Northeast and Northwest. Housing rehabilitation grants and loans were budgeted at $316,000 during the first year and $347,000 during the second year of the CDBG. Besides the CDBG-funded programs, there were two sizable section 8 housing developments to provide 271 new units of low- and moderate-income housing for the elderly and the handicapped.[16] The programs represented a large commitment by the city to improving its housing stock in the target neighborhoods, and they continued in spite of objections by area landlords, developers, and real estate interests. The council voted to include the projects despite reserva-

14. Section 312 is explained in note 5, chapter 1. Section 115 of the urban renewal program was passed in 1965 to provide grants of up to $3,500 to low-income households for rehabilitation in urban renewal and code enforcement areas. These grants, along with the basic urban renewal program, were consolidated into the CDBG.
15. In July 1977 this figure was raised to $6,000 maximum.
16. See note 35, chapter 3, for an explanation of section 8.

Table 7-4. *Capital Projects Started in Carbondale, Illinois, under the Block Grant*
Thousands of dollars

Project	Program year	
	First	*Second*
Renovation of building for senior citizens	55	0
Construction of Helen Street sewer (Northwest and Northeast)	61	75
Housing insulation grants	0	16
Northwest area street and infrastructure	175	750
Eurma C. Hayes Neighborhood Facility improvements	0	8
Drainways-greenways program	27	20
Safety devices for the blind	6	0
Barrier elimination	0	2
Total	324	871

Source: Carbondale CDBG applications. Figures are rounded.

tions because of its sensitivity to HUD preferences, which were strongly in favor of housing opportunities for low- and moderate-income people. Table 7-4 presents the major new capital improvement programs.

The emphasis on housing rehabilitation resulted primarily from two factors. First, the northeast community had become critical of the housing demolition that had taken place under urban renewal. Its people preferred rehabilitation. Second, the private sector provided neither interest nor money to expand the supply of low- and moderate-income housing, and HUD was not making public funds available for this purpose.

Other capital expenditures included a major new sewer that, although located in the Northwest, would benefit both the Northeast and the Northwest. The project was necessary because the Illinois Environmental Protection Agency had directed that no more sewage could be pumped into the city's plant on the southeast side of town. Local officials welcomed the CDBG money as a source of funds for this new project that was forced on them.

The large second-year allocation for infrastructure improvements in the Northwest is also noteworthy. In the first-year program only 6 percent of the total grant was designated for capital programs in the Northwest, compared with 22 percent in the Northeast, but in the next year a significant geographic shift in the city's priorities was accomplished. Local officials maintained that the political prêssures arising from the belated urban renewal focus on the Northwest were sufficient to direct new money there. The fact that CDBG emphasized prevention or elimination of slums and blight facilitated the increase.

An additional point regarding the social-physical and new-old dichotomies in programs is relevant here. Carbondale has been pictured as relatively liberal on the social programs, choosing a level of social funding considerably higher than the national pattern. Even in Carbondale, however, the burden of proof was on the social programs and their supporters. Capital improvements, being tangible, were much easier to defend. Moreover, many of the capital programs had a relatively fixed price and ending date. The social programs represented a more open-ended commitment, and with federal and state funding uncertain, it was a commitment that made local officials very nervous.

Social Targeting

The social targeting effects must be considered within the geographical framework discussed previously. Carbondale decisionmakers perceived the CDBG program as basically an opportunity to continue the model cities and urban renewal programs. It was also seen as requiring that benefits be directed toward low- and moderate-income recipients, and no attempt was ever made to avoid these requirements. In Carbondale these perceptions readily translated into a geographical orientation; that is, the CDBG program had to be directed toward continuing the city's efforts in the Northeast and expanding its commitment to the long-neglected Northwest. But groups from other parts of the city also wanted CDBG money.

In the first year a wide variety of requests arose for new programs, many of which would not have primarily benefited low- and moderate-income residents. Some would have spread the benefits throughout the city. A few of these were funded, including the Women's Center and a citywide information retrieval system located in the city library. The recipients, however, were under constant pressure from the city staff to justify their CDBG money by demonstrating a high level of use by low- and moderate-income people, preferably in the two target areas. After the second year the Women's Center and the information retrieval system were dropped from CDBG funding because they did not meet the benefit requirements. Another citywide program partially funded by

CDBG money, the Senior Citizens Center, continued to receive CDBG funds because evaluation showed that over 75 percent of the participants were low and moderate income and that a large proportion came from the two target neighborhoods.

It is possible to be reasonably precise about the direct users of the social programs since Carbondale gathers income data on them. Carbondale is not in a metropolitan area, so city officials used Jackson County income data for comparison. Following the HUD definitions, those having 80 percent or less of the county's median income were put into the "low and moderate" income category. By this definition, approximately 75 percent of the benefits of the social programs went to low-income recipients, and the remaining 25 percent went to moderate-income recipients.

The Eurma C. Hayes Center in the Northeast provided almost all the social services of the CDBG program. The Hayes Center hummed with activity from 7 A.M., when the first infants and preschoolers were dropped off by their working parents, until 10 or 11 P.M., when the last teenage or adult group meeting closed for the day. It housed a nursery for infants, a headstart and kindergarten program for preschoolers, an outpatient clinic for those needing medical or dental care, an employment agency for those looking for work, a recreational and cultural center for teenagers, a counseling and referral center for those needing psychological and social services, and an arts and crafts center for senior citizens.

The size of some of these programs can be more readily conveyed by the budgetary figures and the numbers of clients served. The two largest activities were the Comprehensive Health Program and the Comprehensive Child Care Program. The health program was budgeted at an average annual rate of approximately $235,000 over the first three years. During this time it served over 2,000 clients annually, with basic health care services ranging from preventive medicine to the outpatient treatment of a wide variety of diseases. The Comprehensive Child Care Program averaged approximately $220,000 a year for the first two years. From 150 to 290 children were regularly enrolled in its infant-care, day-care, evening-care, and preschool programs. The other programs were much smaller by comparison, but the result was that a lot of people were coming and going from the Hayes Center each day.

Most of these programs were funded wholly or in major part with CDBG funds. Most of the Hayes Center programs were open to anyone, but fees were based on a sliding scale of income. The managers of the Hayes Center encouraged people of all income and racial categories from all over the city to use the center, and to some extent this mixed use did take place. The State Employment Service, for example, rented a suite of offices to serve the entire city. Citywide civic and educational meetings were also scheduled intermittently in the Hayes Center. Given Carbondale's still largely segregated housing patterns, however, and the income requirements attached to most of the major social services offered in the Hayes Center, the bulk of the participants were the low- and moderate-income black residents of the Northeast, followed by the low- and moderate-income white residents of the Northwest.

When compared with the model cities and urban renewal expenditures in the Northeast, the movement of the community development program into the Northwest represented some spreading of funds over a wider and generally higher income group. Overall, however, committing the bulk of the CDBG money to the Northeast and Northwest meant that a large share of the benefits would go to lower-income groups.

Conclusion

CDBG provided the opportunity for the consolidation and maturation of community development institutions in Carbondale. Program capacities and expertise were already there, but they developed considerably under the block grant. The young, enthusiastic, and often inexperienced people from the model cities days gained experience. In addition, city officials generally agree that the CDBG approach lessened their dependence on HUD guidance and approval of project details. The block grant program fit more smoothly into the city's planning, management, and budgeting systems than did the categorical grant program because it enabled the city to spend money on a broader range of local needs. In general, local officials felt that in the first two years the block grant had allowed Carbondale officials more initiative and flexibility than had the categorical grant program.

The CDBG process as a whole, including the housing assistance plan, had one additional institutional effect. The application that included multiyear program summaries increased Carbondale's ability to develop comprehensive, communitywide planning and to execute these plans. Planning was already important and reasonably advanced in Carbondale before the advent of the CDBG. But drawing up the community development plan and the housing assistance plan forced the city to take a more careful look at its plans to define the entire range of development needs for the city as a whole, particularly in assessing the direction of community development efforts in the Northeast and Northwest. The phasing out of urban renewal and model cities also meant that the city had to assess carefully the resources available for meeting its long-range planning goals when federal funds might be phased out. The housing assistance plan forced some of the same kinds of discussion of fundamental questions in relation to the development of low- and moderate-income housing in the city.

This is not to suggest that there were no controversies. A series of disagreements occurred between the city staff and various groups and individuals in the city, usually centering on the question of how much control of the CDBG program would reside in city hall. The antipoverty and model cities programs had operated with considerable autonomy under grass roots citizen policymaking boards and had staffs that answered to those boards more than to the city officials. City Manager Carroll Fry was not happy with this arrangement and he constantly sought to bring the staff operations under his wing and to place the policymaking power over the programs in the city council. Fry largely succeeded in doing this but not everyone was happy with the results. He and the city council maintained that this was the only way the city manager could be held accountable for the way the programs were administered and the only way the programs in turn could ultimately be held accountable.

Substantively, the CDBG generally gave more flexibility to local officials to establish priorities and carry out programs. Local officials took the "block grant rhetoric" at face value. They determined local priorities and were able to maintain many of them even in the face of considerable evidence that the city was out of line with the implied limits on spending for social services. For the most part this meant few new program departures and an emphasis on programs that fit easily into the framework of decisions and directions already taken when the CDBG program started.

The block grant did increase Carbondale's sensitivity to HUD preferences in some areas, such as low- and moderate-income housing, because it was looking ahead to future discretionary funding. Carbondale had become heavily dependent on federal funds, turning to Washington for the creation and support of virtually all the city's programs other than the traditional and basic local services such as fire and police protection and the provision of water, sewers, and streets. Now it had to face a future of possible declining grant support. For Carbondale and other small cities, this meant that at the end of the first three years some difficult choices had to be faced.

In general, Carbondale officials were cautiously optimistic about the future although still apprehensive about their funding sources and the reductions they faced. They were cautiously optimistic because they thought there was a chance that Congress would change the law to the benefit of small cities or that Carbondale would be able to compete favorably for discretionary grants. They were apprehensive because of the obvious uncertainty of funding and the probable reduction of funding in any case. This mixture of optimism and apprehension was felt all the way down through program personnel to some of the clients.

Anticipating the fund losses, the city council made the policy decision to protect the Comprehensive Child Care and the Comprehensive Health Care programs as the only social programs likely to survive, and even these faced funding reductions. They also reduced the plans for new streets in both the Northeast and the Northwest. The housing rehabilitation program was retained at about the same funding levels.

In 1977, when Congress debated changes in the law, Carbondale and other small cities brought their problems to Congress. Carbondale officials made several trips to Washington and wrote letters in an effort to obtain special consideration for the small cities. They were not successful in getting hold-harmless extended, but Congress did specify that smaller cities could qualify for multiyear discretionary grants. Priority in awarding such grants was to be given to "a unit of local government which has a comprehensive community development program with a provision for lower-income housing."[17] In addition the secretary of HUD was instructed to give special consideration to those jurisdictions currently carrying out comprehensive community development programs, a pointed reference to cities like Carbondale. In the fourth year Carbondale received a three-year grant under these criteria of $2.7 million, enabling the city to continue some programs while phasing down others.

17. P.L. 9-128, October 12, 1977, title 1, Community Development, sec. 106(e)(3), 91 Stat. 1119.

CHAPTER EIGHT

The Process and Its Outcomes

THE PRECEDING case studies permitted in-depth accounts of the local dynamics of the block grant process and decisions made during the transitional years of the community development block grant. In this chapter findings from the cases and from a larger field research sample (see chapter 1) are combined in an effort to examine the devolution of decisionmaking authority under the CDBG and to identify and compare those features of the block grant that were common to communities receiving grants.

The Changing Federal Role

Did the block grant result in reduced federal controls compared with the predecessor programs? Earlier it was noted that studies of urban renewal came to somewhat different conclusions about federal control of that program, depending on the city studied and where in the urban renewal process the research focused. The model cities program elicits more general agreement: it was intended to be primarily a "mayor's program" and was operated as such.

In neither the case studies nor the field network evaluation study (FNES) did we examine federal controls over the pre-CDBG programs in a way that makes it possible to present a direct before-and-after comparison of such controls. However, from our examination of legislative intent, administrative implementation, and local perceptions, we conclude that at the beginning the block grant resulted in greater local discretion over development decisions.[1]

Some important features of the CDBG legislation produced greater

VICTOR E. BACH contributed to the preparation of this chapter.

1. Paul R. Dommel and others, *Decentralizing Community Development* (U.S. Department of Housing and Urban Development, June 1978), chap. 3.

local discretion. The most significant changes in urban aid processes under the CDBG were the scrapping of discretionary funding in favor of a formula system; limiting federal review of applications to a seventy-five-day period and establishing a veto-only review procedure; eliminating virtually all federal requirements for the structure of the local decision process; and establishing a local certification process to assure local conformity with a variety of compliance requirements that cut across a wide range of federal grant programs. Substantively, local discretion was given greater scope by establishing a set of federal objectives that were sufficiently broad, ambiguous, and potentially conflicting as to permit considerable room for local as well as federal interpretation; eliminating the explicit target area approach of model cities and urban renewal; and creating a long list of eligible activities to meet physical, economic development, and supporting social service needs. Even the Senate, which took the most aggressive stand on maintaining federal controls, agreed to having the federal hand rest more gently on block grant recipients.

The administrative preference for implementing the block grant was a policy of hands-off—no federal second-guessing of local decisions. Local discretion was strengthened not only by this overarching tenet of the New Federalism but also by the fact that the first local applications had to be submitted to the Department of Housing and Urban Development (HUD) within five months of the start of the program. While this compressed application schedule might have adversely affected local development "planning," it gave local officials broad authority to act quickly on some important issues. By the second year, when the application could be prepared in a more deliberative manner, some of the most important decisions had already been made at the local level, thereby further narrowing the limits of HUD's influence over important early decisions on local processes and programs.

At the local level community development officials perceived a loosening of federal controls over community development decisions in the first year of the block grant. One official in Chicago noted that "HUD is essentially divorced from dealing with substantive issues," compared with its previous role of "aggressively raising policy issues." A similar assessment was made by a development official in Los Angeles who said: "The current program is light years away from the categorical grant program." In Sioux Falls, South Dakota, an official said: "Never in my eighteen years in the housing field has so much real decisionmaking been possible right at home." These comments, taken from the FNES, were reflected more broadly in the data for the forty-four communities of the field study sample (the sample total was sixty-one) that had had significant experience with the programs consolidated into the CDBG. In nearly all these communities, field researchers reported a reduced HUD role in making program decisions. These findings on the direction of HUD influence over program choices were also supported in the case studies. Few of HUD's interventions made a major difference in the local program; the five jurisdictions did largely what they chose to do. But some local officials felt that HUD's initial low level of involvement would not last and that as the program matured, the block grant would be subjected to a gradual "recategorization."[2]

Local Decision Processes

A major objective of the New Federalism in general and of the CDBG in particular was to strengthen general-purpose local governments (1) by giving them more flexibility in the use of federal funds and (2) by reducing the fragmentation of local decisionmaking that had been fostered by categorical programs that sometimes provided aid directly to semiautonomous, special-purpose agencies. The principal beneficiaries were to be elected officials or chief executives chosen by them, such as city managers. But achieving this goal required more than just a national legislative intent; local factors were certain to influence the form and dynamics of the decisionmaking processes that would emerge in the recipient communities.

Managing Conflict

The CDBG program, in ending the target area approach of urban renewal and model cities and creating a broadly defined set of eligible activities, was certain to arouse the appetites of a larger number of constituents in a community than could be readily satisfied by the funds available. It fell to local officials to manage this potential conflict. It would not be possible for local officials to simply say, "The feds want it this way," and thereby shift political costs to the federal level. Thus one of the first tasks of local elected officials was to structure the local CDBG decision process to maximize their political advantages or mini-

2. Quotations and other information in this paragraph are from ibid., pp. 72–74.

mize political costs. The process in turn would influence the kinds of decisions made and the distribution of benefits among local constituents. Since the CDBG was established by merging several grants, there were existing processes and constituencies in many of the recipient communities. In such cases alteration of the processes and patterns of allocations was likely to create classes of "winners" and "losers," thus making the establishment of a new bargaining arena the crucial, and potentially hazardous, first step in implementing greater local discretion.

The general pattern was that the local chief executive became the principal architect of the local CDBG process.[3] In some instances, as illustrated by the Chicago and Carbondale cases, the local chief executive was already the dominant influence in local decisions, and the structure of any new process would reflect that dominance. In Allegheny County the Board of County Commissioners had anticipated the CDBG by establishing a process that they would dominate. Local legislatures were assured a role since they had to approve an application before its submission to HUD, but their usual role was to accept decisionmaking structures proposed by the executive. A factor giving the executive an advantage was the short time, five months, provided for both organizing the CDBG process and preparing the application for the first year; executive officials were able to move more quickly.

One of the dominant features of the organization of the CDBG decisionmaking process was the uncertainty caused by the transition from the categorical programs to the block grant. The transition had an unsettling effect on local bureaucrats, interests, and constituencies associated with the predecessor programs. Generally the anxieties afflicted interests associated with the model cities program more than they did those clustered around the urban renewal program. Established as a five-year demonstration grant, model cities had already reached the closing phase in many places, and its future was uncertain; by contrast, urban renewal and neighborhood development programs had become routine functions in many cities. The continuity of the agencies that had been responsible for the earlier programs was at stake, and their leading officials usually became or tried to become key participants in deciding CDBG program priorities and funding.[4] In some jurisdictions the special-purpose agency was entirely shut out of the process, as illustrated by the Allegheny

3. Ibid., pp. 141–45; and Richard P. Nathan and others, *Block Grants for Community Development* (U.S. Department of Housing and Urban Development, January 1977), pp. 384–93.

4. Dommel and others, *Decentralizing Community Development,* pp. 128–32.

County Redevelopment Authority. Sometimes officials were able to maintain their influence, if not their programs, in community development functions. In Allegheny County model cities activities were scheduled to end, but the former director was appointed temporary head of the county's Planning and Development Department, and a number of model cities staff accompanied him to the new department. Thus former model cities officials influenced some of the early decisions about the block grant program. In Chicago the heads of the urban renewal and the model cities programs were appointed cochairmen of the Coordinating Committee, under which the key CDBG negotiations took place, and were able to continue both their influence and their programs.

The pattern of administrative survival is not sufficiently clear in the five cases to support generalization, but the larger monitoring sample shows that urban renewal agencies did better than model cities organizations. By the end of the second year of the block grant only five of twenty-seven model cities agencies still existed, while twenty-three of thirty-seven urban renewal agencies survived as separate organizations.[5] The FNES data, however, also showed that nearly two-thirds of these agencies had little or no influence in CDBG decisions.[6]

Threats to established programs and constituencies represented only part of the turbulence and uncertainty that accompanied the changeover to the block grant. Because the CDBG could potentially operate throughout the community, new constituencies—government agencies, individuals, community groups—could be drawn in. In the case of urban counties, municipalities were likely to become contestants.

The most common type of new claimant was the neighborhood-based organization requesting particular improvements for its area.[7] Some groups were well prepared and aggressive, such as the civic associations in Houston that began to phone the mayor's office soon after the CDBG was first announced, whereas others—such as the Metropolitan Area Housing Alliance in Chicago, the senior citizen groups in Allegheny County, the housing coalition in Phoenix, and the women's groups in Carbondale—became involved only as the program gained visibility and gave some promise of responding to needs that had not been specifically addressed by the categorical programs.

The demands of newly activated interests could be expected to gen-

5. Ibid., pp. 128–29.

6. Nathan and others, *Block Grants for Community Development,* p. 405.

7. Ibid., pp. 455–80; and Dommel and others, *Decentralizing Community Development,* pp. 141–45.

erate conflicts that were potentially costly for the local chief executive and other holders of local elective offices. The competition was particularly evident from neighborhoods that had been left out of the earlier programs. Even in machine-controlled Chicago the public release of the draft first-year application was delayed until after the primaries and final mayoral election had been held. In some cities, however, elected executives tended to view the CDBG more as a potential resource than a burden: note Haley's account of the importance of the CDBG in Commissioner Staisey's bid for reelection and Bach's account of the central role of the CDBG in Mayor Hofheinz's political calculus vis-à-vis Houston's minority voters. Whether local executives viewed the CDBG as an opportunity to reward key constituencies or as a potentially costly and unavoidable area of competing demands, it was clear from the start that the program would call for sensitive distributive decisions that needed to be coordinated and continually reviewed at the top.

Another set of new constituents and crucial participants was the established line departments of local government whose jurisdictionwide functions overlapped some of those functions that would normally be part of local CDBG implementation.[8] In many communities the block grant altered the relationship between the local chief executive and the line departments in a way that often concentrated more power in the executive. One aspect of this greater centralization was that the chief executive acquired a broadened coordinating role in order to link the flexible block grant funds with other resources used by these departments or to substitute CDBG money for local tax revenues and thereby avoid tax increases or add to local surpluses. Where the CDBG meant substantially increased federal funds or where the money now came through the chief executives rather than a semiautonomous renewal agency, executives controlled a substantial source of "new" money to be allocated through a process in which many of them were the dominant influence. In Phoenix Hall reported that the lure of new, uncommitted funds and the potential for interdepartmental conflict over program allocations were important reasons for executive consolidation of CDBG responsibilities in the city manager's office. In Houston conflict over program allocations also was an important reason for executive centralization.

Because the line departments were crucial to program execution, however, the political success of the program for local elected officials was

8. Nathan and others, *Block Grants for Community Development,* pp. 398–407; and Dommel and others, *Decentralizing Community Development,* pp. 128–32.

tied to successful implementation by the line agencies. Thus a centralized, relatively conflict-free process for making allocation decisions could be unwound by serious flaws in program execution by various operating departments of local government. Local departments of planning, real estate, public works, parks, housing inspection or code enforcement, and human resources played an important role in carrying out those CDBG activities over which they maintained normal responsibility. In addition the speed with which the first-year applications had to be prepared put a premium on data and intelligence available from departmental staff. The departments also could be relied on for "off the shelf" proposals that could be readily acted upon and executed. Thus line departments were usually assured a role in the execution of the CDBG, whether the role was wanted or unwanted, and their support in the enterprise was essential to successful implementation.

Citizen Participation

Formal citizen participation was an important part of local processes, and local executives made use of their discretion to structure that participation in a way they thought would support their broader objective of having a relatively conflict-free process. As stressed in chapter 2, the CDBG required no formal structures for citizen participation. Under the law it was sufficient that residents be given an opportunity for involvement during the preparation of the CDBG application and that public hearings be held by the local government to allow citizens to express their views of the draft application. HUD's regulations did not go beyond that. The CDBG potentially opened up citizen participation to whole jurisdictions and seemed likely to enhance the leverage of more affluent residents. At the same time, many communities were left with the remnants of earlier participation structures in which lower-income residents had played a prominent part. Local executives could choose under the CDBG to continue them, abolish them, or replace them with something else.

As shown by the cases, the formal structures of citizen participation under the CDBG, whether new or carried over intact from the predecessor programs, were less influential than what they replaced because of greater competition from other constituencies. In Phoenix and Chicago, where existing citizen mechanisms were retained, they received an increasingly small share of attention. At the public hearings the model cities councils in Chicago and the neighborhood development program committee in Phoenix had to compete for funds with residents and community groups that had not been represented in the earlier grants.

In Carbondale, Houston, and Allegheny County, where the older participatory bodies were replaced, the result was to expand access to a broader range of interests. First, there was a shift from neighborhood representation to representation of at-large interests. Second, there was a shift from selection of participants by election, as was done under model cities, to appointment by the local executive, sometimes in collaboration with the legislature. Third, the new groups included a larger number of community elites and increased representation of higher socioeconomic groups. This was most evident in Allegheny County, where the model cities organization was dismantled and the County Planning Commission was designated the official citizen advisory committee for the CDBG program. In Houston Mayor Hofheinz attempted to avoid representation of subareas on the citizen task force by inviting several citywide public interest organizations to send representatives; these included such organizations as the League of Women Voters, the Houston Council on Human Relations, the National Association for the Advancement of Colored People, greater Houston civic associations, and others. The new groups lacked the political muscle that the Model Neighborhood Resident Commission had had under Moses Leroy. In Carbondale the prior participatory bodies were bypassed in favor of a new steering committee for which the mayor invited nominations from key organizations and selected the participants, a group that Jackson says turned out to be primarily middle class in composition and outlook. Despite Jackson's allusions to the strength of citizen participation traditions in Carbondale, the city manager chose to ignore citizen advisory bodies that had already gained experience, sometimes in encounters with the manager. Instead, he chose a new, untried structure that would take considerable time to become an effective advisory resource.

Local executives in all three jurisdictions showed an obvious preference for participants representing jurisdictionwide interests as a way of avoiding politically harmful conflicts. Thus they consigned existing structures to the fate of the folded-in categorical programs with which they were identified. In that sense the reaction of local executives in Carbondale, Houston, and Allegheny County was a natural consequence of the expanding geographic scope of the block grant and of the considerably greater latitude for local decisionmaking. These three jurisdictions reflected the pattern found in the monitoring studies: communities with citizen participation structures established under the earlier programs generally chose to replace them with a more broadly representative mechanism; only a few communities maintained existing structures.[9] But the form of citizen advisory structures did not determine the degree of citizen influence. As reported in the monitoring studies, "even the most elaborate [citizen participation] structure was not necessarily indicative of substantive or influential citizen activity."[10]

The cases universally note the dominance of local government executive staff in taking the important program initiatives, with the formal citizen advisory bodies taking a subsequent "legitimizing" role. Nor did the frequent regional or neighborhood meetings at which residents could state their priorities and specific proposals turn out to be effective avenues of grass roots influence, except where the staff chose to distill the testimony and translate it into specific initiatives. The only instance in which this proved effective was in Allegheny County, where the consistent turnout of an organized elderly constituency was difficult to ignore during an election year. As a rule, the cases show that testimony was heard at the meetings but not acted upon. Even in the two jurisdictions where citizen advisory groups maintained a continuous presence and a recognized role in program deliberations—Houston and Carbondale—executive staff had an acknowledged upper hand in setting the program agenda, particularly under the compressed time available for the preparation of the first-year application.

Generally the ability of citizen representatives and community groups to influence program decisions depended less on their formal relation to the technical staff responsible for the preparation of the plans than on their informal access to elected officials. This pattern was most evident in those instances where staff and community positions on a given issue were in conflict and elected officials, called upon to arbitrate the dispute, sided with citizen interests. Jackson refers to this as the "safety valve" function served by the city council in Carbondale, as manifested in the disputes concerning the Women's Center and expansion of senior services. The Phoenix city council served a similar function in repeated staff attempts to shift the locus of the city's housing rehabilitation program from census tract 1162, the location chosen by the Housing Commission, to a less impoverished, more manageable neighborhood. In Houston the

9. Nathan and others, *Block Grants for Community Development*, pp. 432–38.
10. Dommel and others, *Decentralizing Community Development*, p. 147.

citizen task force brought its complaints about the initial draft application directly to Mayor Hofheinz and won on nearly all counts. And in Chicago, despite the "midnight method" of program planning shrouded in bureaucratic secrecy, constituent groups could call on their aldermen to serve as advocates for their specific interests.

This pattern of responsiveness on the part of local elected officials was found in both the cases and the field studies, and it justified to some extent the commitment of reformers at the federal level to supplanting special-purpose agencies with decisionmaking by general-purpose local governments. The success of some important interest groups in CDBG decisionmaking—particularly the activist housing groups in Phoenix and the municipalities in Allegheny County—strongly depended on their alignments with elected officials. It should be emphasized, however, that what community representatives were able to influence usually constituted a relatively small portion of an otherwise executive or staff-dominated package of program decisions.

Continuity and Change

An important question arising from the shift to a block grant is whether the greater local discretion and the larger set of local participants with different demands resulted in different development choices. The purpose of this section is to trace the patterns of continuity and change in local program choices under the CDBG. It is on the question of program continuity and change that the case studies become an important complement to the monitoring findings.

The pattern found in the FNES sample was a phasing down of urban renewal and model cities projects, with a simultaneous increase in new, visible, and popular activities that emphasized housing rehabilitation and related neighborhood projects, such as street, sidewalk, and park projects, in areas of the community not previously included in urban renewal or model cities target areas.[11] Some communities spent a significant share of their grant on general communitywide improvements. By the second year even communities with the heaviest involvement in urban renewal and model cities directed more than half of their block grant money to new activities.[12] The case studies qualify and contradict

11. Ibid., pp. 166–97; and Nathan and others, *Block Grants for Community Development,* pp. 255–85.

12. Dommel and others, *Decentralizing Community Development,* pp. 193–94.

in important ways these overall patterns, based on the level of allocations, and improve understanding of the local factors that tend to account for the differences. The cases suggest that the new CDBG projects show a good deal of continuity in nature and in form with the categorical programs they replaced. Implicitly this also means that the block grant did not produce a wave of local strategic innovations, and the broader local discretion was applied, at least initially, to adapting familiar programs to local demands and conditions.

Early decisions made in Chicago, Phoenix, and Carbondale indicated that there would be considerable continuity in the basic development objectives of their block grant programs. In Chicago the appointment of the heads of the model cities and urban renewal programs as cochairmen of the Community Development and Housing Coordinating Committee reflected Mayor Daley's priority commitment to those departments with vested interests in the earlier categorical programs. That decision, and the retention of existing citizen participation structures, signaled the city's commitment to program continuity rather than to change under the block grant. The cochairmen of the Coordinating Committee started deliberations by negotiating an appropriate split of funds between their own respective agencies while leaving a slush fund for other departmental interests represented on the committee. Thus Rubinowitz concludes, *"Plus ça change, plus c'est la même chose."* In Phoenix the initial decision to continue the Booker T. Washington neighborhood development project, which was still in its early stages, meant that the centerpiece of the block grant program would be a carry-over from the categorical programs. That decision also gave a competitive edge for the remaining share to such interests as the Housing Coalition that were in a position to press rapidly for their priorities, while it hampered the ability of less-organized interests to influence the decisions. In one of Carbondale's early decisions, city staff recommended and the Citizens Steering Committee agreed to a 65:35 split between physical and social programs, approximately the same proportions that went to such activities under the predecessor programs; it was, of course, understood that the share for social service programs symbolized in large part a commitment to model cities continuation in some form.

For Houston and Allegheny County, business as usual was not possible because of the physical development emphasis of the CDBG. Houston had participated only in the model cities program and the city had concentrated nearly all its money on social services. The city's program had to change direction. The mayor's early organizational decisions to place CDBG planning within a new division of his office and to create a new citizen task force were clear signals of discontinuities for model cities interests and an announcement that the CDBG was essentially a new ball game. Allegheny County had participated in both urban renewal (through the Redevelopment Authority) and model cities, but the county's first-year allocation was a hold-harmless grant based entirely on its model cities experience. Like Houston, Allegheny County made major organizational changes. It created a new Department of Planning and Development to administer the CDBG program, disbanded the model cities agency and citizen group, and named the County Planning Commission the citizen advisory unit.

Thus among the five case studies, some of the earliest decisions indicated substantial continuity of activities and organizations in three communities and major changes in two. But among all five cases and the larger monitoring sample there was a strong tendency for communities to borrow heavily from federally inspired models for neighborhood revitalization.

Urban Renewal and Housing

In the FNES sample less than 15 percent of the funds in both the first and second years went for the continuation of urban renewal projects. Of the forty communities with urban renewal experience, thirty-two allocated some continuation funds but usually below the level of previous categorical funding. These aggregate data, however, obscure some important local factors that influenced decisions to continue or discontinue urban renewal spending. Phoenix, as a latecomer to participation in the federal categorical programs, had embarked on its single neighborhood development project shortly before the appearance of the block grant program, at which point the project was still in its preliminary stages. Commitments of local officials to continue the project were sufficiently strong to account for both the extremely short time frame in which the city was able to plan its first-year CDBG activities and the increase of funds to the project during the early years of CDBG. Except for Houston, which had no urban renewal project, the other case jurisdictions had already circumscribed their commitments to their redevelopment projects. This contrast between Phoenix and the other cases suggests that local commitments to continuation of the categorical redevelopment projects *sometimes* depended more on the stage these projects had reached when the block grant began than on any inherent discontent of local officials with the substantive objectives of the categorical programs. In Carbondale, officials had already decided to open up a new urban renewal area, and when that program ended they decided to use block grant funds to undertake the new renewal activities.

Nor are the discontinuities between the older renewal projects and the new CDBG development priorities necessarily as sharp as suggested by the shifts in funds found in the monitoring sample. There were important links in both strategy and implementation. The strategic link is most apparent in the CDBG emphasis on neighborhood conservation efforts, which included housing rehabilitation activities and public improvements concentrated in specific residential areas. These conservation programs resembled earlier categorical counterparts consisting of federally funded, concentrated code enforcement activities; housing rehabilitation loans and grants; and planned public improvements in chosen project areas. These kinds of programs were CDBG priorities in many of the communities of the field study sample, including Phoenix, Carbondale, Allegheny County, and Chicago. This suggests that the earlier development programs had provided important conceptual models that guided thinking and priorities under the block grant.

This tendency to adopt federally inspired models was also apparent in the local design of housing rehabilitation assistance, the largest single program activity funded under the block grant.[13] Under the CDBG program, communities established rehabilitation loan programs similar to the federal 312 program; grants to homeowners patterned on the former section 115 grants of the urban renewal program; interest subsidies that adopted the approach of the homeownership (section 235) and rental (section 236) housing programs established in 1968 but that had largely disappeared; and loan guarantees patterned after programs of the Federal Housing Administration and the Veterans Administration.[14] But while adopting the earlier mechanisms of federal aid, local officials frequently made major changes in program details to meet local demands and conditions, reflecting the greater local discretion that accompanied the block grant. The primary alterations tended to be raising the income level of eligible participants and, in the case of rehabilitation grants, providing a

13. Ibid., chap. 6.

14. Section 312 is explained in note 5, chap. 1, and section 115 in note 14, chap. 7. Section 235 of the Housing and Urban Development Act of 1968 assists lower-income families in purchasing new or rehabilitated homes by subsidizing the interest rate below the market level. Section 236 of the same act reduces the rent of lower-income tenants by subsidizing the interest rate the building owner pays on the mortgage.

much higher level of aid than had been possible under the federal assistance program.

Even while drawing on earlier models of federal urban aid, local governments have used the CDBG to significantly expand the scope of local government involvement in housing policy. Historically the largest part of the local housing market has involved nonsubsidized development by the private sector, with public sector involvement in zoning, subdivision, and building code enforcement, and rent control in some cities. More recently some local governments have sought to slow down the conversion of rental units into privately owned condominiums.

A number of major housing subsidy programs funded by the federal government operated through the private sector—for profit and nonprofit—including such programs as rent subsidies, section 235 homeownership and section 236 rental housing interest subsidies, and direct loan programs for housing the elderly and the handicapped. Direct involvement in subsidized programs by the local public sector has generally been confined to federally funded urban renewal, public housing, rehabilitation under the 312 program, and section 8 rental assistance.[15] The local organizational unit involved has frequently been a semiautonomous renewal agency or public housing authority; general-purpose local government involvement in such programs has usually been more limited.

In many cities the CDBG changed the public sector role in important ways. Organizationally, consolidating urban renewal into the block grant has often meant reducing the power of, or eliminating, the semiautonomous renewal authority and shifting more housing development activity to the general-purpose local government. Substantively, the general-purpose local governments have used the more flexible CDBG money to play a larger direct role in local housing policy and development, usually through the establishment of major housing rehabilitation activities that use one or a combination of the approaches noted above. It should be added, however, that because of complexities in setting up the local financing mechanisms and the lack of an experienced staff who understood the intricacies of housing rehabilitation, most communities experienced considerable delay in implementing these activities.[16] Through the

15. Section 8 is explained in note 35, chap. 3.

16. Dommel and others, *Decentralizing Community Development,* pp. 240–43; *CDBG Execution: Problems and Prospects* (U.S. Department of Housing and Urban Development, April 1979); and Paul R. Dommel and others, *Targeting Community Development* (HUD, January 1980), app. 4.

housing assistance plan the general local government has also been required to take a more comprehensive view of local housing needs and to state how it plans to meet these needs.

Model Cities

The block grant resulted in some major discontinuities for social services previously funded by model cities, in terms of both the declining share of CDBG funds going to such activities and who received such services. Because the CDBG program emphasized physical development, allocations for social services were expected to drop below the level that had been supported by model cities. Further, the legislative history of the block grant was interpreted by some federal and local officials to mean there should be a ceiling of 20 percent on social service spending. In cases where model cities had been a major part of a community's grant experience, some HUD area offices permitted social service funding to go above the 20 percent limit. But even communities that had a very large model cities program usually chose to go below 20 percent; officials in many of these jurisdictions simply preferred physical development to social service spending. Cities that had not participated in model cities generally chose not to fund such activities at all; they did not want to get committed to any new operating costs that would have to be funded from local taxes if the block grant was not continued. For the monitoring sample, the average share of second-year funds allocated for social services by former model cities was 17.4 percent, compared with 5.1 percent for those without model cities experience.[17]

Four of the case jurisdictions (Phoenix was the exception) had model cities grants and were alike in that the continuity of model cities activities hinged largely on their being sustained by block grant funding. Except for a relatively small number of projects that could readily and inexpensively be folded into the regular operations of line departments, such as occurred in Allegheny County, the kinds of activities that characterized model cities were not picked up under local revenues but were absorbed as part of the block grant. The original intent of the model cities program was to serve as a demonstration or proving ground for local program innovations; the successful activities would then be supported by local governments from their own revenues. Some were reluctant to use local funds for such transitions, however, and the CDBG became the lifeline for model

17. Dommel and others, *Decentralizing Community Development*, p. 261.

cities activities. The reasons for the reluctance varied: cities with fiscal pressures—as in Chicago and Carbondale—did not want to divert local tax revenues to model cities activities. In Houston fiscal strains were not evident, but a prevailing local conservatism toward funding human services and reservations about the quality and management of model cities activities accounted for the qualified mayoral commitment to model cities programs, even in the face of the politically strong black constituency that supported them. Moreover, the concentration of model cities activities in target subareas made it difficult to justify the use of general funds for their support without expanding the services to other needy areas.

Even where model cities services as such were curtailed, similar kinds of community services were frequently continued under the CDBG on a broader geographical basis. This spreading of model cities social services to new areas was characteristic of both the cases and the monitoring sample as a whole.[18] Houston and Allegheny County cut service delivery in the model neighborhoods but expanded similar services to other areas. As a result, high-priority services—usually day care and services for the young and the elderly—were evened out. The survival of activities generally reflected the continuing influence of the model cities administrators who had a base in CDBG decisionmaking and a role in providing services. The geographic expansion of these services reflected the need to meet new demands for the services from groups in areas that had been left out of model cities. In the case of Phoenix there was a striking absence of any vocal grass roots constituency favoring the funding of human services programs under the CDBG or any agency interest in advocating service commitments. The predominantly physical, or hardware, orientation of the Phoenix approach to the grant can be seen as a consequence of the city's local political culture and its nonparticipation in the model cities program. Consequently Phoenix did not have the kinds of agency specialists and neighborhood constituencies activated by model cities programs elsewhere and possessing vested interests in human services programs.

Targeting

The most significant discontinuity of the block grant program was the end of the target area approach of the renewal programs (urban renewal and the neighborhood development program) and model cities. This carried with it the expectation that there would be a wider distribu-

18. Dommel and others, *Targeting Community Development,* pp. 133–35.

tion of benefits, and there was. One of the first outcomes of the block grant decision process was geographic spreading of activities, usually in the form of highly visible housing rehabilitation assistance and related public works activities (streets, sidewalks, parks, street lighting, and so on).[19] And as already noted, some communities also chose to expand the area for social services that had been confined previously to the model cities neighborhoods. Thus while there may have been considerable continuity in the kinds of activities undertaken under the CDBG, the distribution of such activities underwent very important changes. In both the case and the field studies, spreading often reflected the fact that the target areas of the previous programs seldom included all deteriorated or declining neighborhoods.[20] Because of the greater flexibility of the block grant, some cities chose to expand their development activities to include needy areas and groups that had been left out of the earlier programs. This meant that the spreading of activities had a rationale based on objective needs as well as satisfying the need of elected officials to respond to a broader range of neighborhood-based organizations and other key constituencies.

Two other factors contributed to spreading. One was the allocation of funds to the line departments, which normally operated throughout the jurisdiction and typically used the block grant funds to augment their normal activities. The other was concern about the feasibility of certain development activities, such as housing rehabilitation, in the worst-off areas, which usually were included in the model cities target area. The need to maximize the impact of limited funds caused local officials to direct some funds to areas of lower risk, and in doing so to favor transitional neighborhoods rather than the worst-off areas. In some communities geographic spreading also meant spending in affluent neighborhoods.

The case studies make it possible to get a better understanding of these patterns. In Carbondale, both physical development and service-related funds from the earlier programs were directed toward the poorer northeast section of the city. With the advent of the CDBG, physical development was expanded to include the relatively better-off though still needy northwest section. Service commitments were maintained in the Northeast, while additional CDBG funds were used to meet other service demands in the city. In Houston funds that had been almost exclusively targeted at the model cities neighborhoods (among the city's worst off) were spread to cover twenty-three CDBG target areas spanning a broader

19. Nathan and others, *Block Grants for Community Development,* p. 261.
20. Dommel and others, *Targeting Community Development,* pp. 151–53.

geographic and socioeconomic range. Although the model city neighborhoods retained their service programs during the first two years of the CDBG, by the third year service funds were similarly dispersed. In Allegheny County many of the service programs that had gone to Turtle Creek Valley were dismantled by the second year of the CDBG in favor of a broader-based constituency, the elderly. Physical development shifted to a wider range of purposes and to a larger number of the county's older towns. The county's neighborhood conservation efforts were targeted at moderate-income residential areas, where property owners could be expected to afford their share of housing improvements, rather than the poorer areas. Chicago canceled most of its outstanding urban renewal and neighborhood development projects and expanded its target area beyond the four model cities neighborhoods to include a number of new CDBG target areas designated for conservation efforts, while park improvements funded by the CDBG were extended to some of the city's more affluent areas.

Phoenix provides an example of CDBG targeting. Although geographic spreading did occur as the city expanded its activity beyond the Booker T. Washington project area, the expansion was confined primarily to the housing and public improvement needs of South Phoenix, the city's most impoverished minority area. This new effort in South Phoenix, however, was also accompanied by some CDBG allocations to the city departments, and this resulted in a dispersed pattern of public improvements, although with relatively little funding.

Despite the tendency toward spreading, none of the five tried to devise a strategy of pure, even dispersion among income groups or neighborhoods. Each concentrated funds for particular purposes or geographic areas while at the same time touching a broad number of constituencies, however lightly, with some share of the program benefits. Project centerpieces were combined with a smaller share of flexible funds to meet demands across the jurisdiction.

Conclusion

The new opportunities opened up by the CDBG tended to evoke a common response. Local executives, seeking to minimize conflict, accommodated new claimants. There is little evidence that development strategies rather than political concerns and distributive benefits were uppermost in their minds at the beginning. Moreover, the apparent effort to incorporate most potential constituencies into the process made the achievement of a development strategy difficult. Put another way, generally the substantive form of the program was left to take shape after process-oriented and political goals had been served.

Local programs showed considerable continuity between the consolidated programs and the block grant. Some communities were committed to continuing or completing activities started under the earlier programs, although the level of the continuing commitment varied among communities. There were also important continuities in the kinds of activities funded, continuities in the sense that, although modified in details, they were conceptually the same kinds of development approaches funded under the earlier programs, most notably neighborhood conservation consisting of housing rehabilitation and related public improvements. Such conceptual continuities and adaptations were found both in communities with prior grant experience and in some communities with no prior experience and where the block grant was new money. As noted, however, in some better-off communities local discretion meant significant spending for communitywide public improvements rather than neighborhood revitalization. Usually spending spread beyond the old target neighborhoods into new areas, often needy themselves.

Several reasons appeared to underpin the adoption of neighborhood conservation as the program centerpiece of many communities. First, as already noted, it enabled local officials to expand development into new neighborhoods, making it politically attractive. Second, it was an approach heavily oriented toward the status quo; it left basically undisturbed the racial and socioeconomic mix of a community. A strategy to develop new housing would have been expensive and would have opened up some very sensitive issues concerning the relocation of lower-income groups. Third, the block grant was sufficiently flexible to enable communities to use the money to pay for the wide variety of activities that constituted neighborhood conservation, activities that might otherwise have had to be funded from local tax levies.

There were statutory development objectives, however vaguely defined, that were intended to guide local strategies. Yet at the outset federal officials gave very limited attention to those features of the law that offered the greatest opportunities for intervention, and where they did give close scrutiny to applications, they generally focused on specific activities that in most cases could only marginally influence program strategies. As a result, local discretion was maximized at the outset.

With time, HUD supervision became more feasible and opportunities for scrutinizing local performance developed as activity actually got under way and federal officials carried out the statutory requirement to review and audit local programs. Furthermore, during the second year questions about HUD's administration of the program started to be raised in Congress and the courts, as noted in chapter 2. These factors encouraged HUD officials both in Washington and in the field to begin giving closer scrutiny to local applications. HUD field officials began to raise questions about the eligibility of individual activities included in the local application. In most instances HUD ended up going along with the activities, but to get its approval, local officials had to submit written justifications to show how the activities related to the national objectives. In most cases these justifications took the form of creative writing by local CDBG officials, but as a consequence, during the second year local officials began to sense an increasing federal role in substantive issues.[21]

Unhappiness also grew because of the amount of paperwork attached to the program.[22] Several factors accounted for this. The CDBG program gave local officials responsibility for some tasks previously carried out by HUD, such as environmental impact reviews. Local officials were also required to submit a housing assistance plan as part of their CDBG application, a requirement that most felt was a waste of time because there were not nearly enough federal housing funds to reach the housing plan goals. Another source of irritation was the performance report, required in some cases before the first year ended, which local officials found of little or no use. Sometimes, however, the grumblings about red tape came from local officials who had not worked with the earlier grants and had no real basis for comparing the CDBG with its predecessors. In any case red tape is not tantamount to control, and the general feeling among local officials in the transitional years of the CDBG was that they had more control over substantive decisions, even if the reduction of red tape had not lived up to expectations.

To summarize, when decentralized decisionmaking is implemented to maximize local discretion and minimize federal controls, the outcome takes on the character of a crap game—you roll the dice and take your chance in the arena of local politics. Of course, leaving outcomes to chance is itself a value or policy preference.

21. Dommel and others, *Decentralizing Community Development*, pp. 74–79.
22. Ibid., pp. 79–81.

CHAPTER NINE

Decentralization: A Moving Target

AS SHOWN in the preceding chapters, some change in the initial hands-off policy began during the second year of the block grant program, indicating that the new division of decisionmaking authority had not been settled unambiguously in favor of greater local discretion. This concluding chapter takes a telescoped look at the post-transitional years to see (1) how federal involvement continued to increase with the coming of the Carter administration and the adoption of an administrative policy designed to achieve increased targeting of community development block grant projects; and (2) how the political context changed again with the election of President Reagan in 1980 in ways likely to affect how the CDBG evolves in the future.

Social Targeting

Chapter 2 pointed out that the Ford administration did not adopt any clear policy on how to implement the social targeting language inserted by Congress into the CDBG legislation. Regulations of the Department of Housing and Urban Development (HUD) required only that communities receiving CDBG funds certify that the local program gave "maximum feasible priority to activities which benefit low- and moderate-income families or aid in the prevention or elimination of slums or blight."[1] The regulations followed the language of the law that made the social targeting and the physical revitalization objectives coequal. They defined "low- and moderate-income families" as those whose incomes did not exceed 80 percent of the median family income of the area, but the legislative term "maximum feasible priority" was not defined.

Any ambiguity ended with the coming of the Carter administration in January 1977. Just one month after President Carter's inauguration the

1. *Federal Register,* vol. 41 (January 28, 1976), p. 4135.

new HUD Secretary, Patricia R. Harris, went before the Subcommittee on Housing and Community Development of the House Committee on Banking, Finance and Urban Affairs and declared her intention to give more emphasis to the social targeting objectives of the law. Her position reflected concern in part over criticism from Congress and over reports by HUD and the National Association of Housing and Rehabilitation Officials that there had been a drop in low- and moderate-income benefits between the first and second years of the program.[2] The benefits issue had also led to several lawsuits by local groups to block local officials from spending CDBG money on activities to benefit upper-income groups.[3] Secretary Harris told the subcommittee:

> We will expect communities to direct development and housing programs toward low- and moderate-income citizens. I do not consider this to be just an objective of the block grant program; it is the highest priority of the program, and we, in the Federal Government, must see to it that the thrust of the program serves that objective.[4]

This statement was followed in April by a directive from Robert C. Embry, Jr., assistant secretary for Community Planning and Development, to the CDBG field staff emphasizing HUD's intention to push hard on social targeting.

> One of the major initiatives that the Secretary wants to begin immediately is the orientation of HUD's efforts toward the achievement of statutory objectives, particularly those objectives that speak to the interest of low- and moderate-income people.
>
> The various program requirements should therefore be interpreted in light of the statutory objectives, particularly the objective of providing decent housing and a suitable living environment and increased opportunities principally for persons of low and moderate income.[5]

2. In the second annual report on the CDBG program, HUD reported that low-moderate benefits had declined from 63.6 percent in the first year to 57.3 percent in the second. See U.S. Department of Housing and Urban Development, *Community Development Block Program: Second Annual Report* (HUD, December 1976), p. 23. Using a different methodology, the National Association of Housing and Redevelopment Officials reported a decline in benefits from 51 to 44 percent between the first and second years. See Mary K. Nenno, "Second Year Community Development Experience," *Journal of Housing,* vol. 34 (April 1977), p. 184.

3. Paul R. Dommel and others, *Decentralizing Community Development* (U.S. Department of Housing and Urban Development, June 1978), app. 4.

4. *Housing and Community Development Act of 1977,* Hearings before the Subcommittee on Housing and Community Development of the House Committee on Banking, Finance and Urban Affairs, 95 Cong. 1 sess. (Government Printing Office, 1977), pt. 1, p. 9.

5. Memorandum, Robert C. Embry, Jr., to HUD field staff involved in the CDBG program, "Management of the Community Development Block Grant Program," April 15, 1977.

Thus the Carter administration became allied with the Senate position advocating more social targeting.

During a House floor debate in May 1977 on extension of the program, Democratic Congressman Henry B. Gonzalez of Texas offered an amendment, which was not adopted, to require communities to spend their block grant on lower-income groups in the same proportion that poverty was used as a factor to calculate their grants.[6] Subcommittee Chairman Thomas L. Ashley (D-Ohio) noted that these percentages might actually result in reduced social targeting in some communities. The more important point of Ashley's opposition, however, was his argument concerning local discretion in community development strategies.

> . . . the proposal will severely limit the flexibility of local governments to solve their particular community development needs.
>
> The proposal really would reinstitute that degree of Federal control which the basic legislation was meant to remove.
>
> Going back to the 1974 act, what we said was that we did not want the Federal Government to be telling the local communities what their needs were, and we asked that the local communities develop a community development plan which would be a profile, if you will, of the needs of each community, and then a plan to be responsive in remedying those needs.[7]

Predictably, the Senate reacted differently. Harris told the Senate Committee on Banking, Housing and Urban Affairs in April that HUD was changing its focus from procedural review to substantive review of community applications. "The basic administrative machinery is now in place. It is time to determine if the funds are being spent to carry out a clear strategy: Are they being used primarily to benefit low- and moderate-income persons?"[8] She said that HUD officials reviewing applications were being directed to seek more thorough, detailed verification before making a final decision on the application. Committee Chairman William Proxmire (D-Wis.) commented at the end of her testimony:

> I want to say that I support very strongly the way you are going about this. The funds must be directed to low-income persons, which must have a sharp improvement of the performance in the past [sic].
>
> It is a matter of record that more money went into high-income census

6. This proposition related to the dual formula being proposed in the legislation. Under the original 1974 formula poverty was weighted 50 percent; in the second formula proposed in the 1977 amendments poverty was weighted 30 percent.

7. *Congressional Record,* daily ed. (May 10, 1977), p. H4244.

8. *Housing and Community Development Legislation of 1977,* Hearings before the Senate Committee on Banking, Housing and Urban Affairs, 95 Cong. 1 sess. (GPO, 1977), p. 114.

tracts than went to low-income census tracts. This is outrageous. We can't accept it, there is no rationalization for it.[9]

Proxmire apparently was referring to HUD's second annual report and the study of the National Association of Housing and Rehabilitation Officials, which found that a significant amount of CDBG activity was going into census tracts where a majority of residents had incomes above the definition of low- and moderate-income.

In the bill to extend the program for three years the Senate committee wrote in a new provision allowing the HUD secretary to reject a local application if it did not give "specific regard to the primary purpose of principally benefiting persons of low- and moderate-income."[10] The language, in effect, gave social targeting primacy among the various national objectives, including decentralization.

House conferees took issue with the new language because it referred only to the social targeting objectives of the law as the basis for rejecting an application, leaving out other objectives concerning elimination of slums and blight and assisting with urgent community needs. The final version was a compromise that preserved the Senate language establishing the basis for rejecting an application but expanded that basis to include any of the three national objectives, not just social targeting.

75–25 Regulations

In the fall of 1977, two weeks after President Carter signed the law extending the CDBG program for three years, HUD proposed new regulations, including its plans for social targeting. HUD took the position that "*all* community development funds are to be used for projects or activities which principally benefit low- and moderate-income persons [emphasis added]."[11] The proposed regulations went on to state that there could be exceptions for up to 25 percent of a community's grant for certain activities to prevent slums and blight and for projects designed to meet needs having a particular urgency. The proposed regulation, subject to public comment and final adoption by HUD, became known as the 75–25 rule. The proposed regulations meant that HUD planned to give social targeting a clear and strong preference over other objectives of the law and to set a benefits standard to guide both HUD and local officials.

9. Ibid., p. 135.

10. *Housing and Community Development Act of 1977,* S. Rept. 95-175, 95 Cong. 1 sess. (GPO, 1977), p. 43.

11. *Federal Register,* vol. 42 (October 25, 1977), p. 56466.

The proposed regulations were issued on October 25, and HUD allowed until November 25 for comments. The 75–25 rule, though just one of many proposed new regulations for the program, drew the most attention. By the time the period for comment expired, a total of 1,327 letters had been received, and many included some comments on the proposed 75–25 rule. Generally the proposal was supported by neighborhood and civil rights groups, whereas it was opposed by local government officials and some members of Congress. One very important dissenter was Subcommittee Chairman Ashley, who wrote two strong letters to Secretary Harris objecting to the 75 percent requirement, which he said ran counter to legislative intent. In his first letter—which was cosigned by the ranking minority member of the subcommittee, Congressman Garry Brown of Michigan—Ashley stated:

> We do not concur in the requirement for a set percentage of funds, at minimum, to be spent for the single purpose of benefiting low- and moderate-income persons. . . . The placement of one purpose as more primary than another is neither consistent with the language of the statute nor with the legislative history.[12]

In the second letter, signed only by Ashley, the language was stronger:

> It appears to me that the 75/25 regulation violates the basic concept of the program. It would move us back to a categorical approach we all recognize is undesirable. . . . [T]he conferees on at least three separate occasions reaffirmed the equality of the three purposes of the grants. With this overwhelming evidence I can only conclude from the Department's insistence on the 75/25 regulation that it believes it can legislate on its own. This is a very grave situation and one that I and many of my colleagues on the Subcommittee will feel forced to explore with you.[13]

Ashley's warnings did not go unheeded. The final regulations, issued on March 1, 1978, were less rigorous in their social targeting requirements than were the proposed regulations. Whereas it had been proposed that all activities must principally benefit lower-income persons, the final regulations gave up this language to state: "All projects and activities must *either* principally benefit low- and moderate-income persons, *or* aid in the prevention or elimination of slums and blight, *or* meet other community development needs having a particular urgency [emphasis added]."[14]

The language of the regulations thus came to reflect the legislative lan-

12. Letter, Representatives Thomas L. Ashley and Garry Brown to HUD Secretary Patricia R. Harris, November 4, 1977.

13. Letter, Representative Thomas L. Ashley to HUD Secretary Patricia R. Harris, December 16, 1977.

14. *Federal Register,* vol. 43 (March 1, 1978), p. 8461.

guage that had been insisted on by the House—that social targeting was only one of three coequal national objectives. HUD, however, through directives to the field staff and through the process of developing the regulations, had signaled its clear intentions to recipient communities that social targeting was to be a major goal of the program. The upshot of the dispute was that HUD was legislatively constrained in its interpretation of the priorities of the national objectives, but the level of benefits to lower-income families could now be considered explicitly by HUD in deciding whether or not to approve an application. HUD did not get all it wanted on the benefits issue, but recipient communities could not readily ignore HUD's preferred policy on social targeting.

There was a cost to HUD in pushing its social targeting policy. The department's relations with the House were strained and the issue reemerged in 1978 during consideration of legislation amending a number of HUD programs. Among the amendments adopted was one by the House Committee on Banking, Finance and Urban Affairs restating its view on the coequality of the national objectives of the CDBG. The committee proposed and the House adopted a change in the act to explicitly state that "the three main objectives of the CDBG program are co-equal and that the Secretary may not disapprove an application because it addresses any one of the primary purposes to a greater or lesser degree than any other."[15] A second amendment was proposed on the House floor by Congressman Brown to assert control directly over HUD's implementation of the program by giving either the House or the Senate the power to veto rules or regulations issued by HUD. The proposal passed easily by a vote of 244 to 140. The Senate version of the bill, more favorable toward HUD, contained no language on the coequality of the national objectives, and the Senate rejected by a vote of 65 to 29 a legislative veto amendment proposed by Republican Senator Harrison H. Schmitt of New Mexico.

In the final version the coequality language was dropped and the conferees watered down the House provision for a legislative veto by either the House or Senate. Instead, they allowed the authorizing committee of either the House or Senate to study and delay implementation of regulations up to ninety days. The committee could also initiate a procedure for rejecting the regulations, but this required the passage of a joint resolution or law by both houses and the signature of the president.

15. *Housing and Community Development Amendments of 1978,* H. Rept. 95-1161, 95 Cong. 2 sess. (GPO, 1978), p. 72.

Geographic Targeting

A clear HUD policy on geographic targeting within jurisdictions also began to emerge. In reaction to geographic spreading, early critics of the CDBG argued that it was unlikely to have a long-term development impact in any particular area of a community. A staff report of the House Committee on Banking, Finance and Urban Affairs, issued in early 1977, concluded that such spreading was not necessarily bad but that "the issue is whether or not areas targeted for treatment in order to renew, rehabilitate or conserve them are being programmed with a variety of activities at a sufficient level to reasonably insure that the proposed treatment will be successful."[16] The report expressed concern about whether "CDBG-funded community development programs are merely a variety of eligible activities scattered throughout the community without regard to sound planning and which could result in little or no long-term impact."[17]

In response, and to express its own policy, HUD's proposed regulations in October 1977 set forth geographic targeting, as well as social targeting, as one of the key principles to be used in local CDBG planning.

> It is HUD policy to encourage the use of block grant funds in a concentrated manner in order to produce substantial long-term improvements in the community. The applicant is specifically encouraged to carry out a strategy for comprehensive neighborhood-revitalization which concentrates sufficient resources to stabilize and upgrade residential areas affected by blight and deterioration.[18]

The final regulations issued in March 1978 emphasized geographic targeting in residential neighborhoods, leaving the choice of activities to local officials. But the specification of residential neighborhoods seemed to imply a HUD preference for housing and housing-related activities. Residential neighborhood targeting thus joined social targeting as a major policy emphasis of HUD.

16. *Staff Report, Community Development Block Grant Programs,* Committee Print, House Subcommittee on Housing and Community Development of the Committee on Banking, Finance and Urban Affairs, 95 Cong. 1 sess. (February 1977), pp. 33–34.

17. Ibid., p. 33.

18. *Federal Register,* vol. 42 (October 25, 1977), p. 56465.

The Effect of Targeting Policies

The new targeting policies, as stated by Harris and Embry soon after they took office and well before the new regulations were drawn up, were implemented just as the third-year applications of many of the recipient jurisdictions were ready for review by HUD area office officials. The impact of the policies was quickly evident at the local level.

Our field research showed that HUD's role and influence in decision-making expanded generally in the third and fourth program years, through both the review of local applications and field visits by area office officials.[19] While the increased involvement occurred in all types of jurisdictions (central cities, suburban cities, and urban counties), it occurred most in suburban communities and most frequently concerned targeting. The more stringent HUD review of applications was directed to assuring that proposed activities met the new targeting policy. HUD did not specify the kinds of activities there should be, although as noted above, the policy on targeting on residential neighborhoods suggested an implied preference for housing.

One general result of the closer HUD scrutiny was an increase in red tape for local officials who were required frequently to supply supplemental documentation to justify how specific proposed activities would benefit lower-income groups. Another general result was that in the third year the substance of local strategies became the principal issue of HUD-local relations. By contrast, in the first two program years procedural issues were dominant.

Substantively, according to the monitoring studies, HUD's social targeting policy had some effect. The estimated level of benefits intended for lower-income groups increased overall from 56 to 60 percent between the second and third program years and reached 62 percent in the fourth year.[20] While the aggregate data indicated only an incremental change, a significant increase came in the suburbs, where the planned level of lower-income benefits increased from an estimated 51 percent in the second year to 63 percent by the fourth year. Most notable was the large drop in the number of sample jurisdictions that allocated less than half of their planned program benefits to the lower-income groups. In the first year

19. Paul R. Dommel and others, *Targeting Community Development* (U.S. Department of Housing and Urban Development, January 1980), chap. 3.

20. Ibid., chap. 6.

fifteen of the forty-one sample jurisdictions where benefits were estimated had low-moderate benefits of less than 50 percent; in the second year this increased to sixteen; in the third year, as the social targeting policy was implemented the number of such jurisdictions dropped to nine, and it declined to only four in the fourth year. Again the decline was most evident among the suburban cities. In the first year seven of twelve suburban cities in the sample allocated less than half of their funds to low-moderate benefits; in the fourth year only one was below the 50 percent level. The change in planned benefit levels in these jurisdictions indicated that HUD's policy preference had had an effect.

The combined effects of geographic and social targeting varied among jurisdictions in an important way. In older, declining cities with extensive concentrations of lower-income groups, the policy effects tended to be minimal. Such cities usually adopted at the outset a neighborhood revitalization approach covering a large area to meet the expanded demands accompanying the CDBG, and a large proportion of the activities went into areas fitting the low- and moderate-income standard. The policy effects generally were greater in better-off communities, where the CDBG was frequently new money and where a significant share of the grant was often allocated initially for communitywide public improvements. In such communities the targeting policies imposed a federal development strategy over local program choices. Some local choices continued to emphasize street, sidewalk, and park improvements, but the largest share of such activities were now concentrated in lower-income neighborhoods.

Geographic concentration of activities in lower-income neighborhoods, however, does not necessarily mean that program benefits go directly to lower-income residents. Public improvements tend to provide *locational* benefits, and all residents of the area, regardless of income, may benefit. In some cases the improvement may be repairing an arterial street through a low-income area and the principal benefits may go to well-off commuters driving through. Social services and housing rehabilitation generally yield *personal* benefits and can be more directly targeted. But social service spending, which tends to give the largest share of benefits to lower-income groups, is limited under the CDBG, and the distribution of benefits from housing rehabilitation is greatly influenced by local implementation decisions, a very important one being the income eligibility standards for assistance. Many jurisdictions adopted grant and loan standards well above the low- and moderate-income level to keep higher-income residents in the neighborhood. Thus a neighborhood stabilization strategy to prevent slums and blight sometimes conflicted with social targeting. What share of the direct benefits went to the higher- or lower-income residents of a mixed neighborhood sometimes depended on who walked through the door of the local CDBG office for a grant or loan. Consequently, while the federal targeting policies imposed a clearer development strategy meeting national objectives on some communities, the actual targeting outcome was dependent in important ways on the standards and processes of local implementation.

A final point on benefits concerns the share of benefits to low- and moderate-income groups under the CDBG in relation to the earlier programs. There had been concern from the outset, particularly from supporters of model cities, that the block grant would provide fewer benefits for low-income persons.[21] The model cities program concentrated its activities in low-income areas and, given the predominance of social services, probably directed most of the direct benefits to low-income persons. Urban renewal in the early years focused on downtown redevelopment, which was often accompanied by the destruction of both low- and moderate-income housing and the displacement of such residents.[22] In its later years and as it evolved in the neighborhood development program, renewal started to shift to residential revitalization, often in neighborhoods with a high proportion of moderate- and middle-income, owner-occupied homes. Thus the renewal programs often benefited income groups higher than those benefited by model cities. Under the CDBG, housing rehabilitation assistance has also gone primarily to moderate- and middle-income homeowners as part of a neighborhood stabilization strategy.[23] This strategy, combined with the de-emphasis of social services, means generally that moderate-income groups do reasonably well under the CDBG, while low-income groups probably derive a smaller share of direct benefits than they did before. At the same time, the geographic spreading that has accompanied the CDBG has meant that benefits are now extended to a greater number of low- and moderate-income persons than had been the case under the predecessor grants.

21. Bernard J. Frieden and Marshall Kaplan, *The Politics of Neglect: Urban Aid from Model Cities to Revenue Sharing* (MIT Press, 1975), pp. 249–56; Frieden and Kaplan, "Community Development and the Model Cities Legacy," Working Paper 42 (Joint Center for Urban Studies of the Massachusetts Institute of Technology and Harvard University, 1976).

22. See James Q. Wilson, ed., *Urban Renewal: The Record and the Controversy* (MIT Press, 1966), chaps. 10–14.

23. Dommel and others, *Decentralizing Community Development,* pp. 243–49; and Dommel and others, *Targeting Community Development,* app. 4, pp. 8–17.

Formula Changes

The 1977 legislative amendments made important revisions in the allocation system. As stated in chapter 2, the 1974 formula—based on population, poverty, and overcrowded housing—favored growing communities and those with high levels of poverty; the chief beneficiaries were communities in the South and West. This formula, however, failed to take into account two important measures of urban distress: loss of population and deteriorating capital infrastructure. These two conditions place a heavy burden on a city's fiscal ability to cope with its development needs. The relationship between the two was noted by George Peterson in a study of city financing problems resulting from population decline.

> The dilemma confronted by the older cities is that few of the costs associated with urban growth are easily reversible into economies of diminution. Once a city's road, sewer, and water networks have been constructed to serve a given population, the cost of maintaining these networks does not decline significantly when population shrinks. On the contrary, as capital infrastructure ages, it becomes more costly to keep in repair.[24]

Population growth, however, usually means growth in the middle-income sector, bringing an expanded revenue base in the form of faster growing income levels and property values.[25] Such growth in a community's resource base puts it in a better position to finance its own development needs.

A study of the CDBG formula done at the Brookings Institution in 1976 recommended that the amount of pre-1940 housing stock be used as a proxy measure of community age and deteriorating infrastructure needs.[26] A second major change recommended in the study was the establishment of a dual formula system that retained the original formula and added a second one incorporating the community age factor and dropping overcrowded housing.[27] Under the dual formula system each entitlement community would receive the larger of the two amounts computed under the two formulas. This meant that no entitlement jurisdiction

24. George E. Peterson, "Finances," in William Gorham and Nathan Glazer, eds., *The Urban Predicament* (Urban Institute, 1976), p. 44.

25. Richard P. Nathan and Paul R. Dommel, "The Cities," in Joseph A. Pechman, ed., *Setting National Priorities: The 1978 Budget* (Brookings Institution, 1977), pp. 286–88.

26. Richard P. Nathan and others, *Block Grants for Community Development* (U.S. Department of Housing and Urban Development, January 1977), pp. 187–89.

27. Ibid., pp. 216–22.

would receive less than its allocation under the original formula, but it might receive more. The study said that the added cost of funding each entitlement jurisdiction at the higher level of the two formulas could be paid for through the reduction of funds for discretionary grants to small communities within metropolitan areas, many of which were well-off suburbs. The discretionary fund was what remained after the formula and hold-harmless entitlements had been paid; thus an increase in the cost of the formula entitlements meant a smaller amount would remain for metropolitan discretionary grants.

The dual formula approach with the community age factor added to one of the formulas was endorsed in recommendations to Congress by both the Ford and Carter administrations. HUD Secretary Carla A. Hills, who pushed for the change against a reluctant Office of Management and Budget in the closing months of the Ford administration, also proposed substituting population decline for population in the second formula. This had the effect of greatly increasing the allocation for such cities as St. Louis and Cleveland, which had suffered major population losses since 1960, the baseline to be used for measuring the losses. The population decline factor was subsequently modified in the legislative proposal of the Carter administration to substitute growth lag, which took into account not only population losses but also slow growth. This had the political advantage of benefiting more jurisdictions, including some suburban cities and urban counties. The second formula proposed by the Carter administration and adopted by Congress included the following factors: pre-1940 housing (weighted 50 percent), poverty (30 percent), and growth lag (20 percent).

The feature of the dual formula that protected entitlement communities against loss did not prevent the outbreak of a sharp regional battle in the House of Representatives when the CDBG legislation was up for renewal in 1977. By this time the computerized data system at HUD had been fully developed and lawmakers could easily see how their districts would be affected by any formula changes. All regions were to receive some boost in the *amount* of funds through an increase in the total authorization for the program. But the dual formula had the effect of boosting the *share* of funds going to the Northeast and the Midwest, while reducing the share of the southern and western regions.

Congressmen from the Northeast and Midwest voted almost unanimously to adopt the change while southern and western legislators were nearly as united in their opposition to the dual formula. On an amendment proposed by two Democratic House members from California to delete the dual formula from the bill, eastern and midwestern congressmen voted 215 to 8 to keep it, while southern and western members voted 132 to 18 to eliminate it. The proposed formula changes had less trouble in the Senate, where northeastern legislators succeeded in giving an even greater tilt toward their region by adding a third formula option. The third formula would have used the percentage rather than the number of older housing units in a city, giving a still greater amount to older cities than the second formula. House-Senate conferees finally agreed to the dual formula approach of the House version.

While the voting division implied a clear split in regional benefits, the effect of the dual formula was not simply a matter of northern cities gaining while southern and western cities remained the same. A total of 259 entitlement jurisdictions were estimated to benefit initially from the new allocation system.[28] Those benefiting were disproportionately in the Northeast and Midwest (205), but 54 southern and western cities also gained from the new system. Overall, the entitlement jurisdictions of the Northeast and Midwest increased their formula share from 49 to nearly 59 percent; the central cities in all regions collectively increased their share of the formula fund from 71 to 76 percent and their share of total funds from 36 to 52 percent.[29] Although the dual formula protected entitlement jurisdictions against a loss in the amount of their grants, this was not the case for small metropolitan communities that had to rely on discretionary funds. (Nonmetropolitan communities did not lose, because the law set aside 20 percent of total funds for them.) If the 1974 formula system had been retained, by 1980 small metropolitan communities would have received almost 30 percent of the metropolitan funds. However, since much of the added cost of the dual formula approach was funded from the metropolitan discretionary pot, their share dropped to less than 10 percent.

Program Implementation

The two principal issues during the early years of the block grant program were decentralization, focusing on the conflict between national

28. Dommel and others, *Decentralizing Community Development,* chap. 2.

29. These data on shares distributed by the original formula differ from those in chapter 2 because of increases in the number of entitlement jurisdictions and changes made in the population data between the times the two calculations were made.

goals and local discretion, and the adverse effects of the formula on the older, declining cities. On the first issue, HUD's targeting policies appeared to increase both the level of its involvement in local decisionmaking and benefits to lower-income groups. The amendments of 1977 responded to the second issue by directing a bigger share of funds to the older cities. Another issue emerged, however, and grew in importance as the program matured. It concerned program execution.[30]

One of the complaints against the categorical grant approach had been the long delay between the time a community applied for a federal grant and completion of the project. In urban renewal it sometimes took seven to ten years even to bring a project to the point where the renewal site had been prepared for sale to private developers. And then it frequently happened that for a variety of reasons a potential developer's interest had waned and the prepared site was left empty or only partially developed.

Decentralized decisionmaking in combination with entitlement funding was supposed to eliminate long delays in project execution. Some procedural complexity is of course inherent in the development process no matter how the intergovernmental procedures are arranged; among the complicating factors are preliminary design work, final engineering, land acquisition (in some cases), and bidding and contracting procedures. But some of the delay had been caused by federal red tape. Under the CDBG it was expected that delay would decrease both because the amount of this red tape would be reduced and because a shift from large-scale projects to small-scale projects was expected to occur.

The indicator of progress that came to be used for the CDBG was a community's rate of expenditure of its funds. About midway through the third program year the General Accounting Office, using this measure, called into question the ability of grant recipients to carry out their development programs in a reasonably timely manner.[31] HUD's third annual report, issued after the GAO report, stated that by the end of January 1978 (about midway through the third program year of many recipients) almost 97 percent of the first-year grants had been spent, about 62 percent of the second-year grants, and 8 percent of the third-

30. Paul R. Dommel and others, *Implementing Community Development* (U.S. Department of Housing and Urban Development, forthcoming).

31. Letter, Henry Eschwege, director of the Community and Economic Development Division, U.S. General Accounting Office, to the secretary of the U.S. Department of Housing and Urban Development, January 24, 1978.

year grants.[32] A Brookings study of expenditure rates for the first three years, done for HUD, reported that among a sample of thirty-nine recipients the jurisdictions spent about half of an annual grant by the end of the year in which it was given, although there were great variations from the average in individual communities.[33]

Partly as a result of the GAO criticism, HUD began to give more attention to program execution and increased pressure on communities to spend their grants more quickly. In 1979 HUD adopted a "use or lose" policy, warning communities that if they were not able to make sufficient progress in implementing their CDBG programs, HUD would begin to reduce their grants. Forty-five communities were given official warnings about the possible loss of funds, but by mid-1980 only Houston, Texas, had actually lost funds under the policy. Houston's fifth-year grant was reduced by $435,000, about 2 percent of its grant; in the sixth year HUD approved the city's grant with the condition that it expend a certain amount of the funds allocated for housing rehabilitation by a certain date or lose part of its grant.

From the outset many of the recipient communities experienced problems with getting their programs under way. The most common reasons were disagreements over details of program implementation, lack of administrative capacity, and problems of coordination with other public agencies (state and local) and the private sector.[34] Even cities with considerable experience with federally funded development programs had trouble. For example, in New York City, which had extensive categorical grant experience, the Department of Housing Preservation and Development had difficulty implementing its housing rehabilitation projects because most of its experience had been with new-housing construction. Predictably, cities that used CDBG funds to continue projects started under earlier programs experienced fewer problems of execution. Fewer difficulties also came in spending on social services than were experienced with physical development activities.

One source of delay was dispersion of authority at the local level. The greater centralization of local authority that characterized the priority-

32. U.S. Department of Housing and Urban Development, *Community Development Block Grant Program: Third Annual Report* (HUD, March 1978), p. 65.

33. Michael J. Rich, "Program Execution under the Community Development Block Grant: An Exploratory Analysis," *CDBG Execution: Problems and Prospects* (U.S. Department of Housing and Urban Development, June 1980), p. 34.

34. Ibid., pp. 9–31; and Dommel and others, *Implementing Community Development*.

setting stage did not extend to program execution. The agency responsible for overall administration of the local CDBG grant was often not the same agency that carried out the activities being financed. A major problem, therefore, was getting other departments that were not HUD's clients to expedite CDBG-funded projects in a way that satisfied HUD's wishes for getting the money spent. For some large city departments, such as public works, the CDBG funds represented only a small portion of the department budget and were given low priority. In other cases city and departmental procedures for design, bidding, and contracting were so cumbersome that there were extended delays. Housing rehabilitation activities were particularly troublesome. Local rehabilitation projects were patterned after federal approaches that had been operated under federal standards and guidelines, but in some cases the jurisdiction receiving CDBG funds had had no experience with these federal programs. In other cases local officials, in designing their own rehabilitation programs under the CDBG, tried to vary the procedures to meet local circumstances and ran into problems. For example, most communities chose to adopt standards of eligibility less restrictive than the federal levels, and agreeing on such standards among local participants caused delays; disagreements also arose over whether the assistance should be a loan or grant. There were also the problems of day-to-day execution, such as promoting the program in the target neighborhoods and providing technical assistance to property owners contemplating rehabilitation; rehabilitation specialists were in short supply in most jurisdictions. Further, there was the problem of deciding on the level of rehabilitation that would be assisted: should it be just code enforcement or should assistance also be given for repairs such as new siding and roofing?

Private sector involvement also caused snags. In some cases private lending institutions were reluctant to participate in rehabilitation projects because this meant investing in riskier income groups and neighborhoods. Sometimes so much private construction work was available in the area that contractors were reluctant to bid on CDBG projects, given the special paperwork and compliance burdens attached to federally funded construction.

In summary, some of the initial expectations, perhaps unrealistic to start with, about local implementation of the CDBG program were not being fulfilled, and pressures began to build on communities to show more visible progress. Some of the impetus for the federal pressure came from the GAO analyses, but it was likely that HUD would have expressed the same concern at about the same time. The more general effect of the use or lose policy was that HUD was drawn into closer oversight of execution of all aspects of the program and closer scrutiny of local management, organization, and procedures. From the perspective of local officials the evolution toward increased HUD oversight of program execution suggested a return to the level and detail of federal involvement that had characterized the categorical programs.

The Effects of Changing Administrations

Decentralization is the central conflict that has run through the CDBG program since it was first proposed in 1971. It was on this continuing issue of local discretion versus federal controls that the Nixon administration was in disagreement with Congress, that Congress was divided within itself, and that the House of Representatives and recipient communities were at intermittent odds with HUD as the program matured.

At the beginning of the program local officials expected the block grant to make a sharp break with the federal controls and complexities of the categorical system. This expectation had been encouraged generally by the philosophy of the New Federalism and specifically by general revenue sharing (enacted two years before the CDBG), which channeled new funds automatically to state and local governments without requiring an application and with no strings attached. But the CDBG program was different. It was not new money. It was put together by consolidating old programs and thus had left behind a programmatic, bureaucratic, and constituent legacy. Further, unlike general revenue sharing, the CDBG included several generally stated but substantive national policy goals, which if pursued with any aggressiveness at the national level, were likely to bring federal program administrators into conflict with those giving priority to decentralization.

Expectations of decentralization were certain to be disappointed, perhaps progressively as the program aged. In addition to the national objectives the legislation included a variety of compliance requirements covering such matters as environmental impacts, equal opportunity, and construction wages, which were likely to become more important as CDBG projects progressed beyond the initial planning stage. As the program matured, both HUD and Congress raised questions about how the money was being spent, and this brought HUD into matters of local management and organization. In communities that had little experience with federal programs before the CDBG, these avenues for federal influence were certain to be perceived as leading to more rather than less federal intervention.

The maturation process, program monitoring, and federal concern for national goals began to converge and have an effect as early as the second year of the program. HUD officials in the Ford administration, while still adhering to a hands-off policy, started to take a closer look at the programs of some communities, including in some cases the question of who was benefiting. As indicated by both the field research results and the case studies, local officials began to express concern about the direction of federal program control.

That direction became more clear in the third year of the program when new federal administrators under President Carter adopted a targeting policy to implement national objectives of the legislation. For some communities the policy had little effect, while for others it meant an important shift from communitywide public improvements to the concentration of spending in poorer neighborhoods. Significantly, the change began early in 1977, before any change in the law, through scrutiny of the grant application process, thereby demonstrating the susceptibility of CDBG policies to changes of administration in Washington.

Since the 1980 elections the political context of the CDBG has been marked by fiscal stringency at all levels of government, a new president committed to a greatly reduced federal role, and a more conservative Senate controlled by Republicans. Further, in the House of Representatives, political power is shifting from the Northeast and Midwest to the South and West. These changes have important implications for the CDBG.

Consistent with his general effort to decentralize and deregulate many areas of federal policy, President Reagan proposed and Congress adopted some major changes in the CDBG law in 1981. The most significant change was the elimination of the seventy-five-day period for review and possible veto of the local application; in effect, this made the block grant very similar to the special revenue sharing proposal of President Nixon ten years earlier. In addition, CDBG discretionary grants by HUD to small communities in metropolitan and nonmetropolitan areas were converted to block grants to state governments. The combination of greatly easing the funding requirements for entitlement jurisdictions and folding the discretionary grants into block grants to the states means greatly reduced HUD control over the entire program.

Without waiting for the legislative changes, HUD, under Secretary Samuel R. Pierce, Jr., took steps to reduce the scrutiny of local applications. On May 15, 1981, it instructed its Washington and field staffs to drop certain review procedures. Review of compliance with the benefits provisions of the law was no longer to be based on percentage standards but on a more general effort to detect any obvious failure to comply with the social targeting objective of the law. There were also new guidelines on social services that could open the way to expand the geographic area for such spending; the previous guidelines were intended to confine services primarily to neighborhoods where the CDBG activities were being concentrated. The new guidelines also sought to cut back on the number of conditions attached by HUD officials to approval of local grant applications, such as a condition stipulating the rate of expenditure to be achieved by a community.

For most communities the new guidelines were applicable to the seventh year of the program. They were unlikely to affect the substance of the seventh-year programs, however, since most plans had already cleared the local preparation process. But the changes may serve the symbolic purpose of letting both HUD and local officials know that the rules of the game are once again changing, this time back toward the hands-off policy that characterized the early years of the CDBG. Thus HUD officials of the new administration learned what their predecessors had learned four years earlier—the legislative language of the CDBG is sufficiently broad to allow a new set of policy preferences to be adopted without any change in the law itself.

In part, HUD was able to press its targeting policy under the Carter administration because it had the support of the Senate. Without that Senate support, particularly the backing of Committee Chairman Proxmire, HUD officials might have been less forceful in implementing its policy. Today there is a Republican-controlled, more conservative Senate that tends to support a Republican president who favors decentralization. It remains to be seen how the Republican administration will treat targeting. In the past, targeting under the CDBG was a liberal policy in that it was designed to redistribute resources to lower-income groups even if at the cost of greater federal intervention. Potentially, however, targeting is fiscally conservative because it may provide a rationale for a smaller, cheaper program by giving funds only to the neediest communities for use in defined neighborhoods.

A more-bang-for-the-buck targeting policy would face political difficulty. The first point at which targeting objectives can be achieved is in determining which communities receive a formula grant. The eligibility criteria of the 1974 legislation provided formula grants to a large number of growing, well-off jurisdictions, particularly in the South and the West, including central and suburban cities and urban counties. This grant spreading was partially offset by the change in 1977 to a dual formula that directed a larger share of the money to older, declining communities. In extending the program again in 1980, Congress held off making any further changes in the formula until the new census data could be analyzed, leaving open the possibility of further formula changes in 1983. But the politics that made the 1977 changes possible have been altered by congressional reapportionment. In 1977 the Northeast and the Midwest, whose cities principally benefited from the dual formula, had 225 of the 435 House seats and succeeded in getting the changes; the 1980 census shifted the balance of congressional power to the southern and western regions, which now have 227 seats. This does not offer bright prospects for either cutting out better-off jurisdictions, many of which would be in the South and the West, or further adjusting the formula to give a bigger share to the declining cities, which are concentrated in the Northeast and the Midwest. Moreover, formula amendments in 1983 could reverse the direction of the changes made in 1977 since southern and western lawmakers have been unhappy about the dual formula, particularly the use of the pre-1940 housing factor.

Whatever the outcome on interjurisdictional targeting, geographic and social targeting in a community can still be pursued through administrative policy. Since it is likely that block grant money will continue to go to communities that do not really need it, the case can be made that they should be required to use the money to improve conditions in their most needy neighborhoods and for their neediest residents. The application of such clear policy standards in the CDBG, however, runs into the conflict between social and geographic targeting and those objectives not necessarily related to redistributive goals—elimination or prevention of slums and blight and meeting the needs of a particular urgent situation. Aggressive federal application of a targeting policy also runs counter to the central procedural policy of the Reagan administration—less federal control.

The Effects of Fiscal Stringency

Besides the policy preferences of national administrations, the changing fiscal fortunes of government may affect the evolution of the CDBG. The program is likely to shrink along with many other federal aid programs.

The extension of the CDBG in 1977 provided for a 4 percent growth in funds for the fifth and sixth years of the program. In 1980 the legislation was extended for an additional three years with about the same rate of growth. Because of inflation, however, there has been a continual loss in real dollars. Now the nominal dollars are going down also as part of the general reduction in federal intergovernmental aid programs.

As the five case studies illustrated, dividing the pie is contentious when the pie is growing. It will be more so as local bureaucracies, nonprofit organizations, and citizen groups compete for fewer CDBG dollars. The more fiscally distressed a city, the greater the contentiousness is likely to be. The local resource base cannot be tapped to make up all of the lost funds. Thus for local officials generally the outlook is for operating in a more hostile bargaining arena. Assuming that there will be less HUD intervention, it will be more difficult for local officials to transfer some of the political costs to the federal level.

The likely competition for funds involves not only CDBG constituents but also constituents of other aid programs, both state and federal. State governments too are cutting spending. Fiscal retrenchment has now gained general acceptance at all levels of government, by officials as well as taxpayers. With the greater local discretion that apparently is being attached to the CDBG, the program may be perceived increasingly as a source of general funds for a variety of non-CDBG activities facing elimination or cutbacks in federal and state assistance. For example, a reduction of funds for social services might mean more pressure on the CDBG for funding such services, despite any desire local officials may have to eliminate such spending from the block grant. Conversely, demands for continued housing rehabilitation and public works spending under CDBG could force greater reductions in social services.

A political escape hatch may exist in the nature of the CDBG. Generally it is a program of small, discrete, and interchangeable activities. It may be possible to trade off these parts to reduce any additional political pressures that may accompany the reduction in funds. A smaller number of houses can be rehabilitated in a given year or fewer streets can be resurfaced; the next year some more juggling can be done among individual activities and neighborhoods. But this also means the potential diluting of the development impact of the CDBG unless the target areas can be reduced to match the shrinking resources. Since many of the neighborhoods brought into the CDBG were lower-income areas left out of the predecessor grants, any geographic shrinkage is likely to cut off some of these neighborhoods.

To conclude, the emerging combination of relaxed federal controls and reduced federal funding may require communities to relearn what the case studies showed was the earliest imperative of the CDBG—the need to manage conflict.

Index

Action-Housing, Inc., Allegheny, Pa., 182, 189, 192
Adams, Charles F., Jr., 8n, 58n
Adrian, Charles R., 197n
AFL-CIO Council, 94
Alinsky, Saul, 141
Allard, William Albert, 85n
Allegheny County block grant: case study characteristics, 9, 11; and citizen participation, 177–79, 181, 183, 186; first-year application, 173–85; fourth-year application, 194; and local decision process, 174–77, 185–86; outcomes, 193–94; program choices, 188–91; program targeting, 191–94; second-year application, 185–88; third-year application, 194; and urban county eligibility, 172–74
Allegheny County, Pa.: categorical aid experience, 169–72; characteristics, 166–69; governmental structure, 167–68
Allegheny County Redevelopment Authority, 169–70, 174–77, 181, 185, 186
Allegheny League of Municipalities, 176
A-95 review: Allegheny County, 181, 187; Carbondale, 211; Chicago, 144, 148; defined, 100n; Houston, 100
Antipoverty program, 32; Carbondale, 221; Chicago, 128, 132–33; Phoenix, 61
Ashley, Thomas L., 30, 36, 245, 247
Austin, Richard, 126–27, 134

Bach, Victor E., 223n, 228
Baker, John, 195n
Banfield, Edward C., 7, 199n
Barrett, William A., 30
Barrow, Timothy, 59, 60
Becker, R. James, 49n
Berman, David, 60n
Better Communities Act, 26, 27, 32, 35, 39, 43, 63
Bilandic, Michael, 124, 125, 143, 161
Binford, Elmer, 164–65
Block grants, 2, 16–17. *See also* Community development block grants
Bommersbach, Jana, 53n
Booker T. Washington project, 56–57, 61, 64, 67, 68, 70, 74, 78
Bowser, Palmer, Jr., 97
BPI. *See* Business and Professional People for the Public Interest
Brock, William E., III, 28, 40
Brookings Institution, 7, 9, 41, 253, 257
Brown, Garry, 30, 247, 248
Brown, Lawrence D., 7n, 23n
Bulla, Robert, 66
Business and Professional People for the Public Interest (BPI), 135, 142, 163–64
Byrne, Dennis, 140n
Byrne, Jane, 125

Calkins, Susannah E., 8n
Camfield, Roland E., 74n
Carbondale block grant: case study characteristics, 9, 11; and citizen participation, 205–11; first-year application, 203–12; and local decision process, 203–05, 221; outcomes, 220–22; program choices, 212–18; program targeting, 218–20
Carbondale, Ill.: categorical aid experience, 200–02; characteristics, 195–97; governmental structure
Carey, Bernard, 124
Carter, Joy, 66, 70
Castillo, John E., 97, 103–05, 113, 116
Castillo, Leonel J., 91, 97
Categorical grant programs: Allegheny County, 169–72; Carbondale, 200–02; Chicago, 125–29; citizen participation in, 15; consolidation of, 25–34; development of, 1–3, 13–17; evaluative approaches to, 5–9; Houston, 89–92; Phoenix, 52, 54, 56, 59–62; revenue

sharing approach to, 17–19. *See also* Model cities program; Neighborhood development program; Urban renewal program
CCUO. *See* Chicago Committee on Urban Opportunity
CDBG. *See* Community development block grants
Charter Committee, Phoenix, 55–56, 60
Chicago block grant: case study characteristics, 9, 11; and citizen participation, 131–34, 136, 140–43, 145–48, 161–64; first-year application, 129–44; housing assistance plan, 134–35, 142–44, 147–48, 159, 163–65; implementation, 144–46, 158–60, 163–65; and local decision process, 130–31, 134–40, 143–44, 146–48; outcomes, 160–61; program choices, 149–54, 162–63; program targeting, 137, 155–58, 163; second-year application, 146–49; third-year application, 159, 161–65
Chicago Committee on Urban Opportunity (CCUO), 128–29
Chicago Financial Assistance to Property Owners program, 151–52
Chicago, Ill.: categorical aid experience, 125–29; characteristics, 120–23; governmental structure, 123–25, 128–29
Chicago-Oakley project, 164, 165
Chicanos por La Causa, Phoenix, 65–66
Cincotta, Gail, 140–41
Citizen participation: Allegheny County, 177–79, 181, 183, 186; block grant requirements for, 31–32, 44, 229–32; Carbondale, 201, 205–11; Chicago, 129–34, 136, 140–43, 145–48, 161–64; federal aid programs and, 15; Houston, 93–94, 98–103, 106, 111, 113, 117; Phoenix, 64–66, 71; urban renewal program, 20
Citizens Advisory Committee, Carbondale, 205–07
Colman, William G., 88n
Commission on Mortgage Practices, Ill., 150
Committee on Banking and Currency, House, 39, 40
Committee on Banking, Housing and Urban Affairs, Senate, 26–28, 39, 42, 245–46, 248, 249
Community Development and Housing Coordinating Committee, Chicago, 130, 131, 134, 136–43, 145–48, 160–62
Community development block grants (CDBG), 2, 5; application process, 29–31, 242, 248, 250, 260–61; case study characteristics, 9–12; citizen participation in, 31–32, 44, 229–32; description of, 3–4; eligibility, 35–39, 222, 262; entitlement areas, 35–39; evaluative studies, 9–12; federal role in, 25–26, 43–46, 223–25, 241–42, 255–57, 259–64; formula system, 39–41, 253–55, 262; funding for, 263–64; legislative history, 25–34, 222, 245–48, 254–55; local decision process, 31, 225–29, 240–41; national objectives, 27–29, 248, 260; performance review, 33–34, 257, 259–61; program choice patterns, 232–41; program implementation, 255–59; targeting policy, 41–43, 238–40, 243–52, 261–62. *See also* Allegheny County block grant; Carbondale block grant; Chicago block grant; Houston block grant; Phoenix block grant
Community Development Citizens Steering Committee, Carbondale, 207–11, 213
Community Development Division, Houston, 95–97, 101, 105, 106, 112, 113, 116–18
Community Service and Research Corporation, Chicago, 137
Compliance certification, 33–34
Comprehensive Child Care Program, Carbondale, 219, 222
Comprehensive Employment and Training Act, 2, 19
Comprehensive Health Program, Carbondale, 219, 222
Congressional-Cities Conference, 203
Conolly, Craig S., 208n

Dahl, Robert A., 7n, 20n, 22n
Daley, Richard J., 11, 121, 124, 126, 130, 131, 134
Dentler, Robert A., 20n, 22n
Department of Community Development, Carbondale, 204
Department of Development and Planning, Chicago, 128, 129, 131, 136, 140, 161
Department of Housing and Urban Development (HUD), 36, 39; Allegheny County programs, 180, 181, 183, 184, 187–89, 193–94; Carbondale programs, 211–13, 222; Chicago programs, 126–28, 134, 143–46, 148, 155, 159, 163–65; Houston programs, 90, 92, 94, 96, 99–103, 105–06, 116–18;

model cities administration, 24–25, 32; performance review role, 33–34, 242; Phoenix programs, 56, 60–61, 64, 65, 72–74, 82, 83; program implementation role, 29, 30, 38, 43–45, 224, 256–57, 259–61; targeting role, 243–52; urban renewal administration, 21, 23
Department of Human Services, Chicago, 128, 147, 161
Department of Planning and Development, Allegheny County, 174–77, 179, 182–87, 190, 192
Department of Urban Renewal, Chicago, 128, 129, 139, 161
Derthick, Martha, 7n
De Vise, Pierre, 121n
Discretionary grants, 3, 37–39, 222
Division of Human Resources, Carbondale, 204
Division of Renewal and Housing, Carbondale, 205
Dixon, Hortense W., 96, 97
Dodge, William, 186
Dommel, Paul R., 8n, 17n, 45n, 223n, 225n, 226n, 227n, 228n, 231n, 232n, 235n, 236n, 237n, 238n, 239n, 242n, 244n, 250n, 252n, 253n, 255n, 256n, 257n
Downs, Anthony, 77n, 121n
Driggs, John, 60, 66
Dual formula system, 253–55
Duppa, Darrell, 47

Eckert, Neal, 207, 214
Economic development activities: Allegheny County, 190, 194; Chicago, 152–53, 163; Houston, 108; Phoenix, 83
Economic Development Commission, Chicago, 123, 128
Embry, Robert C., Jr., 117, 244
Emergency Home Repair Program, Phoenix, 67, 75, 78–79
Environmental impact studies, 33, 34
Eribes, Richard A., 47n, 49n
Eschwege, Henry, 256n
Everett, Ray, 54n

Federal Housing Administration (FHA), 67, 75, 78, 101
Fefferman, Hilbert, 20n
Feins, Judith D., 123n
FHA. *See* Federal Housing Administration
Field, John O., 199n
Field network evaluation study (FNES), 7–9, 224–25, 227, 232, 234
Finney, Leon, 141, 142
Flaherty, James, 184, 186
Flannery, Michael, 144n
FNES. *See* Field network evaluation study
Foard, Ashley A., 20n
Focus on Renewal, Allegheny County, 178
Foerster, Thomas, 184
Ford, Gerald R., 13
Formula entitlement system, 37–38, 253–55
Foxhall, Nene, 85n
France, Erwin, 130, 136, 138–39, 147
Frieden, Bernard J., 23n, 24n, 25n, 32n, 252n
Fry, Carroll J., 198, 203–05, 207–09, 221

GAO. *See* General Accounting Office
Gautreaux case, 126–28, 134, 142–43, 159
General Accounting Office (GAO), 256, 257
Gonzalez, Henry B., 245
Goodall, Leonard E., 50, 51n, 54n, 60n, 61n, 89n
Goodstein, Jeannette, 49n
Gosnell, Eldon, 205
Graham, Milton, 60

Haley, Leon L., 228
Hall, John S., 47n, 77n, 228
Hance, Margaret, 53, 56, 73–74
Hanna, Richard T., 35
Harris, Patricia R., 164, 244, 245, 247
Hayes, Eurma C., Neighborhood Center, 201, 219–20
Hayes, Richard, 208–10
Heller, Walter W., 16
Henry, Nicholas, 49n, 77n
Heston, R. W., 87n
Hill, Lewis, 130, 136, 138–40, 142–44, 147, 164, 165
Hills, Carla A., 105–06, 254
Hofheinz, Fred, 91–97, 105–06, 112–13, 117–19
Hold-harmless grants, 37–40; Allegheny County, 171, 174, 178; Carbondale, 203, 222; Chicago, 128
Housing activities: Allegheny County, 180, 184–86, 188, 189, 192, 194; as block grant program choices, 235–36; Carbondale, 215–17, 222; Chicago, 149–52, 159, 162–64; Houston, 103,

107–09, 111–12, 118; implementation of, 258; Phoenix, 74–75, 78–79; targeting effects on, 251–52
Housing Act of *1949,* 19
Housing and Community Development Act of *1974,* 2, 13, 19; benefit distribution provisions, 29–31, 35–36, 39–41, 222, 254–55, 260, 262; decision process provisions, 31–32; implementation provisions, 248, 260; national objectives, 27–29, 42–43, 248; performance review provisions, 33–34; social targeting provisions, 42, 245–46
Housing assistance plans: Allegheny County, 176; Carbondale, 205, 221; Chicago, 134–35, 142–44, 147–48, 159, 163–65; Houston, 94, 99–101, 105–06; impact of, 237, 242; Phoenix, 80; requirement for, 30
Housing authorities: Allegheny County, 169, 170; Chicago, 126–29; Houston, 92, 93
Housing Commission, Phoenix, 65–72, 75
Housing Services Division, Phoenix, 69
Houston block grant: case study characteristics, 9, 11; and citizen participation, 93–94, 98–103, 106, 111, 113, 117; first-year application, 91–104; implementation, 103–04, 111–13, 115–16, 118, 257; and local decision process, 91–94, 105, 115; outcomes, 111–15, 118; program choices, 103–04, 106–09, 115–17; program targeting, 110–11, 114, 115, 117–18; second-year application, 104–06; third-year application, 115–18
Houston-Galveston Area Council, 94, 100
Houston Residents Citizen Participation Commission (HRCPC), 102–05, 111, 117
Houston, Tex.: categorical aid experience, 89–92; characteristics, 84–87; governmental structure, 88–91, 112–14
HRCPC. *See* Houston Residents Citizen Participation Commission
HUD. *See* Department of Housing and Urban Development
Human Resources Department, Houston, 116
Hunt, William, 184

Jackson, John S., III, 230–31
Johnson, Lyndon B., 16
Johnson, Wesley, 58n
Jones, Stuart E., 85n
Jones, Walter L., 97

Kane, Robert P., 180–81
Kaplan, Harold, 20n, 22n
Kaplan, Marshall, 23n, 24n, 25n, 32n, 252n
Kaufman, Michael T., 51n, 59n
Kestnbaum, Meyer, 16
Keyes, Langley C., 7n
Koch, Edward I., 1n

Laird, Melvin R., 16
Lang, Richard O., 135n
Larson, David, 136, 138
Leadership and Education for the Advancement of Phoenix (LEAP), 61, 65, 66
League of Women Voters: Allegheny County, 178; Chicago, 134, 142, 146; Houston, 93, 94
Legal Assistance Foundation, 142, 163
LeGates, Richard T., 21
Leroy, Moses, 90, 93, 101–02, 105, 117
Lovell, Catherine, 1n
Lucas, Robert, 141
Lutheran Service Society, 178
Lynn, James T., 30, 32

McCleskey, Clifton, 89n
McComb, David G., 84n
McConn, James J., 118–19
McEnany, Michael V., 92, 98–99
McGaw, Dickinson, 52n
McQuade, Walter, 20n, 22n
Magida, Arthur J., 43n
Manvel, Allen D., 8n
Marris, Peter, 7n
Mayer, Harold M., 125n
Mee, Joy, 67
Meeker, David, 43–45, 102
Menafee, Hawkins H., 90n
Metcalfe, Ralph H., 124
Metropolitan Area Housing Alliance, Chicago, 136, 140, 142–43, 150
Meyerson, Martin, 7
Milberger, Jack, 175, 177, 179, 186
Mills, Wilbur D., 17
MNRC. *See* Model Neighborhood Resident Commission
Model Cities Administration, Chicago, 128, 131, 139
Model cities program, 3–4, 16, 19, 38, 46; Allegheny County, 170–71, 175, 176, 179, 188–89; Carbondale, 201, 204–06, 213–14, 221; Chicago, 125–

28, 132–33, 136, 138, 145–49, 151, 153–54, 156, 159, 160; citizen participation, 32; development of, 23–25; Houston, 89–90, 94–97, 102, 104–06, 110–11, 115; targeting policy, 41, 42; transition from, 226–27, 232–34, 237–38
Model City Department, Houston, 90, 93, 95, 97, 112
Model Neighborhood Resident Commission (MNRC), Houston, 90, 93, 94, 101–02
Monte, Donald, 204, 207, 209, 210
Moore, Aubrey, 60
Moore, John L., 36n
Moore, Robert L., 99
Moorhead, William S., 35–36
Muller, Thomas, 86n

NAACP. *See* National Association for the Advancement of Colored People
Nathan, Richard P., 8n, 17n, 29n, 36n, 37n, 41n, 43n, 44n, 58n, 203n, 226n, 227n, 228n, 231n, 232n, 239n, 253n
National Association for the Advancement of Colored People (NAACP), 117, 178, 183
National Association of Counties, 35, 175
National Association of Housing and Rehabilitation Officials, 244, 246
National Council of Senior Citizens, 178
National Environmental Policy Act of *1969,* 34
National League of Cities, 31, 36, 64, 203, 206
Neal, Earl, 134
Neighborhood conservation activities: Allegheny County, 180, 182–84, 186, 189–90, 192, 194; as block grant program choices, 235, 241; Chicago, 149–50, 160; Houston, 109; Phoenix, 74–75
Neighborhood development program, 3, 22–23, 41–42, 226; Chicago, 126–28, 151, 159, 160; Phoenix, 56–57, 60–61, 64, 67, 68, 70. *See also* Urban renewal program
Neighborhood Housing Services: Chicago, 152; Phoenix, 67, 75, 78
Nenno, Mary K., 244n
Newcomb, Charles S., 135n
New Federalism, 1–3
Niskanen, William A., Jr., 77n
Nixon, Richard, 1, 17, 24, 25, 29, 31
Northeast Congress, Carbondale, 201, 206, 207
Northeastern Illinois Planning Commission, 140, 144
Northwest Homeowners Association, Carbondale, 202, 212

O'Brien, Patricia, 141n
Office of Management and Budget (OMB), 36, 254
OMB. *See* Office of Management and Budget
Open Doors for the Handicapped, 178
Open spaces. *See* Parks and recreation activities

Packwood, Robert W., 28, 40
Parks and recreation activities: Allegheny County, 187, 191–92; Chicago, 138–39, 149, 157; Houston, 109, 117; Phoenix, 56, 69, 72, 81–82
Partee, Cecil, 147
Partnership for Health Act, 16
Pechman, Joseph A., 253n
Pelinsky, Al, 186
Pennsylvania State Clearinghouse, 181
Performance review, 33–34
Peterson, George E., 253
Phoenix, Ariz.: categorical aid experience, 52, 54, 56, 59–62; characteristics, 47–52, 57–59; governmental structure, 52–56, 61
Phoenix block grant: case study characteristics, 9, 11; and citizen participation, 64–66, 71; first-year application, 62–70, 72–73; implementation, 69–74, 80–83; and local decision process, 62–64, 71, 82; outcomes, 79–83; program choices, 74–77, 81–82; program targeting, 77–79; second-year application, 71–73; third-year application, 82–83
Phoenix Forward, 66
Pierce, Robert, 184, 186
Pierce, Samuel R., 261
Pittman, Dennis K. E., 182n, 192n
Planned variations experiment, 25
Planning Commission, Allegheny County, 177–79, 183, 187
Policy Planning Division, Houston, 92–95, 97, 105
Polikoff, Alexander, 134–35, 142
Powledge, Fred, 7n
Pressman, Jeffrey L., 7n, 80n
Proxmire, William, 44, 96, 245–46, 261
Public hearings. *See* Citizen participation
Public housing: Allegheny County, 170; Chicago, 126–28

Public improvement activities: Allegheny County, 180, 187–91; Carbondale, 213, 215–18; Chicago, 154, 157, 162–63; Houston, 103–04, 107, 109, 111–13, 118; and targeting, 251. *See also* General development activities
Pulliam, Eugene, 54
Putnam, Wayne, 66–67

Rakove, Milton, 124n
Reagan, Ronald, 4, 260
Recreation activities. *See* Parks and recreation activities
Redevelopment activities. *See* Economic development activities; Neighborhood conservation activities; Neighborhood development program; Urban renewal program
Regional Housing Study and Action Group, 141–42
Reichley, A. James, 2n
Rein, Martin, 7n
Residential Restoration and Preservation Program (RRPP), Phoenix, 67, 69–71, 74–75
Revenue sharing programs, 2, 16–18, 25–26, 35
Rhone, James, 63–65, 69, 71, 72
Rich, Michael J., 257n
Rosenfeld, Raymond A., 42n
Rosenthal, Donald B., 42n
Rossi, Peter H., 20n, 22n
RRPP. *See* Residential Restoration and Preservation Program
Rubinowitz, Leonard, 233

Sallee, Rod, 87n
Schmitt, Harrison H., 248
Section 8 program: Chicago, 135, 143, 148, 164; defined, 73n; Houston, 99, 101, 105–06; Phoenix, 73, 78
Section 312 program, 4, 73, 215
Senior citizen activities, 178–79, 183, 184, 192–93
701 planning grants, 175, 176
75-25 rule, 246–48
Shade, William L., 195n
Smyser, Craig, 89n
Social service activities: Allegheny County, 171–72, 178–79, 188, 189; as block grant program choices, 237–38; Carbondale, 213–15, 218–20, 222; Chicago, 125, 153; Houston, 96, 98, 99, 103–06, 108, 111–13, 115–16; Phoenix, 76; targeting impact, 261
Southern Illinois University, 196–98, 202, 207, 212
Southwestern Pennsylvania Regional Planning Commission (SPRPC), 181
Sparkman, John J., 26, 39, 40
SPRPC. *See* Southwestern Pennsylvania Regional Planning Commission
Staisey, Leonard, 174–76, 179, 180, 183, 184
Stalls, Robert A., 204
Strong, George W., 92–97
Subcommittee on Housing and Community Development, House, 244, 247
Subcommittee on Housing, House, 29–30

Taft, Robert, Jr., 26, 40
Targeting, 34–35; Allegheny County block grant, 191–94; Carbondale block grant, 218–20; Chicago block grant, 155–58, 163; geographic, 41–42, 238–40, 249–52, 262; Houston, 110–11, 114, 115; impact of, 238–40, 250–52; interjurisdictional, 35–41, 261–62; intrajurisdictional, 41–43, 238–40, 262; Phoenix, 77–79; 75-25 regulations, 246–48; social, 42, 240, 243–48, 250–52, 262
Thompson, James R., 124
Thompson, Richard E., 17n
Tower, John G., 28, 40
Trimble, John, 210n
Turtle Creek Housing Development Corporation, 184–85

Urban Community Development Revenue Sharing proposal, 18, 19
Urban counties, 35–36, 172–74. *See also* Allegheny County block grant
Urban League: Chicago, 142, 146; Houston, 93, 94; Pittsburgh, 178
Urban renewal program, 3, 19, 39, 46; Allegheny County, 170, 174, 181; Carbondale, 200–02, 205, 212, 215, 221; Chicago, 125, 138, 150, 151, 159; development of, 19–23; federal role, 20–22; funding system, 22–23; Houston, 89; project implementation, 256; targeting policy, 41, 43; transition from, 226–27, 232–37. *See also* Neighborhood development program
Urban Task Force Grant, Phoenix, 75
U. S. Conference of Mayors, 31

Voice of the People, Chicago, 137–38

Wade, Richard C., 125n
Waner, John O., 134, 164
Waterston, Albert, 80n
Weiss, Robert W., 6n
Wentz, John, 55, 62, 63
Whiting, Leroy, 138
Widnall, William B., 30, 35
Wildavsky, Aaron, 7n
Wilson, Glenwood, 62, 63, 69
Wilson, James Q., 20n, 199n, 252n
Women's Center, Carbondale, 211, 214–15, 218
Woodlawn Organization, The, Chicago, 141, 142
Workable Program, Carbondale, 205, 206
Wright, John W. D., 195n

Zimmer, Jonathan, 182n, 192n